Photographic Warfare

STUDIES IN SECURITY
AND INTERNATIONAL AFFAIRS

SERIES EDITORS

Sara Z. Kutchesfahani
Director, N Square D.C. Hub
Research Associate, Center for International and
Security Studies at Maryland

Amanda Murdie
Dean Rusk Scholar of International Relations
and Professor of International Affairs, University
of Georgia

SERIES ADVISORY BOARD

Kristin M. Bakke
Associate Professor of Political Science and
International Relations, University College
London

Fawaz Gerges
Professor of International Relations, London
School of Economics and Political Science

Rafael M. Grossi
Ambassador of Argentina to Austria and
International Organisations in Vienna

Bonnie D. Jenkins
University of Pennsylvania Perry World Center
and The Brookings Institute Fellow

Jeffrey Knopf
Professor and Program Chair, Nonproliferation
and Terrorism Studies, Middlebury Institute of
International Studies at Monterey

Deepa Prakash
Assistant Professor of Political Science, DePauw
University

Kenneth Paul Tan
Vice Dean of Academic Affairs and Associate
Professor of Public Policy, The National
University of Singapore's (NUS) Lee Kuan Yew
School of Public Policy

Brian Winter
Editor-in-chief, *Americas Quarterly*

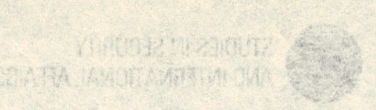

Photographic Warfare

ISIS, EGYPT, AND THE ONLINE BATTLE FOR SINAI

KAREEM EL DAMANHOURY

THE UNIVERSITY OF GEORGIA PRESS
Athens

© 2022 by the University of Georgia Press
Athens, Georgia 30602
www.ugapress.org
All rights reserved
Set in 10/12.5 Minion Pro by Kaelin Chappell Broaddus

Most University of Georgia Press titles are
available from popular e-book vendors.

Printed digitally

Library of Congress Cataloging-in-Publication Data

Names: El Damanhoury, Kareem, author.
Title: Photographic warfare : ISIS, Egypt, and the online battle for Sinai / Kareem El Damanhoury.
Other titles: Studies in security and international affairs.
Description: Athens : The University of Georgia Press, [2022] | Series: Studies in security and international affairs | Includes bibliographical references and index.
Identifiers: LCCN 2022001410 | ISBN 9780820361628 (hardback) | ISBN 9780820361635 (paperback) | ISBN 9780820361611 (ebook)
Subjects: LCSH: IS (Organization) | Terrorism—Religious aspects—Islam. | Islam and state—Egypt—Sinai. | Visual communication—Political aspects—Egypt—Sinai. | Terrorism and mass media—Middle East. | Psychological warfare—Egypt—Sinai. | Sinai (Egypt)—History.
Classification: LCC DT137.S55 E43 2022 | DDC 953/.1—dc23/eng/20220401
LC record available at https://lccn.loc.gov/2022001410

To Egyptian soldiers who've sacrificed their lives for their country and to victims of terrorism everywhere

CONTENTS

List of Illustrations   xi
Acknowledgments   xv

Introduction   State and Non-state Actors' Visual Arsenals   1
Chapter 1   Contextualizing the Sinai Conflict   20
Chapter 2   The Military-Photography Nexus   38
Chapter 3   The Visual Framing Battle   81
Chapter 4   The Visual Semiotic Battle   116
Chapter 5   An Analytic Framework of Visual Contestation   153
Appendix   Coding Sheet and Intercoder Reliability   173

Notes   179
Bibliography   185
Index   199

ILLUSTRATIONS

MAP

MAP 1.   Map of the Sinai Peninsula   21

FIGURES

FIGURE 1.   The analytic framework of visual contestation   10
FIGURE 2.   The number of photographs by Wilayat Sinai   17
FIGURE 3.   Number of Wilayat Sinai's claimed attacks   34
FIGURE 4.   Wilayat Sinai and the Egyptian military's photographs   40
FIGURE 5.   Wilayat Sinai's claimed attacks and the group and military's photographs   43
FIGURE 6.   Timeline of several key military attacks in North Sinai   45
FIGURE 7.   ISIS's attacks and Wilayat Sinai and the military's photographs   51
FIGURE 8.   Monthly Egyptian military's counterterrorism ops and photographs   53
FIGURE 9.   Wilayat Sinai's death images   60
FIGURE 10.   Timeline of key military operations in Iraq and Syria   62
FIGURE 11.   Timeline of reported ISIS leaders killed in Iraq and Syria   72
FIGURE 12.   Timeline of key tensions between Wilayat Sinai and local tribes   75
FIGURE 13.   Wilayat Sinai's visual frames   82
FIGURE 14.   Wilayat Sinai's military visual frames   83
FIGURE 15.   Wilayat Sinai's nonmilitary visual frames   84
FIGURE 16.   The Egyptian military's visual frames   99
FIGURE 17.   The Egyptian military's military visual frames   99
FIGURE 18.   The Egyptian military's nonmilitary visual frames   100
FIGURE 19.   Display of human characters in Wilayat Sinai's photographs   119
FIGURE 20.   Display of human characters in the Egyptian military's photographs   120
FIGURE 21.   The analytic framework of visual contestation   154

PHOTOS

PHOTO 1.	*Al-Masry Al-Youm*'s reporting on the third gas pipeline explosion	3
PHOTO 2.	Bassem Youssef's interview with a masked individual	4
PHOTOS 3–5.	Screengrabs from video production by Ansar Bayt al-Maqdis	5
PHOTO 6.	Sinai Bedouin workers employed by Israeli oil company	25
PHOTO 7.	A plane arriving at Ophira Airport	25
PHOTO 8.	Bulldozers leveling houses in Yamit settlement	26
PHOTO 9.	Detonation of an ISIS IED in Sinai	44
PHOTO 10.	The Egyptian military showcasing ISIS's confiscated cameras	58
PHOTO 11.	ISIS's detonation of an IED against a military vehicle in Sinai	86
PHOTO 12.	ISIS militants attacking a checkpoint in North Sinai	87
PHOTO 13.	ISIS showcasing tribal fighters' confiscated belongings in Sinai	89
PHOTO 14.	Two martyred ISIS media operatives in Sinai	91
PHOTO 15.	ISIS hisba man overseeing the burning of cigarettes in Sinai	94
PHOTO 16.	A group of so-called spies who repented to ISIS in Sinai	95
PHOTO 17.	A house in Rafah reportedly destroyed by the Egyptian military	96
PHOTO 18.	An ISIS militant reading the Qur'an in Sinai	98
PHOTO 19.	The military destroying hideouts in Sinai	102
PHOTO 20.	Egyptian soldiers on the front lines in Sinai	103
PHOTO 21.	The military discovering an illegal tunnel in Rafah	104
PHOTO 22.	Egypt's then–minister of defense in a hospital visit	107
PHOTO 23.	Food distribution by the military in North Sinai	109
PHOTO 24.	A social/public distance shot of ISIS militants	123
PHOTO 25.	A social/public distance shot of Egyptian soldiers	124
PHOTO 26.	A social/public distance shot of two ISIS militants under arrest	124
PHOTO 27.	An intimate/personal distance shot of a martyred ISIS militant	126
PHOTO 28.	An intimate/personal distance shot of Egypt's then–minister of defense	127
PHOTO 29.	A high-angle shot of ISIS militants distributing *al-Naba'* newsletter	131
PHOTO 30.	A high-angle shot of Egyptian soldiers discovering weapons	131
PHOTO 31.	A low-angle shot of ISIS militants targeting jets	133

PHOTO 32.	A low-angle shot of Egypt's then–army field of staff	133
PHOTO 33.	An old man exhibiting a negative facial expression	135
PHOTO 34.	A martyred ISIS militant exhibiting a positive facial expression	136
PHOTO 35.	A man happily holding a food package	137
PHOTO 36.	A middle-aged man looking straight to the camera before being shot	139
PHOTO 37.	A martyred Egyptian officer looking straight to the camera	139
PHOTO 38.	A point-of-view shot of an ISIS militant firing	143
PHOTO 39.	An over-the-shoulder shot of an ISIS militant reading *al-Naba'* newsletter	143
PHOTO 40.	A point-of-view shot of an Egyptian soldier checking an underground tunnel	144
PHOTO 41.	A point-of-view shot showing Egyptian airstrikes in North Sinai	145

TABLES

TABLE 1.	Interactions between photographic outputs and military conditions	41
TABLE 2.	Interactions between visual strategies and military conditions	42
TABLE 3.	Wilayat Sinai's framing categories	84
TABLE 4.	The Egyptian military's framing categories	100
TABLE 5.	Characteristics of Arab and Egyptian societies	117
TABLE 6.	Levels of dependence on visual semiotic devices in Sinai photographic warfare	121
TABLE 7.	Intercoder reliability for coding variables in content analysis	177

ACKNOWLEDGMENTS

I never would have been able to complete this book without the help, support, and generosity of my mentors and colleagues at the University of Tennessee, the University of Denver, Georgia State University, and beyond. Denver's College of Arts, Humanities, and Social Sciences provided needed resources for the book. The views presented here, nonetheless, are those of the author alone and do not represent those of the funding source. I would particularly like to thank GSU communications professor Carol Winkler who took the time to discuss, review, and provide indispensable insights toward the book's development. For supporting the creation of this book, I also owe a debt of gratitude to professors Shawn Powers, Cynthia Hoffner, and Hyunjin Seo as well as DU's College of Arts, Humanities, and Social Sciences' former dean, Daniel McIntosh; the college's former associate dean, Ingrid Tague; DU's Media, Film, and Journalism Studies department chair, Lynn Schofield Clark; Yennhi Luu; Allison McManus; Mohannad Sabry; Omar Said; Lisa Bayer; Nathaniel Holly; and Elizabeth Adams.

I also want to acknowledge the patience and support I received from my life partner, children, and family in Egypt who too often listened passionately as I shared my ideas, put up with my absence, and motivated me to complete this project.

Photographic Warfare

INTRODUCTION
State and Non-state Actors' Visual Arsenals

Egypt is burning! My mother sobbed as she repeated this phrase over and over again to me while dozens of fellow conscripted soldiers stood in line behind me, waiting for their turn to use the phone. I had entered basic training two days before the first spark of the 2011 Egyptian revolution in Tahrir Square. Besides the daily three-minute call to my family, a portable battery radio was the only way I could get updates on the popular uprisings outside the walls of the military base. On January 28, 2011, now known as the Friday of Rage, I saw military tanks and armored vehicles heading out of the base, but headed where I was not sure. Later, I came to understand that the police had retreated the same day and the military had begun to deploy troops across the country. It was not long before many of my squad mates were dispatched to Sinai to secure the northern part of the peninsula. Although the Egyptian revolution to me remained a purely aural experience, others of my fellow soldiers soon became part of an intense, violent conflict in Sinai against a militant force that would later affiliate itself with ISIS,[1] the so-called Islamic State of Iraq and al-Sham (the Levant).

Outside my military encampment on February 5, 2011, Sinai residents near the Egypt-Gaza border could see a huge blaze in North Sinai's capital, al-Arish, about seventy kilometers away. An explosion had damaged a pipeline transporting gas to Israel. This sabotage, as the governor of North Sinai described it, disrupted the gas supply to Israel, which had occupied the Sinai Peninsula until 1982. The identity of the perpetrators, however, remained an open question, with some government officials suggesting a potential link to Palestinians entering Sinai through underground tunnels.

The gas pipeline from Sinai to Israel was part of a largely controversial deal that the two countries had struck several months after the conclusion of the Second Palestinian Intifada. In late June 2005, Egyptian oil minister Sameh Fahmi and Israeli minister for national infrastructure Benyamin Ben-Eliezer met in Cairo to sign a fifteen-year deal that required Egypt to supply to Ashkelon 1.7 billion cubic feet of natural gas per year from al-Arish. In 2008, the Israeli-Egyptian company Eastern Mediterranean Gas (EMG) began pumping gas through Sinai to Israel's state-owned company Israel Electric without publicly announcing the cost. Additionally, Hussein Salem, the co-owner of EMG, was a close associate of former president Hosni Mubarak. The lack of transparency about the Israeli gas deal sparked widespread opposition in the Egyptian population. By late 2008 a Cairo court annulled the deal, but a subsequent ruling overturned that decision. By 2010, 40 percent of Israel's gas exports came from Egypt.[2]

When Mubarak stepped down on February 11, 2011, in response to the Arab Spring uprisings and the Supreme Council of the Armed Forces (SCAF) assumed control, the Egyptian-Israeli gas deal resurfaced as an issue of public concern in revolutionary Egypt. Essam Sharaf, then head of the Egyptian government, decided to revise the gas export contracts in April 2011. Shortly thereafter, the attorney general ordered the arrest of Sameh Fahmi and Hussein Salem for allegedly squandering $714 million in public funds for selling gas to Israel at an artificially low price.

In the same month, several individuals instigated the second gas pipeline explosion in North Sinai. Although the perpetrators remained unknown, their actions were very much in line with growing discontent over the gas deal. The former Court of Cassation vice president Mahmoud al-Khodeiri, who later headed the parliamentary legislative committee, even called on the unknown individuals to destroy the pipelines again if the Egyptian government did not halt the gas deal.

Pipeline explosions became a frequent headline in Egyptian media in the months that followed. The "masked individuals," as the media often identified them, exploded pipelines in North Sinai ten times in 2011 alone, despite the military's deployment of twenty-five hundred troops to deter such actions. While Hamas denied its involvement in the incidents, other potential suspects emerged. Following the seventh explosion, in November 2011, the Egyptian security forces arrested the leader and members of al-Takfir wal-Hijra (Excommunication and Immigration Group), claiming they were behind the attacks. After the tenth explosion, in late December 2011, security forces found a written statement at the explosion site that claimed another group, Ansar al-Jihad (Supporters of Jihad), was responsible, but security officials were unable to confirm the facts. More importantly, neither the reported arrests nor the military presence stopped the ongoing pipeline explosions in Sinai.

By 2012, the Egyptian media had transformed the explosions into a recurring image event. Like many activist groups who had used the media as a delivery system to create "mind bombs,"[3] the pipeline bombers drew widespread attention from the Egyptian population. The image of the flames lighting up the sky in Sinai widely circulated on online news websites, in newspapers, and on TV stations after each explosion. Together, the dominant media coverage and the recurrence of the attacks aroused even more public curiosity about the perpetrators.

Over time, the masked individuals associated with the bombings became a meme. Twitter and Facebook users shared sarcastic posts about both their identities and their evasion of authorities. Some called on the masked individuals to run for the Egyptian presidency, citing their ability to transform words into action. Others mocked the SCAF and the government for their inability to stop the perpetrators, suggesting they use Bluetooth to rid the nation of the pipelines. Caricaturists also utilized the masked individuals and joked about the ease with which they exploded the pipelines. In early 2012, leading Egyptian satirist and television show host Bassem Youssef, known as the Jon Stewart of the Arab World, undertook a nine-minute mock interview with a masked individual. Introducing the masked person as the winner of the national explosive award, Youssef showed a photoshopped image of the masked individual's son "Torch" in diapers and with a scarf covering his face. He also played a comic advertisement for a "Masked without Borders" organization, specializing in "exploding" youths' talents. After four more pipeline explosions in the first four months of 2012, the news about the Egyptian national gas company EGAS's decision to terminate the Israel gas deal in late April boosted the publicity of the unknown masked individuals even further. Two months later, an Egyptian court sentenced Sameh Fahmi and Hussein Salem to fifteen years in prison, sentenced several other Egyptian oil and gas officials to serve jail time of between three and ten years, and ordered all defendants to pay a fine of more

PHOTO 1. *Al-Masry Al-Youm* news website's reporting on the third gas pipeline explosion. Published July 4, 2011. Source: *Al-Masry Al-Youm*.

PHOTO 2. Bassem Youssef's interview with a masked individual on his satirical show *Albernameg*. Published on official YouTube page January 21, 2012. Source: *Albernameg*.

than four hundred million dollars. The Egyptian media helped create a public relations campaign for the masked individuals before they even revealed their identities.

At the peak of the publicity effort, the masked individuals finally revealed themselves. The Ansar Bayt al-Maqdis (Supporters of Jerusalem) group emerged in July 2012 with a thirty-minute video production claiming responsibility for the pipeline explosions and championing their role in revoking the natural gas deal. Almost half of the video featured exclusive shots of the masked, armed militants as they planned their operations, undertook surveillance at the attack sites, fixed the explosive devices to the pipelines, cheered and prostrated as the explosions lit up the sky, and drove away upon accomplishing their mission (see Photos 3–5). The video incorporated sound bites from al-Qaeda's leader, Ayman al-Zawahiri, praising the pipeline attackers; interviews with gas experts censuring the deal with Israel in mainstream media; and footage of Egyptian civilians revolting against Mubarak's regime and the SCAF. The Ansar Bayt al-Maqdis video framed the group's acts as a means to preserve Egypt's natural resources and fight the Egyptian military's corruption.

The Sinai pipeline explosions were critical for setting the stage for a new form of conflict between militants and the Egyptian state, with images as weapons. With its first video production, Ansar Bayt al-Maqdis began to bypass the mainstream media coverage and the framing of Sinai, militant attacks, and Islamist ideology. The group's media department allowed the militants to construct their own messages, reach out to their target audiences, and wage an online media campaign against the government and security forces. The Egyptian military soon responded by establishing its own online media hub. In October 2012, it created official pages for the Armed Forces Spokesman on Facebook and Twitter to disseminate military statements, photographic albums, and videos. Over the years, the direct photographic warfare over the Sinai Peninsula has intensified as Ansar Bayt al-Maqdis has morphed into a powerful, deadly

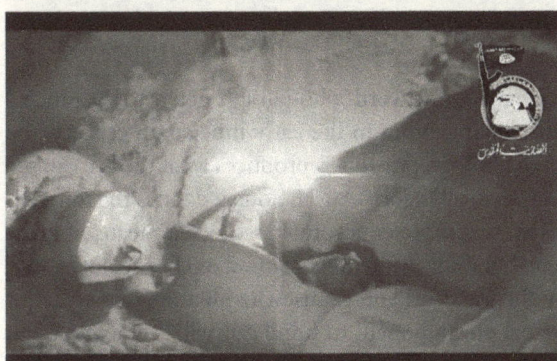

PHOTOS 3–5. Screengrabs from the "And If You Return, We Shall Return" video production by Ansar Bayt al-Maqdis, July 24, 2012. Source: Ansar Bayt al-Maqdis.

ISIS branch by the name Wilayat (Province) Sinai and the Egyptian military has ramped up its counterterrorism operations.

Photographic Warfare captures the peak of the visual conflict between Wilayat Sinai and the Egyptian military in 2016–17. This photographic war dictated the two competing lenses through which the Egyptian populace could see the bombings and fighting in the isolated northern part of Sinai, where the majority of the state's counterterrorism security operations have taken place. The Egyptian military's images constitute the official account on the Sinai conflict and dominate the media coverage in the country and abroad. Wilayat Sinai's visuals, on the other hand, challenge the government's narratives, justify the group's actions, and present an alternative picture of the peninsula. This book compares how the two opposing accounts constructed visual messages, interacted with one another, defined the Sinai conflict, and competed to shape the perceptions of the public. This book also creates a visual archive of the online media campaigns by Wilayat Sinai and the Egyptian military at a critical juncture, when ISIS-led violent attacks peaked on the peninsula.

Photographic Warfare: A Definition

Coming from the Greek language, the word "photograph" refers to the process of writing with light. Since its invention in the early nineteenth century, the camera has been the tool of photography that reproduces what the eye can see as light falls onto a subject. Critical theorist Susan Sontag defines the function of a photograph, broadened to a more conceptual level, as "a means of making 'real' (or 'more real') matters" that individuals cannot or choose not to see.[4]

War, which military theorist Carl von Clausewitz identifies as "an act of violence intended to compel our opponent to fulfill our will,"[5] emerges as an important matter for photography to depict. The battle between ISIS and the Egyptian military in Sinai represents one in a long line of historical conflicts captured in visual form. A few decades after Nicéphore Niépce's innovative photographic experiments in France, the 1846–48 Mexican-American War became the first military conflict to be captured on camera. The British Crimean War and the U.S. Civil War of the nineteenth century subsequently established photography's significance as a key component of war efforts by nation-states. Twentieth-century conflicts further reinforced the importance of visual artifacts in wartime. After all, photography's ability to capture the atrocities of war, arouse emotions, create outrage, carry ideological messages, retain meaning, and serve as affective projectiles renders it an appealing instrument of states' media operations in times of conflict.[6]

Over time, participants in warfare photography have expanded beyond the state and its counterparts to include individuals, militant groups, the media, corporations, organizations, and other non-state entities. Low-cost digital photography on twenty-first-century battlefields has also allowed non-state actors to increase their ability to compete over the perceived realities of war. This book thus defines photographic warfare as the strategic development of visual *content* and *form* by two or more opponents in a conflict. The various participants either through intention or happenstance influence viewers' perceptions of what is real in the conflict in ways that serve the communicators' goals.

Building an Approach to Understanding Photographic Warfare

The full meaning of wartime photography is uninterpretable without consideration of the situational context of the related conflicts. Some argue that the situation itself determines discourse, given that context supposedly has the power to shape communications,[7] while others suggest that "rhetoric is a *cause* not an *effect* of meaning."[8] *Photographic Warfare* rejects the extreme views of both camps, choosing instead to build on conceptions of context and communication as interactive.[9] Such a view serves as an interpretive lens for competing photographic campaigns in times of military conflict.

Moreover, framing is key to understanding how communicators, such as the opposing sides in a wartime conflict, develop content. Erving Goffman's sociological school of framing accounts for linkages between people's construction of meaning and various communicators' selection of and emphasis on particular aspects of an issue. This approach generates context-specific frames.[10] Robert Entman adds to Goffman's perspective by defining framing as a process of selection and emphasis. He also introduces a communication framework that can assess interactions within frames through four associations: problem definition, causal interpretation, moral evaluation, and treatment recommendation.[11] *Photographic Warfare* works from Goffman's sociological understanding of framing and expands on Entman's framework to demonstrate how the various interactions between opposing frames can influence emphasis and selection.

Photographic Warfare also utilizes social semiotics to further expound on the form and symbolic meanings of communicative texts. Building on the Saussurean conception of semiotics as the study and understanding of signs in society, linguistic theorist Michael Halliday develops a systemic functional grammar that identifies three metafunctions of language: interpersonal, ideational, and textual.[12] Examining visuals as another semiotic mode, Roland Barthes identifies some structural components of the image (e.g., distance, focus, framing, etc.) but calls for an inventory of those techniques to facilitate their incorporation in a "cultural lexicon of technical 'effects.'"[13] In *Reading Images*, Gunther Kress and Theo van Leeuwen expand on Halliday and Barthes's work by proposing a grammar of visual design applicable to Western culture.[14] Theories of subjectivity and proxemics further complement visual grammar with insights on the construction and composition of visuals from an American/Western standpoint.[15] Exploring the assumptions of such Western-based models of visual grammar in a non-Western context, this book brings dimensions from Geert Hofstede and Edward Hall's cultural frameworks into the interpretation of semiotic differences.

Dissecting the Pillars of Photographic Warfare

Photographic Warfare dissects the context, content, and form of visual conflict. First, it offers a nuanced look at the military situational factor to understand which elements interact with photographic campaigns. Most existing scholarship narrowly focuses on how attacking or being attacked influences media response. In times of war, states have typically complemented their military operations with a large pool of photographs. But militant groups have not conformed to a set media response during military confrontations.[16] Take ISIS, for example, which reduced its overall photographic output when facing immense military pressure; yet some of its key provincial media offices increased their productivity and reliance on the "about-to-die" visual trope.[17] The same group disseminated photographs on Twitter in the aftermath of major attacks like the 2015 Paris bombings. This book accounts for shifting image frequencies and visual tropes but also traces the use of additional elements in the photographs and, more importantly, adopts a broader view of context. It systematically examines other factors in the situational military context, such as loss of leaders and introductions of new groups into the battlefield. Recognizing the intercontinental presence of contemporary militant groups in several countries, this book also treats both states and non-state actors not as isolated entities but as parts of broader regional or international collectives. *Photographic Warfare* thus reveals the impact of local and regional military conditions on Wilayat Sinai's and the Egyptian military's photographic campaigns.

Second, this book investigates the dynamics of contested visual content between states and non-state militant actors. Although many scholars compare the visual framing of conflicts across media outlets,[18] the literature on state and non-state actors' media usage tends to be one-sided. Such work showcases the thematic evolution in states' visual campaigns over time,[19] while more recent work identifies prominent visual frames and icons in militant groups' online campaigns.[20] The exclusive focus on one side's media practices, however, ignores other communicators altogether and assumes no interactions exist between their contents. This may well result in misunderstanding and even misjudging the entire visual conflict. Although few researchers have addressed this shortcoming by investigating competing visual campaigns in the Palestinian-Israeli conflict, the Arab Spring uprisings, and the Syrian civil war,[21] they have examined the broader work of protesters and artistic spectators of conflict in the visual sphere, including in open spaces, popular culture, and state-controlled/influenced media. What yet remains missing is an in-depth analysis of the online visual field constructed by both the state and the militant group's media content. Building on the nascent body of literature that compares online visual framing on both sides of a conflict,[22] this book takes a step further by exploring the ensuing conversation between the opponents' photographs. *Photographic Warfare* thus recognizes the broader communicative context and identifies how the frames of ISIS and the Egyptian military define the conflict by means of contestation and interaction.

Third, this book raises cross-cultural considerations about form in visual campaigns. Assumptions about motives and impacts of semiotic techniques, such as viewer distance, camera angle, eye contact, facial expression, and subjective shots, are mostly derived from Western respondents and samples.[23] Do those assumptions apply to Arabic culture? Some scholars analyze the semiotic elements in mainstream Arab media and in ISIS campaigns but tend to refer to the same standards of Western semiotics. Such approaches can overlook unique semiotic applications that are culture-specific. A distinction as simple as writing from right to left in Arabic and from left to right in Latin languages can yield cross-cultural differences in assigning meaning to images. Realizing the important role of culture in photographic warfare, this book identifies non-Western visual semiotic tropes in an Egyptian context by emphasizing how Wilayat Sinai and the Egyptian state's photographic campaigns align with and differ from the standards of Western frameworks.

Bringing all three pillars together, *Photographic Warfare* proposes an interactive model that recognizes visual contestation as a communicative phenomenon in the online environment. This analytic framework reveals different aspects of the situational context that can interact with the level of photographic quantity and the nature of visual messaging strategies that states and non-state actors utilize. It demonstrates how visual frames interact within and across opposing photographic camps. It also pinpoints how visual semiotic elements can constitute culture- and campaign-specific constellations that intersect with the visual choices of the opposition. The analytic framework of visual contestation guides systematic analyses of visual conflicts between states and militant groups. The model's applications can thus transcend the immediate context in Egypt to a wide range of media contestations with ISIS, al-Qaeda, and/or other right-wing and far-left violent extremist groups across the world. Figure 1 offers an overview of the model.

The book chapters serve as in-depth analyses of the three pillars of photographic warfare: context, content, and form. Focusing on the Sinai conflict, they investigate the ensuing media interactions between ISIS and the Egyptian military across all three domains. The chapters lay the groundwork for a concluding discussion of the analytic framework and its implications for understanding digital contestations between states and non-state militant actors in

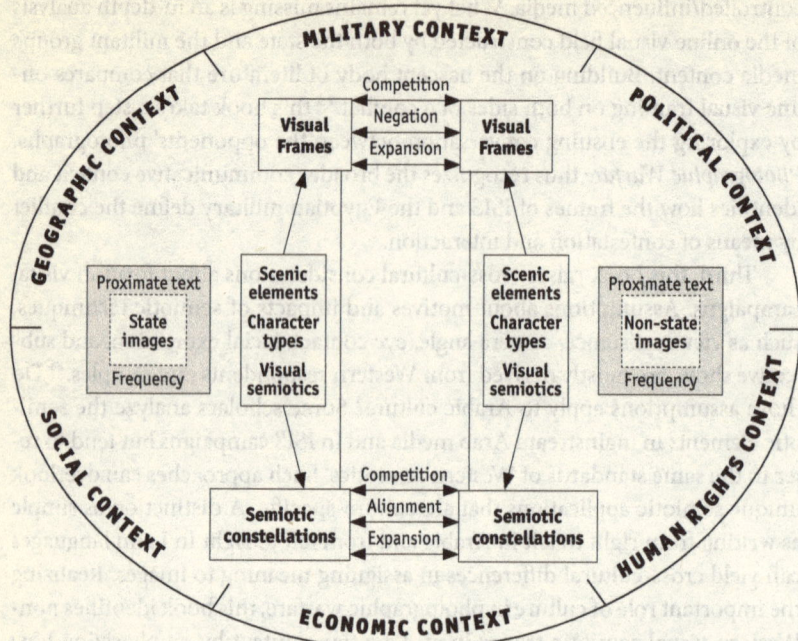

FIGURE 1. The analytic framework of visual contestation by state and non-state actors.

twenty-first century warfare. In essence, *Photographic Warfare* presents a comprehensive approach to the understanding and dissection of visual conflicts from various angles.

Case Study: The Online Battle for Sinai

The decision to focus on the photographic warfare between Egypt and ISIS in the Sinai Peninsula resulted from multiple considerations. Most importantly, the visual contestation at play between those two competing sides meets the definition of photographic warfare. The Egyptian military and Wilayat Sinai have engaged in a prolonged battle for several years. To complement their war efforts, each side has been prolific in its strategic visual communication campaign online, selecting and emphasizing certain aspects of the conflict and its participants as well as incorporating compositional elements with symbolic meanings. But three other factors further drive this book's emphasis on visuals in Sinai: militant Islamist groups' overdependence on visual media, Sinai's strategic importance as a major determinant of stability in the Middle East, and the Egyptian state's media censorship in response to the Sinai insurgency.

ISIS's Visual Campaign

Visuals dominate the contemporary media landscape, serving as important catalysts of presence in today's networked society. Worldwide photographers take over one trillion digital images each year, with the vast majority using smartphone cameras. The twenty-first century signals a pictorial turn that privileges sight as the leading sense, turns viewers into picture-minded people, transforms the real world into images well-trained spectators can perceive, and hails imagery as the recurrent mode of activist engagement.[24] The historic adage "seeing is believing" further captures the perspective that viewing something brings some proximity to the truth.[25] Hence, online communicators engaging and interacting with the public often utilize images as a significant communication tool.

Islamist militant groups have increasingly used visuals as a key element in their media campaigns in order to document their battles, spread fear among enemies, and engage supporters. As early as the 1980s, Afghan Mujahideen leader Abdullah Azzam incorporated photography in his publications. The Mujahideen also used video cameras to document some of their military operations. In the 1990s, prominent Chechen rebel leader Commander Khattab described visuals as a means to multiply the impact of killing Russian soldiers by showcasing operations and spreading fear among Russian civilians. Chechen rebels further introduced ultraviolence as a salient feature in their videos, transforming beheadings and executions of Russian soldiers into media spectacles. In the 2000s, al-Qaeda leader Abdelaziz al-Muqrin expressed his regrets at not recording the 2000 attack on the U.S.S. *Cole* and called on the group's followers to document their operations.[26] Ever since, al-Qaeda and its successors have used their own cameras, operators, and editors to inoculate their followers against opposing media.

Recognizing the existence of such a global context, ISIS has utilized photography as a dominant mode of presentation, and imagery has played an integral role in the group's media campaigns and in targeting audiences. ISIS also embedded its photographs in its Arabic newsletter *al-Naba'*, its English-language magazine *Dabiq*, its French-language magazine *Dar al-Islam*, its Russian-language magazine *Istok*, its Turkish-language magazine *Konstantiniyye*, and its multilingual magazine *Rumiyah*.

Taking advantage of advanced communication technologies and accessible social media platforms, the group also introduced new ways of packaging its photographs into daily provincial news briefs and photo reports. Between October 2014 and October 2015, for example, ISIS disseminated nearly fifteen thousand images and over seventeen hundred photo reports.[27] It also disseminated around fifty-two thousand images between January 2015 and August

2016 on Twitter, while its supporters published another fifty thousand images on pro-ISIS Telegram channels in the second half of 2017.[28] Despite the sharp decline in ISIS's media products after its major territorial defeats, photography has endured as the group's favored medium.[29] Such a refined and rigorous photographic campaign is the outcome of years of development in militant groups' media operations and adoption of communication technologies.

Ample evidence points to the role of visuals as potential catalysts for violent action. Following the Manhattan truck attack that killed eight civilians in October 2017, for example, the U.S. federal criminal complaint revealed the ISIS-inspired driver had thirty-eight hundred images and ninety videos featuring ISIS productions on his cell phone.[30] Another complaint revealed that an ISIS-inspired man who detonated an explosive device in a New York subway tunnel in December 2017 acted on an ISIS video calling for attacks in the West.[31] These recent incidents are not anomalies. Half of the individuals prosecuted for terrorism-related offenses in the United States between 2001 and 2011 had visual media products of some kind in their possession at the time of arrest.[32] Similarly, the British law enforcement agencies recovered almost three hundred fifty videos produced by al-Qaeda, ISIS, and other groups on the digital devices of forty-eight convicted terrorists between 2004 and 2017.[33] Furthermore, law enforcement agents connected the thirty-three images displayed in al-Qaeda's *Inspire* article "Make a Bomb in the Kitchen of Your Mom" with several attacks, including the Boston Marathon bombings in 2013.[34]

Sinai as a Launchpad for Militant Groups

Sinai's religious weight, contemporary political significance, and geographic location render it a distinctive location for ISIS's military and media operations. First, Sinai's religious significance spans the three Abrahamic faiths: Judaism, Christianity, and Islam. In the Hebrew Bible, Sinai is one of the most sacred places on earth and the site of the revelation of the covenant to Moses. Jesus, Mary, and Joseph passed through Sinai on their journey to Egypt, a vital event in the establishment of Christianity. In Islam, the Qur'an explicitly mentions Sinai by name twice and Mount Sinai ten times by the name al-Tor. During the leadership of the second Caliph Umar ibn al-Khattab (634–44 CE), Sinai was also the gateway for the Arab conquests in Egypt and North Africa. Islamist militant groups have built on Sinai's religious significance in Islam to strengthen rhetorical and ideological appeals associated with the defeat of neighboring Israel and the liberation of Palestine.

Second, Sinai's contemporary political significance arises from its history as a site of contention and collaboration in the Arab-Israeli conflict. Sinai was the battlefield in the prolonged conflict between Egypt and Israel that culminated with the 1973 war, leading to the full liberation of Sinai from Israeli forces in 1982. Nonetheless, the Camp David Treaty between Egypt and Israel restrained the Egyptian military presence in Sinai, allowing only civil police and UN forces in Zone C, or eastern Sinai, along the border. This military annex has also played a role in weakening the Egyptian state presence in Sinai over the years. Only recently has Israel allowed the deployment of Egyptian military forces in Zone C to assist in fighting the Sinai insurgency. Furthermore, Israel has reportedly conducted drone strikes against militants in Sinai since 2013.[35] The shifting relationship between Egypt and Israel in relation to Sinai has created political tensions and serves as a primary justification for violent militant action against Egyptian security forces.

In addition, Sinai's unique location as an intercontinental bridge to Asia and the Levant has provoked local insurgent groups to repeatedly attack their enemies. Israel has indeed been a target of the Sinai insurgency for over a decade. When the Sinai-based Jama'at al-Tawhid wal-Jihad (Monotheism and Jihad Group) carried out three bombings on South Sinai resorts in October 2004, it mainly targeted Israeli tourists, killing over twenty.[36] The Sinai-based Ansar Bayt al-Maqdis not only bombed the pipelines carrying gas to Israel but also claimed responsibility for several cross-border rocket attacks on Eilat between 2012 and 2014. Sinai's border with Gaza and Israel renders it a hotspot for militant insurgency with regional aspirations.

Thus, Sinai has been of special importance to ISIS's ideology and military goals since the group decided to expand beyond Iraq and the Levant in 2014. ISIS has claimed its status as an Islamic caliphate, fighting off "crusaders" represented by the U.S.-led coalition and its collaborators. Sinai also gives ISIS a strategic foothold closer to Israel and boosts its anti-Jewish rhetoric. In its official pledge of allegiance to ISIS in November 2014, Ansar Bayt al-Maqdis vowed to keep fighting the Jews, describing them as Islam's biggest enemy. Four days after that pledge, Abu Bakr al-Baghdadi, in his first official audio speech as a self-declared caliph, mentioned the word "Jews" twelve times and accepted the group's transformation into the Wilayat Sinai (ISIS's Sinai Province) in a bid to fight the Egyptian security forces, support Jerusalem, and terrorize Jews. Over a year later, ISIS released another audio speech in which al-Baghdadi mentioned the word "Jews" eleven times and explicitly threatened Israel. The ISIS leader proclaimed: "We haven't forgotten Palestine for a second, and we will not forget it. . . . We are getting closer to you day after day and you'll be harshly punished. You'll never feel blissful in Palestine, oh you Jews. It will never be your land or home. And Palestine will not be but a grave for you."[37]

Operating under the ISIS banner, Wilayat Sinai claimed to have targeted the al-Ouga border crossing with Israel, the Eshkul Israeli settlement, and the Egyptian military forces stationed closer to the border with Israel multiple times. Egyptian security forces, however, were ISIS's primary target in most of the seven hundred attacks in Sinai between November 2014 and March 2017.[38] By way of justification, Wilayat Sinai has highlighted Egypt's collaboration with the Israeli military, the aftermath of airstrikes on the civilian population in Sinai, and the status of Egyptian security forces as apostates. In 2016 and 2017, the group also claimed that Israeli planes and helicopters launched airstrikes in North Sinai over a dozen times. Subsequently, Wilayat Sinai stepped up its intelligence operations in the peninsula, as evidenced by the killing of the Egyptian military commander of Bir al-Abd city and the assassination attempt against the ministers of defense and the interior in their secret visit to Arish in December 2017.

Sinai has also received much attention in ISIS's media operations. In May 2016, ISIS launched a coordinated visual campaign in which fourteen Iraqi, Syrian, and Libyan provinces released videos to praise Wilayat Sinai militants. The videos highlighted the Egyptian-Israeli military collaboration and reiterated Sinai's importance as the gateway to Jerusalem liberation. Wilayat Sinai has also served as one of the most productive provinces beyond Iraq and Syria in terms of media products in the past few years. As ISIS suffered territorial losses, Wilayat Sinai's media products were relatively more prevalent than those coming from other provinces. Following President Trump's recognition of Jerusalem as the capital of Israel, ISIS chose Wilayat Sinai's video release "The Religion of Abraham" as the main platform for its first media response, condemning Hamas, the Palestinian authority, and Egypt for their acquiescence.

Taken together, Sinai offers ISIS a rich environment from which to attack the strongest Arab military, threaten Israel, and bolster its own ideological resonance. By tapping into the Crusades and the 1948 Nakba (Catastrophe) master narratives in Islamist thought,[39] ISIS uses Sinai to foreground Israel as a target and the liberation of the third holiest Muslim site (Jerusalem) as a goal. With the announcements of Syria and Iraq's liberation in late 2017, U.S. military leaders have further discussed publicly ISIS's aspirations to establish a larger presence in Sinai and Libya as the next phase. A few months before the declarations, however, about 80 percent of Wilayat Sinai militants were foreigners, according to the spokesman of al-Tarabin tribe that fights alongside the Egyptian military in North Sinai.[40] With smuggling networks connecting Sinai to Libya, Sudan, and Gaza, Wilayat Sinai boasts a pipeline of foreign fighters. Further, the escalating tensions surrounding the status of Jerusalem after its U.S. recognition as Israel's capital adds to Sinai's relevance as a new front line for foreign ISIS fighters. Thus, focusing on the visual campaign of Wilayat Sinai as a key ISIS province is imperative to understanding how the group has adapted to major territorial losses in Iraq and Syria.

Government-Imposed Media Blackout

In response to ISIS's military and media operations in Sinai, Egypt has broadened its censorship methods to control the information coming out of the peninsula. Egypt imposed a media blackout on North Sinai, where the clear majority of the state's counterterrorism security operations have occurred. Since the end of 2013, news reporting from North Sinai has become a risky endeavor for Egyptian and foreign journalists alike. Security forces assaulted some reporters, arrested others, and even accused a few of acting as agents of terrorism.[41] To bolster the country's grip on the information flow during the war on the Sinai insurgency, in August 2015 Egyptian president Abdelfattah al-Sisi approved an antiterrorism law that punishes journalists for false news on terrorist attacks and counterterrorism operations. The law imposes a fine of between two hundred and five hundred thousand Egyptian pounds (equivalent to $12,000–30,000) and can bar the offending journalist from practicing the profession for up to one year. The law defines false news as "contradicting the official statements released by the Ministry of Defense."[42]

With the passage of the new law governing media operations, the Egyptian military's reporting on Sinai has become indisputable, with the result that the media's independent reporting on such operations has sharply decreased. Journalists have become largely unable to verify the number of counterterrorism operations, militant groups' attacks, and deaths as well as the scale of military activity. Instead, Egypt-based media outlets rely upon the military's information and figures as officially presented. The only exceptions to the Egyptian military's frames are a few media outlets operating in Turkey and Qatar, such as *al-Sharq*, *Mikamilin*, and Al Jazeera Arabic. The result of the reconstituted media context is that the Egyptian military spokesman's Facebook page has become the main source of news on the Sinai conflict, as it regularly disseminates statements, images, and videos to over seven million followers.

Nonetheless, Egypt's censorship methods have not hindered accessibility to Wilayat Sinai's online media products. Wilayat Sinai continues to disseminate its visuals on ISIS's official Telegram channels and encrypted apps, which then recirculate in pro-ISIS channels and on other social media platforms. In fact, Egypt ranked third among Arab countries for accessing ISIS online content at one point, after only Saudi Arabia and Iraq.[43]

Thus, the Egyptian government has emerged as an actively engaged participant in a media war against ISIS. The state consistently vows to eradicate what it describes as the enemies of the nation and religion in Sinai. ISIS, on the other hand, produces ample media products celebrating attacks against Egyptian soldiers, whom it also deems apostates and enemies of the religion. In other contexts, such advocacy campaigns can mobilize for consensus through various means. But during wartime, putting out an abundance of contradictory information war can further magnify both sides' opposing narratives and thus result in a much more dangerous conflict, as evidenced by the "Syrian data glut."[44] Examining the Sinai photographic warfare between ISIS and the Egyptian state yields understandings of how opposing visual messages compete in a polarized digital media environment. It also highlights visual strategies and techniques that can guide the government, NGOs, grassroots initiatives, and communication respondents in future efforts to develop alternative frames and narratives.

Examining the Sinai Photographic Warfare

This book analyzes all Sinai-related images that ISIS and the Egyptian military disseminated online during the peak of the insurgency in 2016 and 2017. This two-year period corresponds to a 175 percent surge in Wilayat Sinai's claimed attacks in 2016, the extension of the Martyr's Right Egyptian military operation in Sinai into three stages in 2016 and 2017, extensive military pressure on ISIS in its heartlands that led to vast territorial losses in Iraq and Syria by the end of 2017, the apparent deterioration in Wilayat Sinai's military capabilities afterward, and the depletion of its photographic output by over 70 percent in 2018–20 (see Figure 2). The ISIS data set comprises all photographs that Wilayat Sinai disseminated on ISIS's official Telegram channel Nashir, which has served as the main hub for dissemination and the most reliable means for collecting ISIS's official media products since late 2015, upon the intensive crackdown on the group's activity on Twitter. The Egyptian military data set comprises over a thousand photographs that the Egyptian military spokesman disseminated on his official Facebook account. This page is the main hub for the military's official news on Sinai and the most reliable means for collecting all of the Egyptian military's photographs; the associated official Twitter account and website post only a fraction of the photographs.

Photographic Warfare applies three main approaches to analyze Wilayat Sinai and the Egyptian military's competing campaigns. First, this book traces the changes in the two photographic campaigns that correspond to contextual military conditions on the ground locally (in Sinai) and regionally (in Iraq and Syria). Second, it uses a qualitative, bottom-up, grounded theory approach to generate context-specific visual frames in the opposing photographs, understand how the individual frames on one side interact together to constitute an overarching message, and examine how the frames from the two sides interact to define the Sinai conflict. Third, it employs a content analysis to compare the visual semiotic elements in the state and the militant group's campaigns and identify how the constituted semiotic constellations interact between

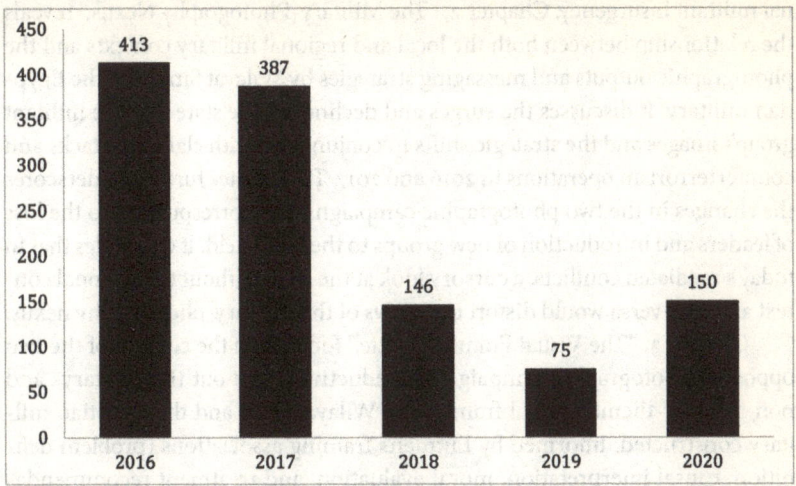

FIGURE 2. The number of photographs posted by Wilayat Sinai on the Nashir Telegram channel from January 1, 2016, to December 31, 2020.

both sides (for the coding sheet and details on intercoder reliability, see the appendix).

A close reading of select visuals further complements the analysis of Sinai photographic warfare. Given the large number of images involved in the two competing campaigns and the underlying goal of dissecting how they visually contest one another, a close reading analysis of every photograph is beyond the scope of this book. The value of this approach as a method for interpreting iconicity and viewer engagement, however, renders it a critical tool to pinpoint key exemplars, enrich the photographic analysis, and highlight how states and militant groups align with and differ from standard visual practices.

Plan of the Book

This book emphasizes the situational context in the first two chapters. Chapter 1, "Contextualizing the Sinai Conflict," underlines the shifting political, economic, social, and human rights conditions in the Sinai Peninsula since the 1967 Israeli occupation. The chapter traces the origin of violence in Sinai to three waves of attacks, in 2004, 2005, and 2006. To elaborate on the model's contextual factors, chapter 1 discusses the role of the security repercussions in the early 2000s, political developments amid the 2011 revolution, former president Mohamed Morsi's ousting in 2013, and the government's crackdown on Muslim Brotherhood supporters amid the emergence and growth of the Sinai militant insurgency. Chapter 2, "The Military-Photography Nexus," reveals the relationship between both the local and regional military contexts and the photographic outputs and messaging strategies by Wilayat Sinai and the Egyptian military. It discusses the surges and declines in the state and the militant group's images and the strategic shifts in conjunction with claimed attacks and counterterrorism operations in 2016 and 2017. The chapter further underscores the changes in the two photographic campaigns that corresponded to the loss of leaders and introduction of new groups to the battlefield. It concludes that in today's mediated conflicts, a cursory look at the local without the regional context and vice versa would distort our views of the military-photography nexus.

Chapter 3, "The Visual Framing Battle," focuses on the content of the two opposing photographic campaigns. It inductively lays out the military- and non-military-themed visual frames that Wilayat Sinai and the Egyptian military constructed. Informed by Entman's framing associations (problem definition, causal interpretation, moral evaluation, and treatment recommendation), the chapter examines how the frames on each side cohered around a unique, broader message. The chapter then further identifies competition, negation, and expansion as three emerging interactive strategies through which the opposing visual frames contested each other in the online environment. It concludes that understanding the media battlefield requires an examination of contested visual frames and the interactions that exist between states and non-state actors.

Chapter 4, "The Visual Semiotic Battle," examines the form of the images in the Sinai visual conflict. It analyzes Wilayat Sinai's and the Egyptian military's use of viewer distance, camera angle, direct eye contact, facial expressions, and subjective shots in the portrayals of different character types. By juxtaposing these applications in the Egyptian context with the assumptions about Western standards of visual grammar, the chapter exposes different ways by which semiotic tools can function in non-Western contexts. The chapter also presents competition, alignment, and expansion as interactive strategies that the state and non-state actors adopted at the level of semiotic constellations. It concludes that visual semiotic battles can exacerbate localized clashes of ideology.

Chapter 5, "An Analytic Framework of Visual Contestation," discusses a comprehensive approach to understanding photographic warfare as a communicative event in the online sphere. Based on the research process examining the media campaign experiences of Wilayat Sinai and the Egyptian military, the model emphasizes that images of non-state militant actors do not exist in a vacuum, situates the visual contestation itself as part of the overall context, and highlights the visual characteristics defining the opposing campaigns. The situational context (military, political, geographic, economic, human rights, and social factors), the immediate context (proximate text and frequency), and image components (scenic elements, character types, and visual semiotics) constitute the model's key variables. The chapter further demonstrates that the interactions between competing campaigns take place at the levels of visual frames and semiotic constellations. It concludes by highlighting the implications of the model for understanding visual contestations in the digital sphere.

CHAPTER 1

Contextualizing the Sinai Conflict

Sinai has a very rich, unique cultural context that warrants a close investigation. But existing cultural frameworks treat the Arab world, and at times the entire Middle East, as a homogenous regional collective. Geert Hofstede's cultural dimensions, for example, present Egypt, Lebanon, Libya, Kuwait, Iraq, Saudi Arabia, and UAE as part of a single culture that is collectivist, masculine, and hierarchical, in contrast to Nordic countries.[1] Similarly, Edward Hall broadly typifies Arab culture as high-context and polychronic, compared to low-context, monochronic nations like the United States.[2] Such taxonomies misconstrue the Arab cultural context by blurring the line between Gulf, Levantine, and North African subcultures, as one example. Even more recent and focused characterizations of Egypt as a national culture steeped in a short-term orientation and significant restraints overlook the distinct history, traits, social fabrics, and experiences of select nomadic communities whose life differs from the majority of the Egyptian population living in the Nile Delta and alongside the riverbanks.[3] This chapter applies a contextual analysis of the geographic, social, economic, political, human rights, and military factors in Sinai as a first step to better understand the conflict and the ensuing photographic warfare between Egypt and ISIS.

The present-day conflict between the Egyptian military and Wilayat Sinai lies against a backdrop of unstable relations between Bedouins and the changing Sinai rulers since the late 1960s. After a brief geographic, demographic, and etymological introduction of Sinai, this chapter highlights the strategic divisions between North and South Sinai in relation to social alienation, waning economies, and the presence of illegal industries since the Israeli occupation. Then, it traces the origins of the Sinai insurgency, identifying three waves of attacks in South Sinai, the subsequent security crackdown, and the human rights violations in the early twenty-first century. It also identifies the role of political turmoil in the aftermath of the Arab Spring uprisings in the evolution of the Sinai insurgency and the intensification of conflict, including the ouster of former president Mohamed Morsi in 2013 and the government crackdown on Muslim Brotherhood supporters.

Sinai: An Overview

Sinai is an Egyptian peninsula that connects Africa and Asia. Some historians link the name Sinai to Sin, the god of the moon in Sumerian civilization, others with the Arabic word *Sen* (tooth) in reference to the shape of its mountains. However, historians do agree about its geographical boundaries. Despite being part of Egypt, the Sinai Peninsula is technically in West Asia, lying alongside the Red Sea and the Suez Canal, which mark the northeastern border of the African continent. A 1906 British-Ottoman agreement created the border that demarcates Sinai from Palestine and the Levant. Sinai's sixty-one thousand square kilometers constitute over 6 percent of Egypt's total area and about 30 percent of the country's coastlines. Sinai spreads from the Mediterranean Sea in the north to Ras Mohamed in the south, as well as from the Gulf of Aqaba, Israel, and Gaza in the east to the Gulf of Suez and the Suez Canal in the west.

MAP 1. Map of the Sinai Peninsula. Source: Library of Congress / Central Intelligence Agency, 1988.

The governmental divisions of the Sinai Peninsula have changed over the years. In 1960, the Egyptian government established a local civilian administration in each of the border governorates, except for in Sinai, which remained under military rule. When Israel occupied Sinai after the 1967 war, it divided the peninsula into two units governed by the military: North Sinai, with its headquarters in al-Arish, and South Sinai, based in Sharm El Sheikh. In the wake of the 1973 Egyptian-Israeli War, however, former Egyptian president Anwar Sadat declared Sinai a single governorate, with al-Arish as its capital, and appointed its first civilian governor in 1974. Five years later, Sadat issued a decree breaking the peninsula into two distinct administrative units, with capitals at al-Arish for the North and al-Tor for the South. The 1979 decree also attached the small parts of Sinai west of the Suez Canal to the Suez, Ismailiya, and Port Said governorates. Ever since, Sinai has spanned the five different governorates, with the vast majority of the peninsula falling in the North Sinai and South Sinai governorates.

The area is home to a heterogeneous mix of people, including a wide range of Bedouin tribes, Egyptians from the Nile Valley, Palestinians who moved to Sinai after 1948, and Bosnians. Egypt's official figures indicate a total population of almost half a million people in North Sinai and over a hundred thousand in South Sinai.[4]

Bedouins, in particular, constitute the most distinctive collective in the Sinai social demographic. The word "Bedouin" is derived from the Arabic word *Badu*, which refers to nomadic people of the desert who originated in the Arabian Peninsula and the Levant. Many Bedouin tribes moved to and settled in the northern and southern parts of the peninsula over the centuries. The population figures, however, do not truly reflect the number of the Bedouins, as thousands hold identification papers but do not enjoy full citizenship rights.[5] Despite the lack of definitive figures, contemporary estimates range from 200,000 to 380,000,[6] up from a population of 40,000 Sinai Bedouins in 1906.[7] For most Bedouins, tribal loyalties, land rights, and communal agreements take precedence over national identity and state borders. Today, the Sinai Bedouins' culture and Arabic dialects remain closer to those of their brethren in the Arabian Peninsula and the Levant than to those of Egyptians of the Nile Valley.

Nonetheless, Sinai Bedouins are not a single homogenous group. Tribal agreements indicate that at least fifteen major Bedouin tribes constitute a collection of peoples who share Sinai. Al-Sawarka and al-Rumaylat compose two key tribes that settled in al-Arish, Sheikh Zuwayid, and Rafah in the North. Al-Sawarka is one of the strongest and most populous tribes in Sinai, with at least seventy thousand members and up to thirteen different clans. Another powerful Bedouin tribe is al-Tarabin, which mainly spans across North Sinai, Nuwaiba in South Sinai, Palestine, and the Negev desert in South Israel. The

Al-Masa'id, al-Dawaghra, and al-Bayyadiyya tribes settled in the West.[8] The Al-Tayaha, al-Ahywat, and al-Azazma tribes reside in Central Sinai, with al-Azazma extending to lands in Palestine and Jordan. In the South, al-Towara, named for al-Tor mountain, is a confederation of several tribes, including al-Alayqat, Muzayna, Awlad Sa'id, al-Sawalha, and al-Jibaliyya. Although the al-Jibaliyya tribe has its origins in the Bosnian and Wallachian slaves whom the Roman emperor sent to Sinai in the sixth century, it has now become a part of South Sinai's Bedouin tribes and a member of the al-Towara confederation.[9] The South Sinai tribes mostly live in the Sharm Sheikh and Dahab regions as well as in the inner mountains.

Understanding the Origins of the Sinai Conflict

The lands of Sinai serve as an important site of contestation in the current conflict between Egyptian security forces and Sinai insurgents due to both economic and national security considerations. Economically, the Sinai Peninsula is vital to Egypt because it borders the Suez Canal, a key source of the country's income since former president Nasser nationalized it in 1956. With tourism serving as another key pillar of Egypt's economy, the Red Sea resorts in South Sinai generate a crucial part of tourism revenue. In 2018, the Egyptian and Saudi governments announced a total of one thousand square kilometers in South Sinai would become part of the transnational, megacity project NEOM. Militarily, Sinai is key to Egypt's national security as it has always been the gateway for Egyptian rulers expanding eastward or for outside forces marching to North Africa over the centuries. In the past seventy-five years, Israel has fought four wars against Egypt in Sinai, in 1948, 1956, 1967, and 1973.

The Occupation Period, 1967–1982

On June 5, 1967, Israel attacked Egypt, destroying almost the entire Egyptian Air Force as it sat on the tarmac. Subsequently, Israeli ground forces marched to Sinai and battled the Egyptian military in both the northern and southern parts of the peninsula. Sinai Bedouins provided Egyptian officers and soldiers with food, water, and aid. They also created volunteer rescue groups to treat and transport the injured. After Israel defeated the Egyptian military, Bedouins hid officers and soldiers from the Israeli forces in al-Arish homes, gave them fake North Sinai identification cards, and worked with Egyptian military intelligence to establish an evacuation center in Beer al-Abd.[10] The war resulted in an Israeli occupation of the entire Sinai Peninsula that humiliated and terrorized many Sinai Bedouins, expelling about half of the prewar population westward to the Nile Valley.

The Israeli occupation between 1967 and 1982 had a differential impact on the North and the South, with the North suffering the most. Israel saw the building of settlements in the North as an opportunity to create a Jewish buffer zone between Sinai and Gaza that would divide the region and disrupt the flow of weapons. To build such settlements, the Israeli army expelled thousands of Bedouins from their tents and lands. On January 14, 1972, for example, then–military commander Ariel Sharon ordered "the destruction of the orchards, the blocking up of the water wells and the deportation of the villagers" to build the Yamit settlement on the Mediterranean and surrounding agricultural settlements in the Rafah area.[11] Later, Israeli forces admitted to expelling nine tribes and almost five thousand Bedouins in that single incident, while tribal leaders put the number closer to twenty thousand.[12]

By contrast, the Israeli occupation came with some benefits for the Bedouins of South Sinai. Prior to the 1967 war, Bedouins in the South were living in poverty and isolation in sparsely populated areas under Egyptian military rule. Under Israeli governance, leaders spent billions of dollars to build roads connecting South Sinai with the coast of Eilat, establish civilian ministries, introduce water, telephone, and electrical utilities, and transform the region into a source of wage labor for thousands of Bedouins. The Israeli Ministry of Defense also employed about twelve hundred Bedouin men in the oil, construction, and tourism sectors in the South, with job openings outnumbering Bedouin men in Abu Rodeis by 1972.[13] In addition, the Ministry of Labor provided vocational courses, the Ministry of Education worked with Bedouins to build schools, and the Ministry of Health established clinics.

The main economic development in the South, however, was in tourism. Israel built the Ophira resort town and its airport as well as the Di Zahav and Neviot settlements, which opened new employment opportunities for Bedouins. In sum, the Israeli occupation resulted in higher standards of living for the South Sinai Bedouins.

Despite working alongside the Israeli administration during occupation years, the Sinai Bedouins played a key role in the resistance movement. In the years leading up to the 1973 war, Bedouins created popular resistance groups, such as the Sinai Arab Organization, that carried out military operations against the Israeli forces, including targeting Israeli jets at al-Arish airport, destroying the headquarters of the Israeli military ruler and the military intelligence building in the same city, kidnapping Israeli soldiers, and confiscating weapons.[14] Further, Bedouin tribes reportedly refused Israel's offer to declare Sinai a state and asserted their allegiance to Egypt and Nasser in a publicized press conference in al-Hasna, North Sinai, in October 1968. During the 1973 war, Bedouins also sided with the Egyptian military, serving as guides through the desert and providing intelligence on the locations of Israeli army units.

PHOTO 6. Sinai Bedouin workers employed by the Israeli oil company Netivei Neft at Abu Rodeis, November 2, 1971. Source: Moshe Milner, Government Press Office of Israel, D324-017.

PHOTO 7. A plane arriving at Ophira Airport, August 21, 1974. Source: Government Press Office of Israel, D391-019.

PHOTO 8. Bulldozers leveling houses in Yamit settlement three days before returning Sinai to Egypt, April 22, 1982. Source: Tel Or Beni, Government Press Office of Israel, D319-021.

The Camp David Accords subsequently laid the groundwork for the end of the Israeli occupation. Less than a year after Sadat gave a historic speech at the Knesset in November 1977 calling for the establishment of peace based on justice, he took part in the Camp David Summit with then–Israeli prime minister Menachem Begin and U.S. president Jimmy Carter in September 1978. Both the Egyptian and Israeli leaders negotiated the terms for a peace treaty, which they signed in March 1979. In compliance with the Camp David Accords, Israel gradually withdrew its forces and settlers from Sinai, culminating in the full liberation of the peninsula on April 25, 1982, although Israeli forces and settlers remained in Taba until 1989.

Israel's withdrawal from Sinai, however, further reinforced its preferential treatment of the South over the North. As they evacuated, Israeli forces razed Northern settlements, including the coastal town of Yamit and its surrounding agricultural lands. In his autobiography, then-newly appointed minister of defense Ariel Sharon describes the destruction of the infrastructure in Yamit and surrounding settlements as a necessity to prevent the creation of an Egyptian city of at least a hundred thousand residents alongside Israel's border.[15] By contrast, the withdrawal from South Sinai and the evacuation of its settlements did not result in similar levels of destruction. The infrastructure in Ophira, Neviot, and Di Zahav was left intact, allowing Egypt to expand the tourism industry in the following years.

The occupation resulted in lasting suspicions of Sinai Bedouins. Despite the role that they played in the resistance movement, some did collaborate with Israeli forces. After all, Bedouins lived in Sinai under an Israeli administration that established schools, ran hospitals, managed the tourism industry, and controlled trade. Many Egyptians in the Nile Valley thus perceived Bedouins as traitors for accepting the occupation and collaborating with the Israeli administration for about fifteen years. The improved socioeconomic conditions for some Bedouins during the occupation fueled distrust and triggered security concerns. These suspicions increased the isolation of Sinai Bedouins and widened their schism from the rest of the Egyptian population.

The Post-occupation Period, 1982–2003

The return of Sinai to the Egyptian state triggered hopes for multiple development projects across the peninsula. Feasibility studies for developments had begun in 1974, as Egypt regained control over parts of Sinai after the 1973 war. Amid the restoration of its authority over the entire Sinai Peninsula, the Egyptian government outlined its plans to repair roads to facilitate transportation, buy existing hotels to boost the tourism industry, install pipelines and infrastructure for an improved water supply, develop power plants to deliver electricity, and build housing units to accommodate the Sinai population. The government also announced a national project in 1994 to allocate seventy-five billion Egyptian pounds for the development of Sinai.

But the Egyptian state failed to fulfill many of its promises. The multistage, long-term national project to develop the entire Sinai Peninsula flopped. According to a Nasser Academy for Military Science study, sector-based planning and the lack of a clear vision stalled this national project and signaled its failure.[16] General Adel Suleiman, who served as an intelligence officer in Sinai, highlighted corruption as another reason behind the failure to implement other development projects in Sinai.[17]

However, the Egyptian government did continue to focus on the development of tourism in South Sinai, with the industry flourishing in the 1990s and early 2000s. Egypt expanded Ophira and its former Israeli airport and transformed Sharm El Sheikh into an international tourist destination. The infrastructure in Neviot and Di Zahav laid the groundwork for Nuwaiba and Dahab to emerge as key towns on the Red Sea. The number of hotels increased from 17 in 1994 to 225 in 2002, which prompted an increase in the South Sinai population by over 70 percent.[18] Although the booming tourism industry provided many new employment opportunities, hotels mainly employed migrants from the Nile Valley while forcefully removing Bedouins from the rapidly expanding coastal territories in South Sinai.[19]

On the other hand, North Sinai suffered from continued economic marginalization after Egypt regained control of the peninsula. The Egyptian regime treated the North as a demilitarized security zone. The agricultural sector suffered due to diminishing rainwater and irrigation from al-Salam Canal not reaching farmlands. The government also resettled Egyptians from the Nile Valley to al-Arish and provided them with economic opportunities, which altered the North Sinai population.[20] As a result, Bedouins did not benefit much from the agricultural jobs. By the mid-1990s, some Bedouins resorted to smuggling drugs and gold through underground tunnels, with weapons becoming another smuggled commodity between North Sinai and Gaza following the Second Palestinian Intifada in 2000.[21]

The post-occupation period deprived Sinai Bedouins of basic human rights, especially in the North. The Egyptian government not only framed Bedouins as potential spies but also treated them as second-class citizens. It denied them land ownership rights, excluded them from government and security positions, and refused to grant some of them citizenship.[22] Some of the Sinai-located members of al-Azazma tribe, for example, have remained stateless for decades. Moreover, the entire Sinai Peninsula did not house a single university in the post-occupation period, which partially explains why only 5 percent of the North Sinai population had achieved higher education by 1996.[23] Further, over 95 percent of the North Sinai population had no access to the public sewage network and over fifty thousand people had no access to water by the mid-1990s.

The Initial Rebellion Period, 2004–2010

Historically, Sinai had no radical Islamist movement. Even when militant groups such as al-Jihad and al-Jama'a al-Islamiyya were carrying out attacks in mainland Egypt between the 1970s and 1990s (e.g., the assassination of former president Sadat, the attack on the Assyut Security Directorate, and the Luxor massacre), Sinai did not suffer such havoc. In October 2004, however, militants carried out three synchronized bombings in the South Sinai resort towns of Taba and Nuweiba, killing thirty-four people and injuring more than one hundred fifty others. The bombings were the first major terrorist attacks in Sinai and the first on Egyptian soil since the 1997 Luxor attack. Subsequently, militants carried out major synchronized bombing attacks in Sharm El Sheikh in July 2005 and Dahab in April 2006, killing over a hundred people in total.

The perpetrators of the attacks were from North Sinai. Following the Sharm El Sheikh bombings, the militant group Jama'at al-Tawhid wal-Jihad Fi Ard al-Kanana (Monotheism and Jihad in Egypt) claimed responsibility for the attack as well as for the 2004 bombings. The statement identified group members from al-Sawarka, Tarabin, al-Masa'id, and al-Tayaha Bedouin tribes. The

Egyptian Ministry of the Interior later attributed the 2006 Dahab attack to the same group. Khalid Musa'id, a dentist from al-Sawarka tribe, founded the group with Nasr al-Malahi, a law graduate residing in al-Arish. They recruited Bedouins and Palestinians in areas that had suffered from unemployment and lack of infrastructure, such as Sheikh Zuwayid and Rafah in North Sinai. After the police killed Musa'id in 2005, al-Malahi assumed leadership and extended the group's ties with militants across the border in Gaza.[24]

At the local level, the 2004–6 attacks signaled an unprecedented rebellion against the Egyptian state in Sinai. The Sinai-based group chose strategic targets in the South that would hamper Egypt's flourishing tourism industry and disrupt Egyptian-Israeli relations. The targets included hotels, campsites, restaurants, and markets in the resort towns of Taba, Nuweiba, Sharm El Sheikh, and Dahab. The group also vowed to continue the war to evict Jews and Christians, deeming them the cause of the spread of evil and prostitution in the Sinai Peninsula. Moreover, the dates on which the attacks occurred carried a clear message of defiance to the Egyptian state. The 2004 bombings that killed twelve Israeli tourists took place on October 7, one day after the thirty-first anniversary of the 1973 war against Israel. The 2005 bombings occurred on July 23, which marked the fifty-third anniversary of the 1952 revolution that overthrew King Farouk, declared Egypt an Arab republic, and installed an Egyptian military ruler. The 2006 bombings took place on April 24, on the eve of the twenty-fourth anniversary of Sinai's liberation. At the time of the attacks, Minister of the Interior Habib al-Adli asserted that the militants' choice of timing was no coincidence.[25]

The Sinai attacks also revealed the expansion of al-Qaeda's ideology in the peninsula. First, the name that the North Sinai–based militant group chose—Jama'at al-Tawhid wal-Jihad—implied a linkage to Abu Mus'ab al-Zarqawi's militancy in Iraq. In 2000, al-Zarqawi was in charge of al-Tawhid wal-Jihad training camp in Herat, Afghanistan. He then founded Jama'at al-Tawhid wal-Jihad in Iraq to fight the American forces and subsequently pledged allegiance to al-Qaeda in 2004. Second, the rhetoric of Jama'at al-Tawhid wal-Jihad in Egypt was pro-al-Qaeda despite any lack of official affiliation. The group explicitly framed the attacks on South Sinai resorts as a response to bin Laden and al-Zawahiri's calls for jihad and retaliation against the U.S.-led coalition's intervention in Afghanistan and Iraq.

In response, the Egyptian state cracked down on North Sinai Bedouins. General Habib al-Adli, who assumed the role of minister of the interior and began clamping down on Islamists one day after the 1997 Luxor attacks, applied his brutal campaign to Sinai after the Taba bombings. The retaliation involved arbitrary arrests, detentions, and torture of Bedouins. Human rights organizations estimated the State Security Investigations apparatus arrested approximately three thousand people from al-Arish, Rafah, and Sheikh Zuwayid after the Taba attacks, including family members to obtain confessions and pressure wanted persons to surrender.[26] Several North Sinai residents maintained that interrogators tortured them in various ways, such as stripping them naked, hanging them by their hands, and shocking them with electricity.[27] The state extended their mass arrest campaigns after the Sharm El Sheikh bombings, resulting in the detention of several hundred more by August 2005. According to the Sinai Prisoners Defense Front, civilian courts sentenced three hundred in absentia, military courts indicted hundreds, and at least one hundred Sinai detainees were still in prisons by 2010.[28] This crackdown fueled resentment among Sinai Bedouins.

Meanwhile, the booming underground smuggling industry was providing economic gains for North Sinai Bedouins. Israel and Egypt imposed a blockade on the Gaza Strip after Hamas seized it from Fatah forces loyal to the Palestinian president Mahmoud Abbas in June 2007. With the blockade severely restricting the flow of goods into Gaza, the underground tunnels became the main source of sustenance. From mid-2007 to November 2008, the number of tunnels linking North Sinai to Gaza soared from twenty to at least five hundred, increasing the scale of illegal trade to over six hundred thousand dollars' worth of goods annually.[29] The devastating 2008 Gaza War bolstered North Sinai's smuggling industry even further, and by late 2010 over a thousand smuggling tunnels delivered food, water, fuel, construction materials, and weapons.[30] The growth of illegal trade between Sinai and Gaza continued to increase, as the related Egyptian-state-imposed punishments were relatively lenient. According to an Egyptian security official, the state's posture toward the smuggling industry not only provided North Sinai Bedouins with a source of income but also halted armed activity in the peninsula temporarily between the 2006 Dahab bombings and the 2011 uprisings.[31]

Yet the tunnels also facilitated a Salafi militancy spillover from Gaza into North Sinai.[32] One key factor contributing to Sinai's Salafi militancy was crossover of Salafi preachers from Gaza to North Sinai. Building on existing grievances in the North, some preachers called for violently resisting the state, supporting Palestine, and denouncing the traditional Sufi orders. Salafism spread among the youth, and some Bedouins called for boycotting and fighting the government. Another contributing factor involved the militants escaping into northeast Sinai in 2009 when Hamas cracked down on Salafi groups in Gaza. The relocated militants regrouped and created a number of factions, some of which eventually merged to form the Sinai-based group Ansar Bayt al-Maqdis. By late 2010, al-Tawhid wal-Jihad, al-Salafiyya al-Jihadiyya, the Mujahideen Council, and Jaysh al-Islam were among the militant groups operating in Sinai and laid the groundwork for a more refined militant insurgency that merged localized grievances with an external Salafi militant ideology.

The Postrevolution Period, 2011–2013

On January 25, 2011, demonstrators took to the streets of Cairo, protesting the brutality of al-Adli's Ministry of the Interior. Three days later, police forces withdrew from the streets, allowing the demonstrators to seize Tahrir Square in downtown Cairo and prompting the Egyptian military to deploy its forces across the country. Over twenty thousand prisoners escaped from Egyptian jails during the revolution. The continuous nationwide protests and escalating demands culminated in former president Mubarak stepping down and transferring power to the Supreme Council of the Armed Forces on February 11, 2011. The council then ruled the country until June 29, 2012, when Muslim Brotherhood candidate Mohamed Morsi took over as the first Egyptian president since the revolution.

In Sinai, violence against Egyptian security forces increased during the revolution. Apart from sporadic Sinai protests on January 25, 2011, attacks against security compounds and the State Security Investigations buildings erupted in North Sinai after police killed a twenty-two-year-old demonstrator in Sheikh Zuwayid on January 27. Among those who escaped from Egyptian jails were Salafi militants who reportedly fled to North Sinai, bolstering the existing network of militant groups. After Mubarak stepped down, attacks against Egyptian security forces continued in Sinai, with a total of nineteen under the rule of the Supreme Council of the Armed Forces.[33] One of the most notable occurred in July 2011, when masked militants carrying black flags attacked a security facility in al-Arish and killed several people. The incident came after a protest by North Sinai Bedouins demanding the release of their relatives in connection with the 2004 Taba bombings. The militants later distributed documents, titled "al-Qaeda in the Sinai Peninsula," in al-Arish, Sheikh Zuwayid, and Rafah, condemning the Egyptian military for the Camp David Peace Accords. Reiterating demands for the release of their detained relatives, armed Bedouins later besieged the Multinational Forces and Observers camp in North Sinai in March 2012.

Israel also became a recurring target for the Sinai militant insurgency in the postrevolution period. As mentioned earlier, Egypt was supplying 40 percent of Israel's natural gas by 2011 through pipelines in Sinai as part of the Gas Supply and Purchase Agreement between the two countries. Between February 2011 and April 2012, North Sinai militants bombed the gas pipelines over a dozen times, prompting the Egyptian state-owned gas company to cancel the deal and stop exporting natural gas to Israel. After the new militant group Ansar Bayt al-Maqdis publicly announced itself and claimed responsibility for the pipeline bombings in North Sinai, it also claimed a couple of cross-border attacks on South Israel. Another newly formed group, Majlis Shura al-

Mujahideen fi Aknaf Bayt al-Maqdis (Mujahideen Shura Council in the Environs of Jerusalem), released a video claiming responsibility for a cross-border attack that killed an Israeli worker in June 2012. The same group claimed four rocket attacks on South Israel in the following months. Following the revolution, the rising Sinai insurgency posed a great threat to Israel.

As a result, the Egyptian military increased its presence in North Sinai in the postrevolution period. In response to attacks on security compounds, gas pipelines, and Israel, the Supreme Council of the Armed Forces launched Operation Eagle in North Sinai in August 2011. For the first time since the Camp David Accords, the military deployed twenty-five hundred soldiers and two hundred fifty armored personnel carriers in North Sinai with the goal of restoring control and deterring the rise of militant groups. Minister of Defense Mohamed Hussein Tantawi announced that the military ensured complete security in Sinai by October 2011.

Nonetheless, a major attack in North Sinai after Morsi came to power on June 30, 2012, prompted another military operation. After about thirty-five militants attacked a Rafah border checkpoint, killing sixteen military officers and soldiers on August 5, the military launched Operation Eagle II. The campaign aimed to reinforce security checkpoints in Rafah, Sheikh Zuwayid, and al-Arish and restore order. In a presser a month later a military spokesman announced the results of the operation—thirty-three militants dead, thirty-eight arrested, thirty-one underground border tunnels destroyed, and weapons and vehicles seized. Meanwhile, Morsi and senior military officials visited North Sinai during the operation in the first presidential visit in decades. He met with Bedouin tribes, promised development projects, and later sanctioned foreign investments in the peninsula. Further, Morsi forced the retirement of the longstanding minister of defense and army chief of staff and appointed Abdelfattah al-Sisi and Sedki Sobhi, respectively, to the vacant positions.

Militant groups in Sinai apparently differed on whether to attack the Egyptian military under Morsi's rule. After the Rafah checkpoint attack, Majlis Shura al-Mujahideen and al-Salafiyya al-Jihadiyya issued statements denying their responsibility for the attack. Despite not commenting on the attack, Ansar Bayt al-Maqdis was the most hostile. The group assassinated Bedouin leaders who endorsed the military after Operation Eagle II. However, attacking the military was still a turning point that no militant group could afford to publicly claim. Later in May 2013, militants kidnapped six Egyptian policemen and one army border guard in North Sinai. But this time militants released them a week later after talks between the military and tribal leaders. Despite these major incidents, Morsi's year in power saw only eleven attacks in total, seven of which targeted security forces in Sinai.[34] The relative calmness in North Sinai throughout June 2013 hinted at potential negotiations between the government and Bedouins.

The Post-Morsi Period, 2013–Present

On June 30, 2013, anti-Morsi mass protests took place across Egypt, demanding the president's resignation after one year in power and calling for a new election. The military released an audio statement the next day, delivering a forty-eight-hour ultimatum to Morsi to satisfy the public's demands. Morsi defied the demand and stressed his legitimacy as the country's president in a televised speech. But after the forty-eight-hour period expired on July 3, al-Sisi announced the ouster of Morsi and the installation of an interim government with Adli Mansour, chief justice of the Supreme Constitutional Court, as acting president.

Attacks in North Sinai skyrocketed to over two hundred in the five months after Morsi's ouster. Assaults on the military and police facilities in North Sinai killed dozens of soldiers in the first month. Five days after the Egyptian security forces dispersed pro-Morsi sit-ins in Cairo, killing at least six hundred by most conservative estimates on August 14, North Sinai militants killed twenty-five soldiers in Rafah. Clashes and attacks in Sinai killed over a dozen individuals in the week to follow. The slaying of five Sinai militants by an Israeli drone strike in August also ignited Ansar Bayt al-Maqdis's highly intensified rhetoric deeming the Egyptian government a traitor and a collaborator with Zionists. Since then, Ansar Bayt al-Maqdis has become more vocal, assassinated security officials, attempted to assassinate the minister of the interior, attacked military posts, shot down a military helicopter in North Sinai, fired rockets at South Israel, and bombed the military intelligence command in Ismailiya as well as the South Sinai, Cairo, and Daqahliya security directorates. By late 2013, the group explicitly reiterated that its fight was against the Egyptian security forces and Israel.

Five months after President al-Sisi came to power, Ansar Bayt al-Maqdis (the peninsula's strongest militant group) announced its pledge of allegiance to ISIS's leader Abu Bakr al-Baghdadi in November 2014 and changed its moniker to Wilayat Sinai. The average number of attacks in North Sinai surged from twelve per month in 2014 to about one per day in 2015, 2016, and 2017, with over twenty-three hundred people killed over the three-year period.[35] Wilayat Sinai was the deadliest militant group in Egypt during that period, claiming responsibility for almost nine hundred attacks. After pledging allegiance to ISIS, the group mainly claimed responsibility for attacks inside the Sinai Peninsula only, while the ISIS Egypt branch claimed those on the mainland. In 2018, however, the majority of attacks in North Sinai went unclaimed and Wilayat Sinai became much less active, claiming an average of eight attacks per month and killing around fifty people in total.[36] Despite a relative surge in militant activities in North Sinai in 2019, Wilayat Sinai has evidently weakened compared to its zenith in 2016 and 2017.

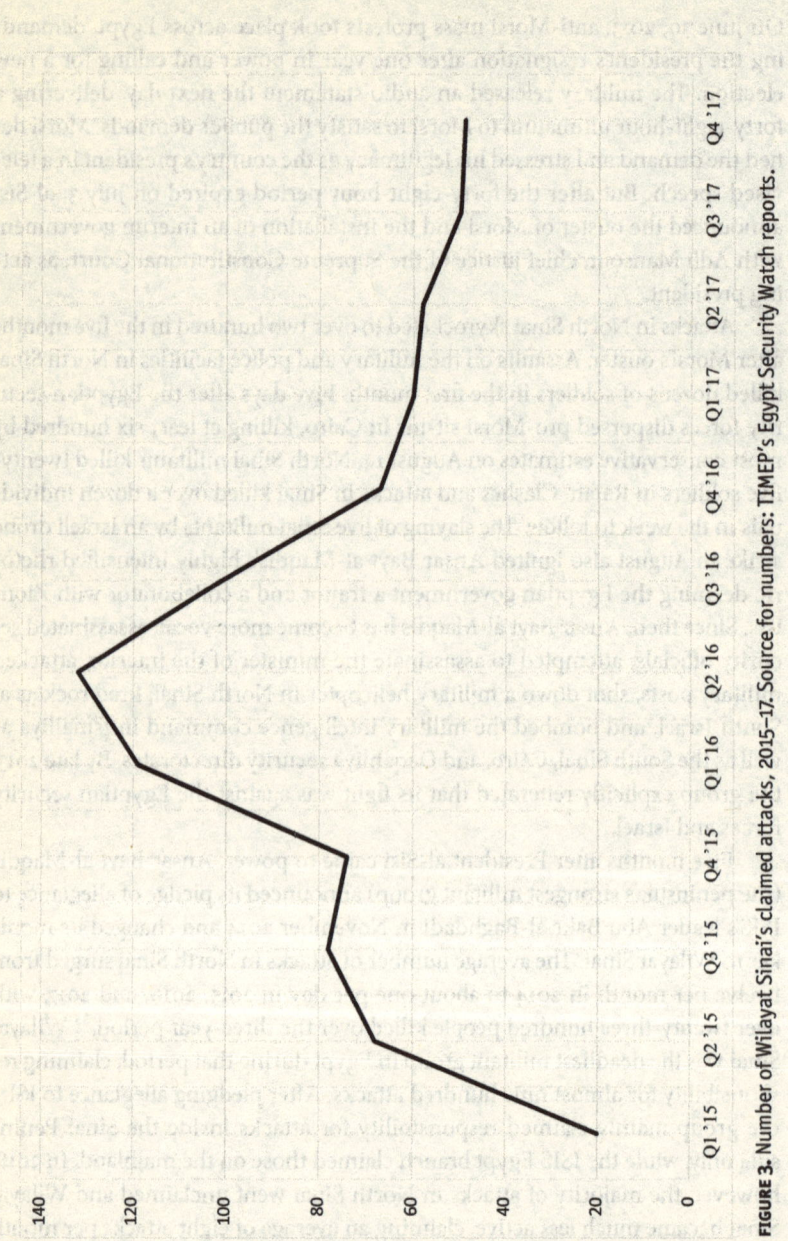

FIGURE 3. Number of Wilayat Sinai's claimed attacks, 2015–17. Source for numbers: TIMEP's Egypt Security Watch reports.

Wilayat Sinai underwent major tactical shifts over time in the peninsula. In the group's attacks in 2015, improvised explosive devices (IEDs) were the main weapon of choice, with at least 130 attacks.[37] The group's most notable attack was the downing of the Russian airliner in October 2015, which killed over two hundred people. Firearms and snipers against Egyptian security forces were also prevalent throughout the same year. IEDs surged in Wilayat Sinai's attacks against Egyptian security forces in 2016, exceeding 220 incidents in North Sinai. Most importantly, Wilayat Sinai's targets expanded beyond security forces and foreign tourists to include local civilians in late 2016. The focus on civilians in Wilayat Sinai's attacks became clear soon after an Egyptian airstrike killed the group's leader Abu Duaa al-Ansari in August 2016. After Abu Hajar al-Hashemi replaced al-Ansari, attacks against Sufi Muslims and Christian Copts increased. The group beheaded two Sufi men accused of practicing witchcraft, including a hundred-year-old cleric in November 2016. Coinciding with two suicide attacks on Cairo churches by the ISIS Egypt branch in December, Wilayat Sinai also started a systematic campaign targeting Christian Copts in North Sinai.

The year 2017 emboldened a shift in both the group's tactical operations and its ideological underpinnings. In the first quarter, Wilayat Sinai claimed three attacks against Christian Copts in al-Arish. By the end of February, around two hundred fifty Coptic Christians had already fled their homes seeking refuge in Ismailiya.[38] Meanwhile, the ISIS Egypt branch continued its assault on churches, killing almost fifty individuals during Palm Sunday service in Alexandria and Tanta. The use of *inghimasi* attacks, in which suicide fighters use small arms and explosives usually until they are killed, also increased in the peninsula. The number of Wilayat Sinai's suicide operations in North Sinai jumped from three in 2016 to eight in 2017.[39] The shift was arguably due to pressure from the Egyptian military, the increasing number of Palestinians in Wilayat Sinai's ranks willing to take their lives, and the change in leadership. The attack on a North Sinai Sufi mosque that killed over three hundred worshippers during Friday prayer in November illustrates the extent of permissible civilian targets for the Sinai insurgency by 2017. Although Wilayat Sinai did not publicly claim responsibility for the attack, the Egyptian attorney general's public statement asserted that the militants were carrying ISIS flags as they shot the worshippers and bombed the mosque. But as military pressure escalated in response, Wilayat Sinai resorted to assassinations and IED attacks to the west of al-Arish in 2018–19, which aligned with ISIS's new strategy to avoid direct confrontation and focus instead on weaker targets.

On the other hand, the military strategy in North Sinai signaled constraints on the Bedouins in the post-Morsi period. A strident curfew and a shoot-to-kill policy governed residents of Rafah, Sheikh Zuwayid, and al-Arish since July 2013. The military started a forced eviction and mass home demolitions in Rafah in the same month as part of an official plan to create a buffer zone to prevent weapons smuggling from Gaza into Sinai. According to Human Rights Watch, by August 2015 the campaign had resulted in the eviction of over three thousand Sinai Bedouin families, who reportedly received neither adequate compensation nor temporary housing.[40] The military's campaign resumed in late 2017, resulting in the eviction of almost all seventy thousand Rafah residents and the destruction of over three thousand homes and commercial buildings by mid-2018.[41] The military's counter-tunnel operations have also resulted in outrage due to disruptions in the profitable smuggling industry. Further, evoking memories of the State Security Investigations after the Taba bombings, the Second Field Army command in Ismailiya and the 101 battalion in al-Arish have purportedly become notorious among Bedouins due to the military's mass arrest campaign in North Sinai since 2013.[42]

Like Wilayat Sinai, the Egyptian security forces also shifted their tactics in Sinai over time. In 2015, security forces were mostly reactive, using traditional warfare tactics against the Sinai militants.[43] They also worked to create a buffer zone at the border with Gaza. Coinciding with Wilayat Sinai's increasing number of attacks in the first half of 2015, the military and police conducted at least sixty counterterrorism operations per month and reportedly killed around fourteen hundred in North Sinai between March and June 2015. Nevertheless, the militants were able to briefly seize parts of Sheikh Zuwayid on July 1, 2015. In the afternoon, the military launched airstrikes that pushed the militants out of the city and spoiled ISIS's plan to control territory in North Sinai. Two months later, in the Martyr's Right Operation, the military reportedly killed over five hundred alleged terrorists, arrested several hundred suspects, and destroyed a few hundred IEDs. Despite reports of large numbers of casualties and arrests, Wilayat Sinai's attacks actually surged between October and December 2015.

The Egyptian military further intensified its Sinai operations in 2016 and 2017. After the number of Wilayat Sinai's attacks peaked in the first half of 2016, the military launched two phases of the Martyr's Right Operation in the same year, conducting almost fifty counterterrorism operations.[44] Unlike during the first phase, however, the military extended its operations beyond just Al-Arish, Rafah, and Sheikh Zuwayid to include Halal Mountain in Central Sinai and other hideouts. Moreover, the military extended its policy at the Rafah-Gaza border to al-Arish and Sheikh Zuwayid by displacing residents around key military locations and government infrastructure. It also attempted to stifle Wilayat Sinai by reportedly killing its leaders, including Abu Duaa al-Ansari and over forty of his aides. Wilayat Sinai's attacks dropped in number between mid-2016 and late 2017, yet they remained deadly. The Egyptian military thus continued to mount pressure on the group by tripling the number of counterterrorism operations in 2017.[45] The Tarabin tribe also spearheaded an initiative in 2017 to unite the Bedouins against Wilayat Sinai militants. As a result, al-Tarabin units fought alongside the Egyptian military in North Sinai, strengthening the counterterrorism operations. Yet again the security presence failed to eliminate Wilayat Sinai, which came close to assassinating the ministers of defense and the interior at al-Arish airport by December of the same year.

A new major counterterrorism campaign in 2018 crippled the Sinai insurgency. By late 2017, President al-Sisi had ordered the newly appointed army chief of staff Mohamed Hegazy to restore security in the peninsula within three months. The military subsequently launched the Sinai 2018 Comprehensive Operation in February. Throughout the year, the military built a six-meter-long wall around al-Arish airport, intensified its operations, and claimed to have killed almost five hundred militants and arrested over five thousand, while Wilayat Sinai's attacks dropped to their pre-2015 levels.[46]

Concluding Thoughts

This chapter laid out the situational context of the Sinai conflict between the Egyptian state and ISIS in North Sinai. The Israeli occupation of Sinai set the stage for growing suspicions against Bedouins and differential economic policies in the North vis-à-vis the South. Egyptian rule over the peninsula upon liberation brought social alienation, economic deprivation, lack of educational opportunities, and underdevelopment to the North Sinai Bedouins. The state's crackdown on the North in the aftermath of the 2004–6 Sinai bombings violated the Bedouins' human rights and further exacerbated their grievances, yet simultaneously allowed them to benefit from illegal trade with Gaza. Hence, when the 2011 revolution erupted, it presented the ideal backdrop for a North Sinai–based militant insurgency to emerge and flourish amid political turmoil. Ever since, militants in Sinai have attacked the Egyptian security forces, who have responded in turn with several multistage counterterrorism operations. Nevertheless, the sophistication of the insurgency's tactics, the severity of its attacks, and the scope of its permissible targets have evolved over the years. Wilayat Sinai thus remains the heart of the insurgency and is likely to remain a serious threat to Egypt's economy and national security as long as it can wage attacks against military and police personnel, civilians, and infrastructure.

CHAPTER 2
The Military-Photography Nexus

The rise of non-state militant actors complicates the situational context and its interactions with photographic warfare. Militant groups run the risk of obliteration in their asymmetric conflicts with state actors. Airstrikes, counterterrorism operations on the ground, leadership decapitations, and state alliances with local, regional, and international actors are among the numerous threats facing militant groups and their survival. Nevertheless, such groups also pose serious challenges to conventional state militaries. Militant groups have a heightened organizational fluidity that makes them difficult to fully defeat, including flexible military tactics to capitalize on variable circumstances, a prolonged commitment to attrition warfare, potential affiliations with other like-minded regional groups, ties to local citizens who can serve as force multipliers, and widespread fear that their major attacks can cause.

The online media environment serves as a key battleground for state and militant groups alike. Both seek to convey their power and resiliency as well as transform conditions on the ground into memorable, favorable messages for their side of the conflict. Digital photography in particular serves as a low-cost and efficient medium to create and disrupt visual narratives. Photography's role as documenting the "real" also helps both sides in a conflict maintain an online presence. Expanding on existing analyses of the military-photographic nexus,[1] this chapter highlights critical aspects of the military context, explores patterns of the online media's response, and traces tactical changes in ISIS's and Egypt's competing visual campaigns over Sinai.

The digital media sphere has been a key site of contestation between Wilayat Sinai and the Egyptian military for years. Wilayat Sinai's predecessor, Ansar Bayt al-Maqdis, posted videos and standard written statements on web forums, but once the group pledged allegiance to ISIS, its media operations evolved tremendously. Wilayat Sinai has produced thousands of high-quality images, most of which serve as components of photo reports and daily news briefs on social media platforms and file-sharing sites. The militant group has also benefited from ISIS's official and unofficial distribution networks. Wilayat Sinai's photographic output has achieved featured visibility in the broader group's *Dabiq, Rumiyah*, and *al-Naba'* publications as well as enhanced circulation on ISIS's centralized platforms. The Egyptian military, by contrast, has utilized its official Facebook page as the main hub to disseminate photographs documenting its operations in North Sinai to millions of followers since late 2012. The circulation of these images has moved beyond the millions of followers on Facebook, with state and private-owned media using them as official documentations of on-ground events in Sinai. Both sides of the Sinai conflict developed photographic campaigns to complement their military action over the past few years.

Together, Wilayat Sinai and the Egyptian military disseminated 1,905 images on their primary platforms related to the Sinai conflict at its peak in 2016–17. Over the twenty-four-month period, ISIS distributed a total of 800 Sinai-related images on its official Telegram channel, while the Egyptian military posted 1,105 on its spokesman's official Facebook page. A monthly breakdown of the photographic output reveals that both the Egyptian military and Wilayat Sinai did change the number of photographs they released over time, but the shifting distribution patterns of the two groups did not statistically correspond to one another (see Figure 4).[2] In short, the number of images put out by one side of the conflict did not always correlate with an accompanying boost or reduction in the media productivity of the other side.

Instead, the level of photographic output of ISIS and the Egyptian military in the Sinai conflict changed in large part due to military conditions on the ground. The military context in Sinai was not the only factor interacting with the contested media campaign, as military events in ISIS's former strongholds of Iraq and Syria also played a key role. The multifaceted nature of the military influences on media efforts in Sinai, as in other conflict zones, does not occur in isolation and does not remain unresponsive to external circumstances. In the particular case of ISIS, which built its self-proclaimed caliphate primarily on Iraqi and Syrian lands and ran a central media organization that filtered, revised, and published content coming from its branches elsewhere, the regional conditions emerged as an important variable to consider when examining localized, provincial media operations. As the rest of the chapter demonstrates, several contextual military factors at the local and regional levels help explain changing photographic output levels and visual strategies. The main situational prompts include the militant group's attacks, the onset of counterterrorism military operations, the completion of counterterrorism operations, the loss of leaders, and the introduction of participating local groups into the battlefield activities. For an overview of how those factors interacted with Wilayat Sinai and the Egyptian military's distribution patterns and photographic strategies, see Tables 1 and 2.

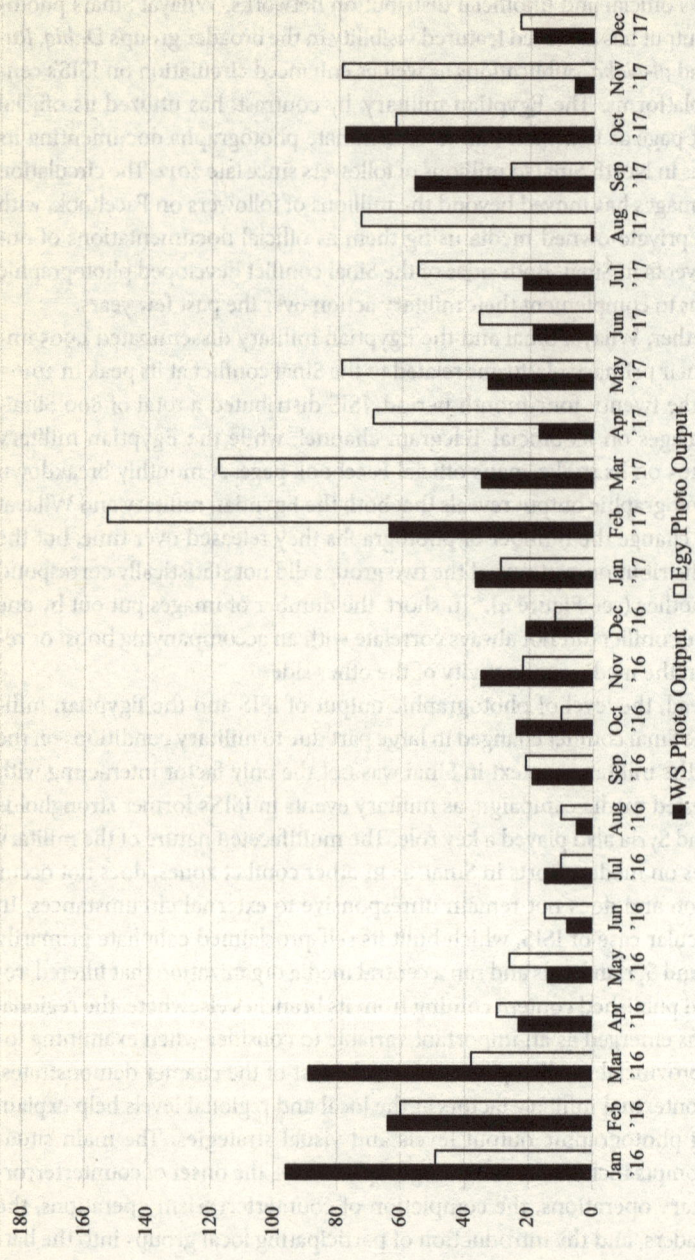

FIGURE 4. Wilayat Sinai and the Egyptian military's photographic outputs, 2016–17.

TABLE 1. Statistical overview of the interactions between photographic outputs and military conditions in the Sinai conflict

	Wilayat Sinai's photographic output				Egyptian military's photographic output			
	Correlation		t-Test		Correlation		t-Test	
	r-Value	Sig.	2016 (n = 413)	2017 (n = 387)	r-Value	Sig.	2016 (n = 303)	2017 (n = 802)
Militant attacks			M = 34.32, SD = 31.13	M = 32.25, SD = 23.45			M = 25.25, SD = 16.42	M = 66.83, SD = 38.75
Local	r(22) = .10	p > .05	t-Value	Sig.	r(22) = −.18	p > .05	t-Value	Sig.
Regional	r(22) = −.07	p > .05	t(22) = 0.19	p > .05	r(22) = −.02	p > .05	t(22) = −3.42	p < .05**
	Correlation		t-Test		Correlation		n-Test	
	r-Value	Sig.	Pre (n = 333)	Post (n = 467)	r-Value	Sig.	Pre (n = 259)	Post (n = 846)
Counterterrorism ops			M = 37.00, SD = 35.90	M = 31.13, SD = 21.10			M = 28.78, SD = 17.44	M = 56.40, SD = 40.65
Local	r(22) = .06	p > .05	t-Value	Sig.	r(22) = .56	p < .01***	t-Value	Sig.
Regional	r(22) = −.07	p > .05	t(22) = 0.51	p > .05	r(22) = −.02	p > .05	t(22) = −1.92	p = .07*

*Marginally significant, .05 ≤ p ≤ .07. **Significant, p < .05. ***Very significant, p < .01.

TABLE 2. Statistical overview of the interactions between visual strategies and military conditions in the Sinai conflict

		Local militant attacks		Local counterterrorism ops	
		Correlation		Correlation	
		r-Value	Sig.	r-Value	Sig.
Wilayat Sinai photographic campaign	Possible death	$r(22) = .50$	$p < .05$**	$r(22) = -.18$	$p > .05$
Egyptian military photographic campaign	Ongoing destruction	$r(22) = -.30$	$p > .05$	$r(22) = .62$	$p < .01$***
	No humans	$r(22) = -.21$	$p > .05$	$r(22) = .65$	$p < .01$***

**Significant, $p < .05$. ***Very significant, $p < .01$.

Local Attacks by the Militant Group

Overall, Wilayat Sinai and its media workers strived to avoid disruptions to their photographic campaign as the group's attacks declined in the peninsula. In other words, the number of Wilayat Sinai's claimed attacks did not correspond to shifts in the group's photographic output in 2016 and 2017. Even when the group's attacks dropped by almost half from 2016 to 2017, its photographic output remained constant, pushing out over thirty images per month. The consistent level of media production reflects the militants' efforts to maintain a steady online visual presence for followers, perhaps as a way to deflect attention from the group's setbacks on the ground.

Unlike the militant group in 2016–17, the Egyptian military's Facebook page increased its photographic output exponentially over time. The increase of almost 300 percent over the two years did not correspond with changes in the militant group's monthly attacks. Even with the visual surge occurring at a time when Wilayat Sinai's attacks were dwindling, the militants' relative inactivity in 2017 did not fully explain the shift in the military's media efforts. Instead, a plethora of other contextual factors, particularly intensified counterterrorism operations, appear to have played a role in the increased productivity.

Nonetheless, tactical shifts in the provincial group's visual media messaging strategies were most noticeable in relation to the number of Wilayat Sinai's claimed attacks. The group's use of the possible death visual trope (that is, the depiction of photo subjects facing impending death with no textual or visual confirmation of their actual deaths)[3] did correlate with the number of claimed attacks. As the display of possible death dropped by 60 percent from 2016 to 2017, Wilayat Sinai's attacks simultaneously dropped in half. A closer look reveals that almost all the possible death images in 2016 depicted Egyptian soldiers in the field positioned within the blast zone range of a detonating IEDs.

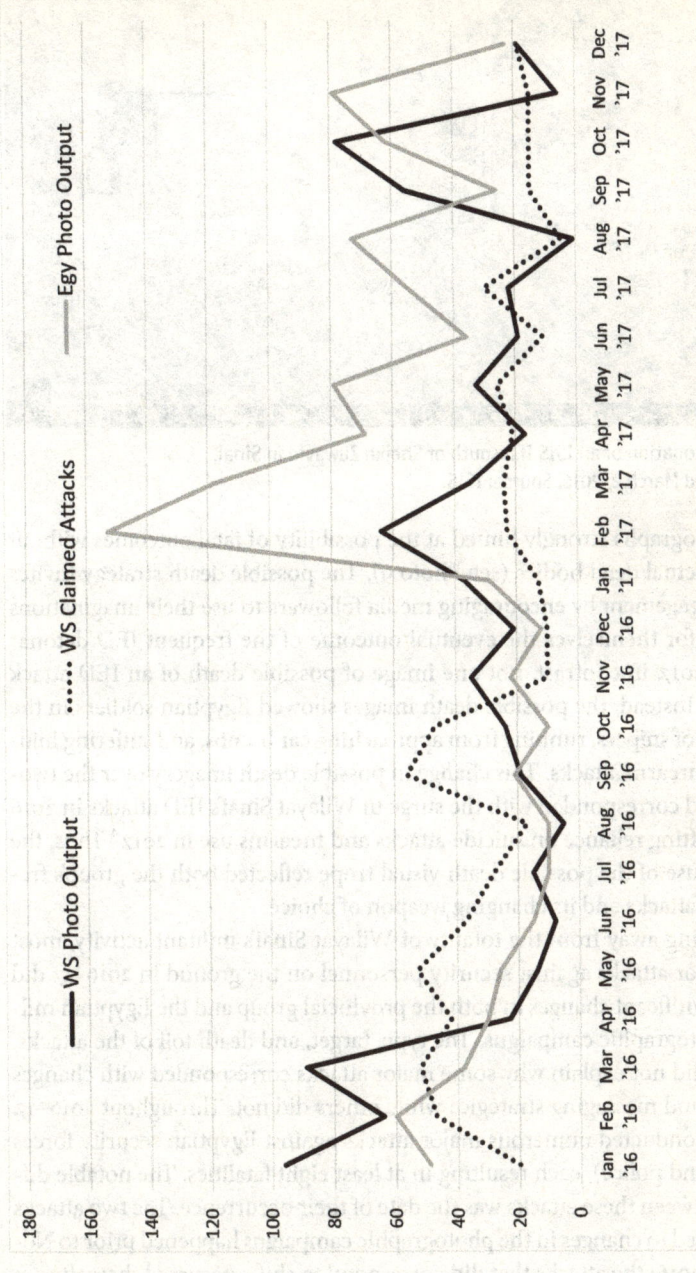

FIGURE 5. Wilayat Sinai's claimed attacks and the group and military's photographic outputs, 2016–17. Source for number of attacks: TIMEP's Egypt Security Watch reports.

PHOTO 9. Detonation of an ISIS IED south of Sheikh Zuwayid in Sinai, disseminated March 2, 2016. Source: ISIS.

Such photographs strongly hinted at the possibility of fatal outcomes without showing actual dead bodies (see Photo 9). The possible death strategy invites viewer engagement by encouraging media followers to use their imaginations to decide for themselves the eventual outcome of the frequent IED detonations. In 2017, in contrast, not one image of possible death of an IED attack appeared. Instead, the possible death images showed Egyptian soldiers in the crosshairs of snipers, running from approaching car bombs, and suffering injuries from firearm attacks. This change in possible death imagery over the two-year period corresponded with the surge in Wilayat Sinai's IED attacks in 2016 and its shifting reliance on suicide attacks and firearms use in 2017.[4] Thus, the militants' use of the possible death visual trope reflected both the group's frequency of attacks and its changing weapon of choice.

Stepping away from the totality of Wilayat Sinai's militant activity, most of the major attacks against security personnel on the ground in 2016–17 did prompt significant changes in both the provincial group and the Egyptian military's photographic campaigns. The type, target, and death toll of the attacks, however, did not explain why some major attacks corresponded with changes in output and messaging strategies while others did not. Throughout 2016–17, militants conducted numerous major attacks against Egyptian security forces (military and police), each resulting in at least eight fatalities. The notable difference between these attacks was the date of their occurrence. The two attacks unconnected to changes in the photographic campaigns happened prior to November 1, 2016; the attacks that did correspond to shifts occurred thereafter.

What changed in November 2016 that could account for the media importance of the major attacks? Wilayat Sinai's attacks dropped by almost 80 per-

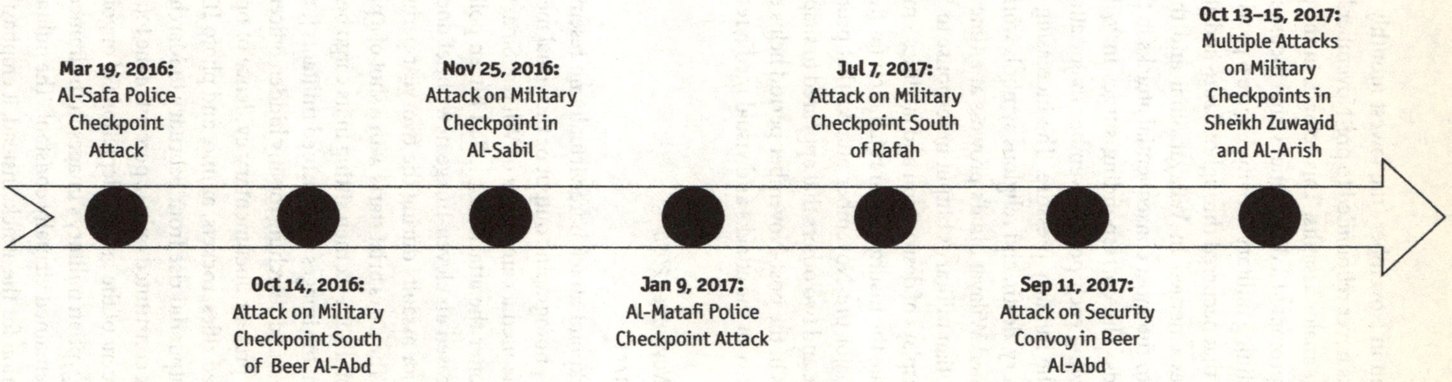

FIGURE 6. Timeline of several key military attacks in North Sinai, 2016–17.

- **Mar 19, 2016:** Al-Safa Police Checkpoint Attack
- **Oct 14, 2016:** Attack on Military Checkpoint South of Beer Al-Abd
- **Nov 25, 2016:** Attack on Military Checkpoint in Al-Sabil
- **Jan 9, 2017:** Al-Matafi Police Checkpoint Attack
- **Jul 7, 2017:** Attack on Military Checkpoint South of Rafah
- **Sep 11, 2017:** Attack on Security Convoy in Beer Al-Abd
- **Oct 13–15, 2017:** Multiple Attacks on Military Checkpoints in Sheikh Zuwayid and Al-Arish

cent to a low of only ten in November (the lowest monthly number of 2016). The frequency of attacks never rebounded to pre-November levels. Yet Wilayat Sinai continued to wage major assaults. This setback in the provincial group's activity on the ground prompted a differential visual focus on major attacks to compensate for the declining military activity. Figure 6 provides a summary of the major Sinai attacks that occurred throughout 2016 and 2017.

Notable differences emerged in Wilayat Sinai and the Egyptian military's visual responses to the most consequential attacks in the pre- and post-November 2016 periods. The corresponding surges in Wilayat Sinai's photographic output following each post-November major attack functioned as a virtual response to the military pressure. The increasing display of explosions, fire, ruined artillery, death, and religious symbols worked to reinforce a spectacle that exaggerated Wilayat Sinai's prowess at a time of actual decline. The upticks in the Egyptian military's output in response to Wilayat Sinai's assaults, along with the displays of destruction and fatalities, emphasized the military's ability to obliterate the insurgency in retaliation for their major attacks. A closer look at two major pre-November attacks that prompted no tactical shifts in media response and two others that appeared to shape the distribution of images on both sides in the post-November period helps explain the multifaceted relationship between the attacks and visual media response.

Major Attacks prior to November 2016
AL-SAFA CHECKPOINT ATTACK

The al-Safa police checkpoint attack bore virtually no resemblance to noticeable changes in level of photographic output or the visual messaging strategies in the competing online media campaigns of Wilayat Sinai and the Egyptian military. Immediately after the attack that killed fifteen policemen in March 2016, Wilayat Sinai released an eleven-image news brief documenting the attack. As with other major assaults during the two-year period, the group created a media spectacle. The news brief starts with a shot of a pickup truck heading toward the checkpoint with six men sitting in its cargo bed. Once the truck arrives at its destination, the images show armed militants jumping out, shooting at the police vehicles, and searching for any hidden officers or soldiers. The last three photographs present documentary evidence of operational success by displaying confiscated rifles, rockets, ammo, and photo IDs. While Wilayat Sinai's photographic output did rise from February to March 2016, the images of the checkpoint attack constituted only 12 percent of the total image output in March and barely 8 percent of the group's depictions of ongoing destruction in the same month. The Egyptian military's images in the immediate aftermath of the al-Safa attack also remained virtually constant. The military put out no images showing its retaliation for the attack; instead, it emphasized the success of a preplanned African conference held three days later and over four hundred kilometers away in Sharm El Sheikh.

BEER AL-ABD CHECKPOINT ATTACK

Also unrelated to a change in the visual media campaigns was the Beer al-Abd military checkpoint attack in October 2016 that killed twelve security personnel. The next day, Wilayat Sinai released a four-image news brief that begins with a shot of security personnel at a checkpoint with Egyptian flags right before the attack. Heavy gunfire erupts in the subsequent two images that show the soldiers fleeing their positions. The brief ends with a one-sided active shooting scene where militants are advancing with their rifles as bullets are flying, while the body of an Egyptian soldier presumably killed in the assault lies on the ground. The four images, representing Wilayat Sinai's only depiction of an armed attack in October 2016, did not tactically shift the group's photographic output as its October levels fit into the steady increase occurring between August and November 2016. The Egyptian military's output in the immediate aftermath of the attack also continued the regular monthly ebbs and flows from August to December 2016. The military's ten images in October display no security operations serving as retaliation for the attack. Instead, five static shots show stationed security forces posed on top of and around tanks and armored vehicles holding their rifles, three images of empty playgrounds in two new schools that the military had opened for the local community, and two of confiscated explosives arranged on the ground. Wilayat Sinai's major attacks in November 2016 onward, however, showed a very different picture.

Major Local Attacks after November 2016
AL-MATAFI CHECKPOINT ATTACK

Killing eight, injuring another twelve, and prompting the military to send in reinforcements to many Sinai checkpoints, the January 9, 2017, attack on al-Matafi police checkpoint boosted Wilayat Sinai's photographic output. Two days after the attack, Wilayat Sinai released a twenty-six-image news brief that gives viewers rare insights into an assault from multiple angles. Taken from the top of a building, the first shot looks at two armored vehicles at dawn parked on opposite sides of the road, with a white pickup facing a nearby two-story police building parked between them. In the next four images, the seemingly quiet scene shifts to a large explosion from three different angles immediately after militants detonate a car bomb inside the white pickup. About eight armed, masked militants, wearing red headbands reminiscent of the battle attire of Abu Dujana, a prominent companion of Prophet Muhammad praised for his courage, then appear in sixteen action shots. They run toward the destroyed police building, conduct an internal sweep, and shoot at police personnel and artillery. The remaining images emphasize the outcome, showing the corpse of a soldier, a police vehicle on fire, and debris. This single news brief constituted 70 percent of the group's monthly output, which marked Wilayat Sinai's highest level of output in over ten months.

Further shifting its messaging strategy in the wake of the successful al-Matafi attack, the provincial group reinforced its visual identity as a destructive and deadly fighting force. In January 2017, Wilayat Sinai almost doubled its displays of ongoing destruction. Almost all of the twelve photographs appear in the al-Matafi attack news brief, showing the explosions and fire at the police checkpoint. The two January images displaying dead bodies also appear in this brief, showing a policeman's corpse. Reinforcing the destructive potential of the militant group, the only display of possible death in the entire month, a policeman as he tries to escape hostile gunfire, was again in this news brief.

The checkpoint attack at al-Matafi also appeared to have prompted an increase in photographic output by the Egyptian military. Compared to only twelve in the previous month, the military disseminated twenty-nine images in January 2017, with over two-thirds released after the al-Matafi attack. Based on the text in the Facebook posts, the images show corpses of militants, confiscated weaponry, burning vehicles, and destroyed hideouts in the immediate aftermath of the military's successful counterterrorism operations. They also display military officials as they engage in their daily routines: Major General Mahmoud Hijazy monitoring and interacting with Egyptian Special Forces at a military base and the minister of immigration visiting injured soldiers in a hospital. Perhaps as a result, January marked the highest output of the Egyptian military's images in eight months.

In its visual response to the al-Matafi attack, the Egyptian military also placed greater emphasis on its own group as a destructive fighting force against the militant insurgency. All three images showing ongoing destruction displayed in January, which constituted the largest number of such Egyptian military images since September 2016, appeared after the al-Matafi attack. The scenes of ongoing destruction reportedly showed militant hideouts and motorcycles burning in flames in the Sinai desert. The military's power was thus on display.

MILITARY CHECKPOINT ATTACK NEAR RAFAH

For Wilayat Sinai, the attack on a military checkpoint south of Rafah served as critical source material for sustaining the provincial group's photographic campaign. The July 7, 2017, attack killed and injured twenty-six checkpoint personnel. Two days later, Wilayat Sinai released a twenty-two-image report documenting how the militants surrounded and destroyed the military checkpoint. The first two photographs show a militant standing on top of a pickup truck laying down heavy machine gunfire at early dawn. Two subsequent images feature an explosion in the distance lighting up the sky, reportedly due to a suicide bombing at the checkpoint. As the morning proceeds, several armed militants appear running toward the checkpoint and shooting as they approach the military building from their surrounding positions. Four photographs in the aggregate serve to claim divine victory by featuring building rubble, destroyed military vehicles, an Egyptian soldier's corpse, and two of the militants prostrated in prayer after taking control of the checkpoint. Meanwhile, the remaining images suggest the military's failure to send timely, adequate support by displaying another large explosion in the distance reportedly after a suicide bombing attack against military forces and showing a drone and a fighter jet in the skies later in the day. This photo report constituted Wilayat Sinai's entire July output and represented an increase in productivity from the preceding month.

Capitalizing on the Rafah attack in the media realm, Wilayat Sinai placed a greater emphasis on presenting itself as a destructive, pious fighting force. The ISIS province displayed seven shots of ongoing destruction at the checkpoint in the single photo report distributed in July. Those images featured two suicide attacks' explosions and militant gunfire during the assault. Further, the image showing the militants praying in gratitude after the attack was one of only five such displays during the entire 2016–17 period.

The same Wilayat Sinai attack played a pivotal role in the surge of the Egyptian military's photographic output. The military disseminated fifty-five images in July 2017, up 65 percent from the previous month. On the day of the assault, the military responded with seven images showing the corpses of five militants who had attacked the Rafah checkpoint with blood all over their bodies, three of those with their pants dragged down or their naked stomachs exposed as they lie motionless in the sand. Despite the lack of visual output in the following week, the military's visual campaign bounced back with thirty-nine images in the last fifteen days of July, featuring reported airstrikes on militant hideouts, blazing vehicles, confiscated weaponry, drug busts, and arrested terrorists and traffickers. Those images in the second half of the month composed the vast majority of the military's monthly output.

The military particularly highlighted its identity as a lethal fighting force against militants in the aftermath of the checkpoint attack south of Rafah. All seven images showing dead militant bodies in July appeared as part of the same Facebook post on the day of the attack, marking the second highest death image count in the military's 2016–17 photographic campaign. The military was quick to visually reinforce that any attempt to attack military checkpoints would be met with the death of the perpetrators. Further recognizing ISIS's media competence and the need for a mass media response, the Egyptian state supported the production of the thirty-episode TV series *al-Ikhtiyar* (The Choice), which aired in summer 2020 and paid tribute to the military officers and soldiers killed in the Rafah checkpoint attack.

Regional Attacks by the Militant Group

Unlike local attacks in Sinai, ISIS's attacks in Iraq and Syria did not appear to produce changes in Wilayat Sinai or the Egyptian military's photographic campaigns in 2016–17. According to START's Global Terrorism Database (GTD), ISIS conducted 2,653 attacks in Iraq and Syria in 2016 and 2017.[5] A comparison of the regional military activity with the localized visual contestation in Sinai revealed no correlation between ISIS's monthly attacks in Iraq and Syria and Wilayat Sinai's levels of photographic output. While ISIS's claimed attacks slightly dropped from 2016 to 2017, Wilayat Sinai's photographic output remained relatively constant over the twenty-four-month period due to a move by the provincial group to exaggerate the visualization of its major local attacks when its militant power weakened. Similarly, no statistical relationship existed between ISIS's monthly attacks and the Egyptian military's photographic output. Further, the number of regional attacks neither shaped nor appeared to even play a minor role in the shifts in visual elements and tropes on both sides. In short, ISIS's regional attacks had no clear influence on Wilayat Sinai and the military's outputs and visual messaging strategies.

A closer look at two of the major attacks in Iraq and Syria further reinforces the lack of relationship between ISIS's regional attacks and Wilayat Sinai's photographic output. On July 3, 2016, an ISIS suicide bomber carried out the group's deadliest attack in Iraq over the two-year period, killing nearly four hundred in the al-Karrada neighborhood of Baghdad. Two days later, Wilayat Sinai continued its regular pattern of disseminating IED attack images. The July images also did not exhibit any major shifts and the output was within the typical range throughout the summer 2016. The Egyptian military's output in July was also consistent with its pattern established before and after of featuring key figures visiting injured soldiers. In short, ISIS's deadliest attack and the worst bombing in Iraq since the 2003 U.S.-led invasion did not prompt any notable changes in either the Wilayat Sinai or the Egyptian military's photographic campaigns.

Similarly, ISIS's deadliest attack in Syria over the two-year period, killing at least 120 members of the Syrian regime forces in Palmyra on December 10, 2016, did not correspond to any major shifts in the visual campaign. The six images Wilayat Sinai disseminated in the twenty-one days after the attack showed two martyred members of the local group and one rocket attack.

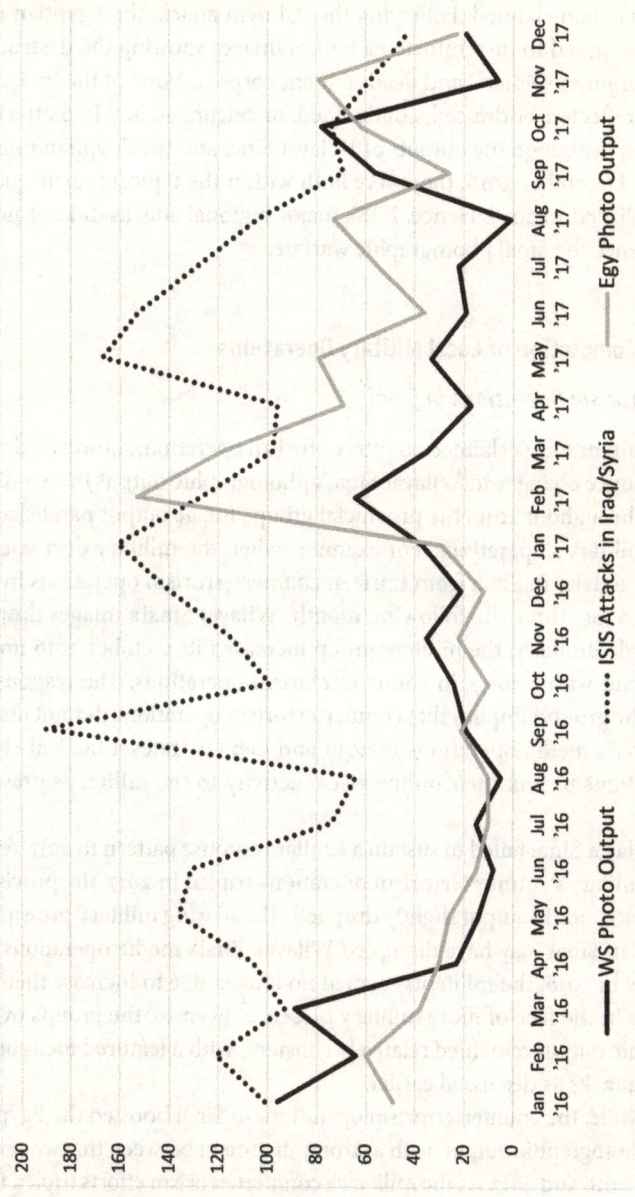

FIGURE 7. ISIS's attacks and Wilayat Sinai and the military's photographic outputs, 2016–17. Source for number of attacks: Global Terrorism Database.

The only unusual thing about the Sinai images was distinguishable from the Palmyra attack. The group issued an image of a martyred militant who had conducted a December 11, 2016, attack on a Cairo church that ISIS Egypt, not Wilayat Sinai, had claimed. Following the Palmyra attack, the Egyptian military also continued to disseminate its typical images showing the destruction of tunnels, injured soldiers, and dead militant corpses. None of the images on either side reflected, addressed, condemned, or celebrated any ISIS attacks in Syria or Iraq. Although the outputs of Wilayat Sinai and the Egyptian military declined in December 2016, they were both within the typical fourth-quarter range established in 2016. Hence, ISIS's major regional attacks did not necessarily influence the Sinai photographic warfare.

Onset and Completion of Local Military Operations

Counterterrorism Operations in Sinai

The Egyptian military's claimed counterterrorism operations, however, did appear to produce changes in Wilayat Sinai's photographic output in two different ways. Throughout 2016, the provincial group's image output paralleled the Egyptian military's operations. For example, when the military decreased its on-ground activity in Sinai from thirteen counterterrorism operations in January 2016 to just three the following month, Wilayat Sinai's images dropped by one-third. Similarly, the militant group increased its October 2016 images to correspond with a surge in counterterrorism operations. The response to events on the ground implies that counterterrorism operations did not disrupt Wilayat Sinai's media operations in 2016 and demonstrates a tactical choice by the militants to link their online visual activity to the military's presence offline.

Yet Wilayat Sinai failed to sustain a similar response pattern in 2017. As the Egyptian military's counterterrorism operations tripled in 2017, the provincial group's photographic output slightly dropped. The soaring military pressure on the ground in Sinai may have disrupted Wilayat Sinai's media operations that year. Unlike in 2016, the militants seemed no longer able to increase their online activity in the face of more military presence. Even so, the group's overall photographic output remained relatively constant, with a featured focus on select major attacks as discussed earlier.

Meanwhile, the counterterrorism operations in Sinai boosted the Egyptian military's photographic output, with a strong alignment between the two prongs throughout 2016 and 2017. As the military's counterterrorism efforts tripled from 2016 to 2017, its photographic output more than doubled. Clearly, the Egyptian military systematically used digital photographs as online weapons to complement its battlefield operations against the Sinai insurgency (see Figure 8).

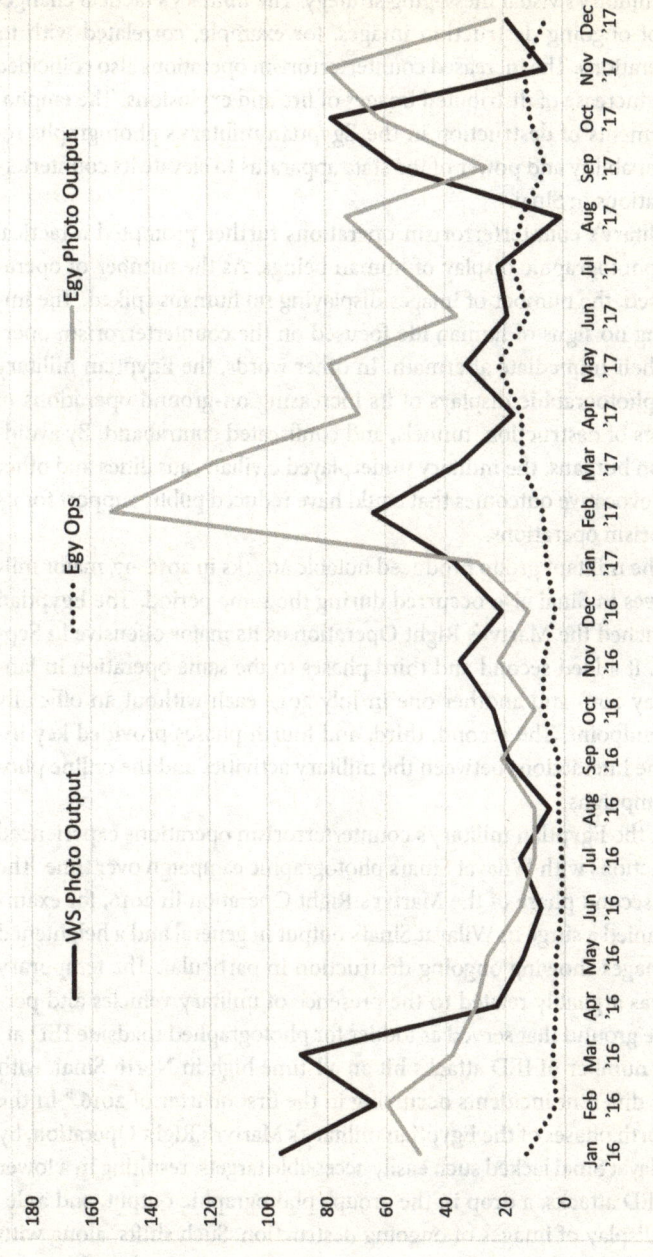

FIGURE 8. Monthly 2016–17 Egyptian military's counterterrorism ops and photographic output levels. Source for claimed counterterrorism ops: TIMEP's Egypt Security Watch reports.

The Egyptian military's counterterrorism operations also appeared to influence the military's visual messaging strategy. The military's tactical changes in the use of ongoing destruction images, for example, correlated with its monthly operations. The increased counterterrorism operations also coincided with a sharp increase of distributed images of fire and explosions. The emphasis on implements of destruction in the Egyptian military's photographs reflected the capability and power of the state apparatus to elevate its counterterrorism operations in Sinai.

The military's counterterrorism operations further prompted a tactical shift in the photographic display of human beings. As the number of operations increased, the number of images displaying no humans spiked. The images featuring no signs of human life focused on the counterterrorism operations and their immediate aftermath. In other words, the Egyptian military limited the photographic displays of its increasing on-ground operations in 2017 to scenes of destruction, tunnels, and confiscated contraband. By avoiding a focus on humans, the military underplayed civilian causalities and other emotionally evocative outcomes that could have reduced public support for its counterterrorism operations.

Just as the militant group produced notable attacks in 2016–17, major military offensives in Sinai also occurred during the same period. The Egyptian military launched the Martyr's Right Operation as its major offensive in September 2015. It added second and third phases to the same operation in January and May 2016 and another one in July 2017, each without an officially designated endpoint. The second, third, and fourth phases provided key insights into the interactions between the military activities and the online photographic campaigns.

Overall, the Egyptian military's counterterrorism operations experienced varied interactions with Wilayat Sinai's photographic campaign over time. The onset of the second phase of the Martyr's Right Operation in 2016, for example, accompanied a surge in Wilayat Sinai's output in general and a heightened display of images showing ongoing destruction in particular. The temporary alignment was arguably related to the presence of military vehicles and personnel on the ground that served as fodder for photographed roadside IED attacks, as the number of IED attacks hit an all-time high in North Sinai, with seventy-four different incidents occurring in the first quarter of 2016.[6] In the third and fourth phases of the Egyptian military's Martyr's Right Operation, by contrast, Wilayat Sinai lacked such easily accessible targets, resulting in a lower number of IED attacks, a drop in the group's photographic output, and a decline in the display of images of ongoing destruction. Such shifts, along with the declining displays of death and religious symbols, temporarily fractured the provincial group's media spectacle of their prowess.

In contrast to the shifting relationship with Wilayat Sinai's media campaign, counterterrorism operations aligned consistently with the military's increased use of its online photographic campaign. The paired increases in monthly operations and photographic output positioned the military to project its own strength in on-ground actions. The military's dissemination of more images in the immediate aftermath of each of the three phases of the Martyr's Right Operation in 2016 and 2017 reinforced the ability of the Egyptian military to control the conflict and set the tone for mainstream media coverage. The increasing displays of ongoing destruction and caring leaders, along with the exclusion of human engagement in the operations, bolstered a narrative that positively characterized the military. A more nuanced examination of each of the three phases of the Martyr's Right Operation helps explain the grounds for patterns of the Sinai photographic warfare and emphasizes the differential visual strategies of Wilayat Sinai and the Egyptian military.

Major Local Military Offensives
SECOND PHASE OF THE MARTYR'S RIGHT OPERATION

The onset of the second phase of the Martyr's Right Operation on January 3, 2016, strongly correlated with Wilayat Sinai's decision to produce a high number of images. In the first week after the announcement that the operation would begin, the group distributed forty-two images showing IED attacks, rocket launchings, shootings, spy executions, militant trainings, and aftermaths of the Egyptian military's airstrikes. On January 4 alone, for example, Wilayat Sinai disseminated eight images from three different locations, beginning with shots of two blindfolded men in orange jumpsuits kneeling submissively on the side of an empty road as two militants point their rifles toward the back of their heads from a close distance in broad daylight. With the captions identifying the two men as spies helping the military, both meet their fate as their bodies splay next to one another after receiving headshots from the militants' rifles. Another two images introduce a different location, showing militants pointing their machine guns to the sky and firing heavily at helicopters. Finally, an image features a militant in the desert affixing a rocket to the sand, before two subsequent photographs confirm the successful launch as the rocket flies in the sky with fire trailing behind it. The images posted in this week made up almost half of the group's output for January 2016, which marked the highest point in the two-year period with almost a hundred images. Viewed a bit more broadly, the first quarter of 2016 was the most productive for Wilayat Sinai in its online photographic campaign over a two-year period.

Visually responding to the second phase of the Martyr's Right Operation, the ISIS provincial group placed greater emphasis on reinforcing its identity as a destructive and devout fighting force. The display of ongoing destruction images was at its peak in January, mainly focusing on the immediate aftermath of

IED attacks against security forces in North Sinai. The remaining images depicted active shootings and fire on the battlefield too. Further, the display of religious symbols was at its highest point in January. Using shots of armed militants making the monotheism gesture, a militant reading the Qur'an during his break, a destroyed mosque, and a dusty Qur'an after airstrikes, Wilayat Sinai presented its members as protectors of religion in the face of sacrilegious forces.

As a reinforcing supplement to the increasing military pressure in the same phase of the Martyr's Right Operation, the Egyptian military's January output was at its second highest point in 2016. January's forty-nine Egyptian military images showed the confiscation of the militants' weaponry and explosive materials, the destruction of drugs and vehicles, the discovery of underground storehouses, the minister of international cooperation visiting sites of Sinai development projects, the minister of defense visiting injured soldiers, and top security officials attending the funeral of an officer who died in the operations. At a broader level, the first quarter of 2016 following the onset of the major offensive was the most productive for the Egyptian military in its online photographic campaign that year.

The military further presented itself as a successful war machine against the Sinai militants during the second phase of the Martyr's Right Operation. In a thirteen-image post on January 21, for example, twelve images feature the outcomes of the counterterrorism operations: confiscated rockets, rifles, ammo, IEDs, electric circuits, motorcycles, and black ISIS flags. The images during and after the second Martyr's Right Operation focused more on the successful outcomes of the offensive, leaving the viewer to imagine aspects of battlefield combat, the strength of the military personnel, and the process of seizing the militants' belongings. Thus, around one-third of the total photographic output in January and February 2016 featured no humans, marking the highest point of images erasing human engagement that year.

THIRD PHASE OF THE MARTYR'S RIGHT OPERATION

Contrary to the second phase of the Martyr's Right Operation, the onset of the third phase on May 25, 2016, corresponded with a decrease in Wilayat Sinai's level of photographic output. For almost three weeks after the Egyptian military announced the operation, Wilayat Sinai disseminated no images whatsoever. Then, the group released only eight images in the subsequent two weeks. Six of the images show two almost identical IED attacks on armored personnel carriers, where a distant police/military vehicle first appears to be moving down the road before two subsequent images of the detonation's aftermath display a large explosion engulfing the security vehicles. The two remaining photographs feature two pistols, a cell phone, a wallet, photo IDs, and a power bank charger that—according to the captions—belonged to the policeman whom the militants had killed. In sum, the onset of the major offensive in Sinai disturbed the provincial group's photography operations.

Wilayat Sinai also appeared to struggle to sustain its identity as a destructive and deadly fighting force amid the third phase of the Martyr's Right Operation. The group's June photographic campaign broke from its previous practices of displaying death and about-to-die images. In June, they used neither of the two. Further, only four images displayed ongoing destruction in the context of the two IED attacks, a significant drop from the previous month. The mounting military pressure on Wilayat Sinai seemed to disrupt the group's media tactics.

The third phase of the operation also corresponded with a slight uptick in the Egyptian military's photographic output. In the first five days after the third phase began, the military circulated eleven images in four different Facebook posts showing tanks, armored vehicles, and soldiers on the battlefield as well as the minister of defense visiting the Second Field Army. A three-image Facebook post on May 28, for example, begins with two shots of armed personnel advancing in the desert as several other soldiers stand atop armored vehicles with machine guns at the ready. The next photograph features two military tanks in an open battlefield firing at distant targets and producing smoke coming out of a distant building. The images in those five days constitute 42 percent of the military's photographic output in May 2016. The military thus complemented its offensive on the ground with a temporary surge in online photographs.

In the wake of the third phase, the Egyptian military also appeared to shift its visual messaging strategies by deemphasizing its self-portrayal as a destructive war machine. Moving away from the tactical display of no human beings in the majority of May images prior to the offensive, the military portrayed its soldiers advancing through the desert in almost all of the eleven images appearing at the onset of the operation later the same month. All images in the following month continued the practice of depicting human engagement, with a sizable majority featuring military leaders opening new schools and visiting soldiers at military bases and in hospitals. Five images in late June, for example, show the minister of defense surrounded by other military leaders as he honors soldiers and officers with plaques for their efforts in Sinai. The military presented its soldiers as courageous on the battlefield and the leadership as embodying a caring attitude toward their subordinates during the third phase of the offensive.

FOURTH PHASE OF THE MARTYR'S RIGHT OPERATION

The onset of the fourth phase of the Martyr's Right Operation further disrupted Wilayat Sinai's media operations. The reinitiated military operation came in quick response to Wilayat Sinai's attack on a Rafah military checkpoint

PHOTO 10. The Egyptian military showcasing ISIS's confiscated cameras and computers in Sinai, disseminated July 27, 2017. Source: Egyptian Army Spokesman.

on July 7, 2017, the deadliest of the thirty attacks the group had claimed that same month. For about a month and a half after the operation began, Wilayat Sinai released only one image, thus marking the lowest level of photographic output for the group in 2016–17.

Unsurprisingly, the fourth phase further hindered Wilayat Sinai's ability to maintain its image as a destructive and deadly fighting force. Instead, the group barely even attempted to present its members as courageous in the face of military escalations. The only Wilayat Sinai image appearing during this low point portrays a smiling militant holding his rifle in a green field, with an accompanying caption eulogizing him as a "martyr" without even disclosing how he died. The lack of details of his death diverged from ISIS's standard practice of valorizing those who martyred themselves for the group's cause.

In contrast to the devastating drop in Wilayat Sinai's production to only a single image between July 17 and September 2, the fourth phase simultaneously boosted the Egyptian military's photographic output. In that same period, the Egyptian military disseminated more than a hundred images, four of which specifically highlight the targeting and disruption of ISIS's local media infrastructure in Sinai by displaying the group's confiscated computers, cameras, scanners, and photocopiers (see Photo 10). The other images mostly focused on airstrikes, arrested suspects, destroyed hideouts, burned drug plantations, newly discovered underground tunnels, and confiscated vehicles and weaponry. The military emphasized its omnipresence on the ground at that time.

The fourth phase brought back the military's self-presentation as a destructive war machine against the Sinai militancy. The display of ongoing destruction of tunnels, vehicles, and hideouts peaked. The military reverted to its emphasis on the immediate outcome of the Martyr's Right Operation, again excluding humans from the scene. A four-image Facebook post on August 9 illustrates the military's pattern of combining an erasure of signs of life with the creation of a destructive spectacle. The post begins with an image of a large burning barn in the distance, a dark plume of smoke rising. The image tagline identifies the barn as a militant hangout. Three images shot from different angles then reveal the source of the fire from the inside, featuring a blazing pickup with its tires melting. With the militants out of sight and their belongings destroyed, the military visually reinforced its power over Wilayat Sinai during the offensive.

Onset and Completion of Regional Military Operations

Military Offensives in Iraq and Syria

The escalation of military pressure on ISIS in Iraq and Syria also marked a significant shift in the contested visual campaign between Wilayat Sinai and the Egyptian military. The regional military pressure on ISIS in its heartlands and main media centers increased dramatically with the onset of the Mosul operation on October 17, 2016, followed by the Raqqa operation beginning the next month on November 6. Wilayat Sinai's output dropped from an average of thirty-seven images per month before the battles to twenty-one in the post-escalation period. Despite the decline, the intensified military pressure by the coalition-backed Iraqi forces and the Syrian Democratic Forces on ISIS's strongholds did not seem to cripple the distribution of Wilayat Sinai's media output. The Egyptian military's photographs, on the other hand, doubled after the onset of the operations. The regional military operations may have prompted a higher level of media productivity by the Egyptian armed forces in an effort to preempt shifts of ISIS forces to Sinai.

Beyond the relatively constant level of Wilayat Sinai's photographic production, the group altered a key element of its visual messaging strategies amid the regional military operations. The display of dead bodies in the group's campaign almost tripled in the post-escalation period. The corpses served as a key indicator of vengeance against a wide range of permissible targets including military personnel, policemen, alleged spies, al-Tarabin Bedouin tribal fighters, and Sufi clerics. Through the visual shift, ISIS presented itself as a deadly threat to both civilians and security personnel in Sinai even as military pressure intensified in Iraq and Syria.

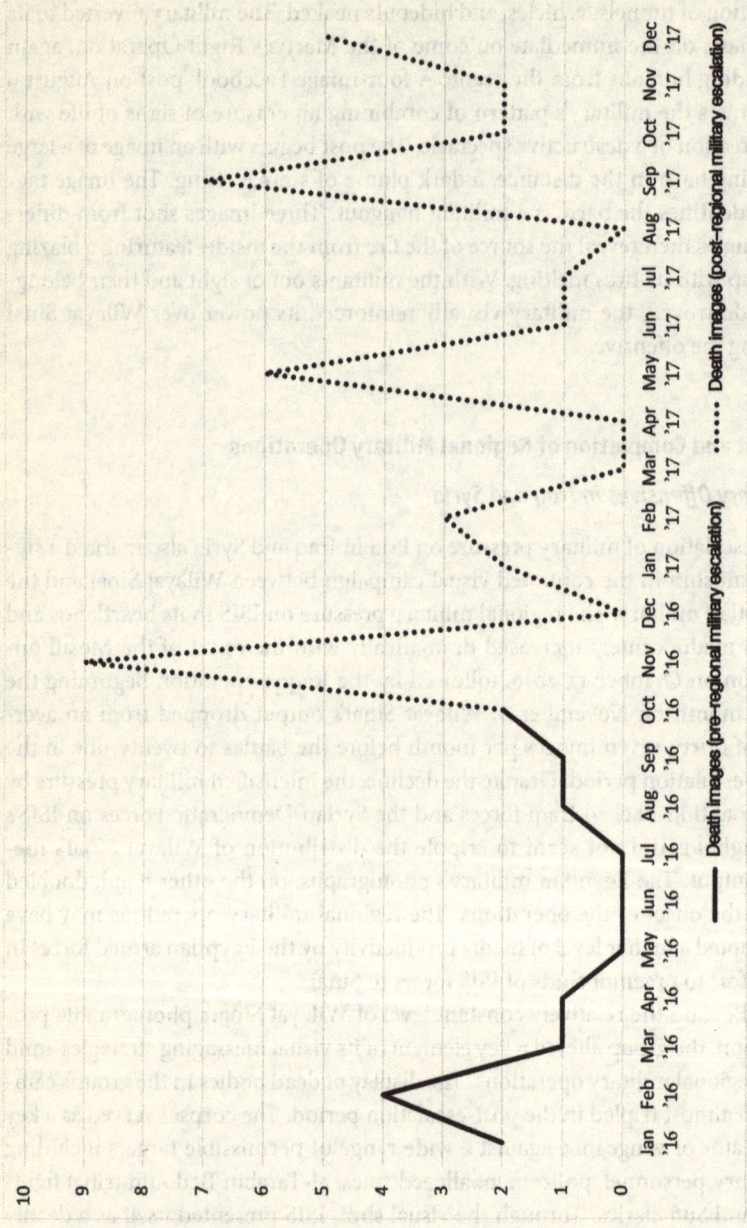

FIGURE 9. Wilayat Sinai's death images, 2016–17.

Meanwhile, regional military operations signaled a different shift in the Egyptian military's visual messaging strategy. The number of images displaying ongoing destruction soared in the post-escalation period. Such images mirrored the state apparatus's media practices after the surge of its own counterterrorism operations in Sinai from 2016 to 2017. The patterned response to planned offensives at the local and regional levels revealed how certain on-the-ground conditions can lead to predictable changes in the visual campaign.

In addition to the interactions between aggregated regional attacks and media campaign activities, certain major military operations had unique relationships with the contested photographic campaigns. Exemplars include when coalition force commanders declared official start dates for the battles of east Mosul, west Mosul, and Raqqa and end dates for the resulting liberation of those respective cities. Such a clear time frame facilitated the identification of any output level and visual strategy shifts during and following the completion of each operation.

While Wilayat Sinai maintained an online visual presence during each of the major regional battles, the defeat of ISIS in Mosul and Raqqa eventually corresponded with a drop in its media output coming out of Sinai. The provincial group temporarily increased its photographic output at the onset of military pressure on east Mosul and Raqqa, perhaps as a means of using its photographic output as an alternative mode of resistance. The increasing displays of death and ongoing destruction served to reinforce the group's spectacle despite the mounting, countervailing local and regional military pressures. But the full liberation of the two cities corresponded to two major declines in Wilayat Sinai's photographic campaign, even though the group was still militarily active in Sinai. The failure to maintain extensive displays of death and destruction after ISIS's regional defeats undermined Wilayat Sinai's image spectacle of the group as a sustainable fighting force. The changes in output levels and nature of content may well relate to the disruption of ISIS's media infrastructure in its main media centers in Mosul and Raqqa.

For the Egyptian military, the major regional operations played a different role. The onset of the Mosul and Raqqa operations did not seem to correspond to any major shifts in the military's images. The military's photographic output reflected only local operations on the ground. Nonetheless, the military's image output remarkably surged at the time when ISIS lost territorial control of its two capital cities. Although the two spikes in photographic output levels coincided with upticks in the number of military counterterrorism operations in Sinai, they may also serve as indicators of 2017 coordination between Egypt and the global coalition to defeat ISIS concurrently in Iraq, Syria, and Sinai. The increasing displays of deaths, ongoing destruction, and security officials in Sinai bolstered the military's online presence by emphasizing its operational success. A closer look at the Sinai visual contestation during the Mosul

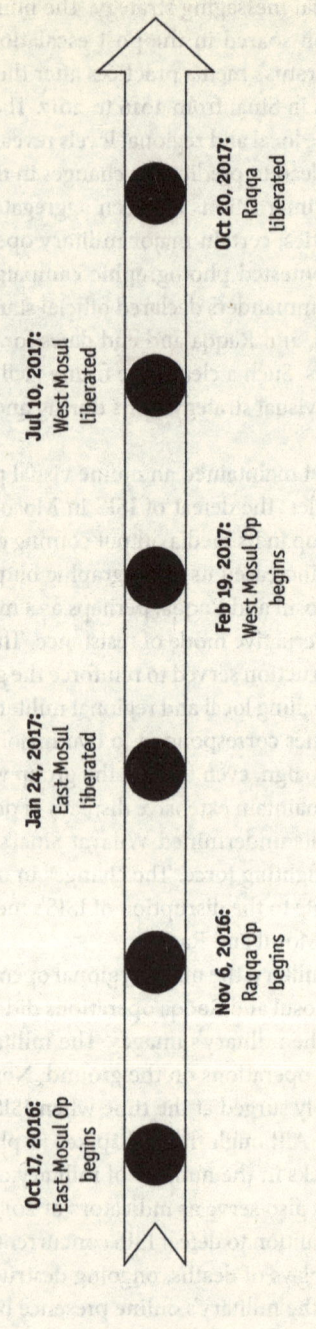

FIGURE 10. Timeline of key military operations in Iraq and Syria, 2016–17.

and Raqqa operations, however, reveals more about the military-photography nexus.

Major Regional Military Operations
EAST MOSUL OPERATION

The onset of the east Mosul operation accompanied a general increase in the level of Wilayat Sinai's photographic output. The same pattern continued throughout the four-month battle that occurred between October 2016 and January 2017, except for the month of December. But even considering the slight drop in December, the group's output was more than in any other month in the third quarter of 2016. The increasing number of images from Sinai presented ISIS as a deadly and destructive force able to sustain itself elsewhere even if the group faced challenges in Mosul.

The launch of the operation also coincided with Wilayat Sinai's self-presentation as a geopolitical player that stands on the side of the Sinai Muslims. One week after the Mosul operation started, Wilayat Sinai disseminated an eleven-image photo report that starts with images of destruction that the group claimed were all the result of Egyptian military's airstrikes. The first eight photographs feature the destruction of deserted one-story buildings adjacent to one another. The devastation ranges from buildings with open craters in their ceilings to others mostly ruined. One shot positions the viewer to peer through an open doorway into destroyed rooms. Devastated agricultural fields then appear in the remaining photographs, showing a large pit in the middle of trees, metal poles bending to the ground, and uprooted tree trunks as they fall to the ground. This display was the first since January 2016 to highlight the outcome of the military's airstrikes on Sinai residents.

As the east Mosul operation continued and the Raqqa operation started in November, Wilayat Sinai's display of deaths reached its highest point in the two-year period, with images showing the corpses of two beheaded Sufi clerics, six soldiers, and one of the group's own militants. The display of ongoing destruction also gradually increased between October 2016 and January 2017, emphasizing gunfire, explosions, artillery, and buildings in flames as part of Wilayat Sinai's attacks. While acknowledging the Egyptian military's air firepower, the group projected itself as a stronger, deadlier force on the ground at a time when ISIS was battling the forces advancing on Mosul.

Wilayat Sinai continued to stress its military and media power even more as ISIS lost east Mosul. Upon the announcement of the full liberation of the eastern part of the city in late January 2017, the group's output leaped again, reaching its highest point since March 2016. That surge accompanied Wilayat Sinai's visual emphasis on the deadliness and the devoutness of its forces as well as its ability to organize workshops and distribute media products on the ground. Less than a month after the liberation, for example, the group released a dozen images featuring certain death, another type of about-to-die portrayals that depict subjects facing impending death where the accompanying text or subsequent images confirm the fatal outcome.[7] Five of those depict several opposing military personnel looking up to the armed militants right before being shot, while the others are confiscated pictures of about twenty enemy fighters whom ISIS identified as dead. The remaining certain death images in February eulogize seven ISIS militants in Sinai by depicting them with their weapons and/or cameras (as a representation of their media involvement) before death. The group's emphasis on certain death that month was all the more striking given that the group had displayed only twenty such images in all of 2016. In the same month, Wilayat Sinai's visualization of nonmilitary activities appeared for the first time in a couple of months to depict a first aid workshop, the distribution of the weekly *al-Naba'* newsletter, and a group of militants praying together. The visual narrative insisted that ISIS's defeat in this major regional operation did not hinder Wilayat Sinai's media operations at all.

The fall of east Mosul also accompanied a boost in the level of the Egyptian military's photographic output. The number of images leaped by over 500 percent in February 2017. The images depicted various scenes ranging from the then–minister of defense and other figures visiting injured soldiers to the former military chief of staff checking on the forces in military bases, the military spokesman in Sinai, and the aftermath of counterterrorism operations. Less than a week after the fall of east Mosul, a five-image Facebook post featured the Egyptian minister of immigration and expatriates' affairs shaking hands with soldiers on their hospital beds, handing them flowers in acknowledgment of their efforts in Sinai, and posing for pictures. The text pointed to the soldiers' willingness to return to the battlefield as soon as possible, despite having suffered injuries, in order to resume their duty of protecting Egypt and its people. The military reached the peak of its monthly photographic output over the two-year period in the wake of ISIS's major regional defeat, perhaps to assure viewers that Wilayat Sinai militants would soon be meeting a similar fate despite the challenges.

In the same period, the military presented itself as a destructive war machine that would bring safety to Sinai in response to the liberation of east Mosul. The military spokesman, Colonel al-Rifai, appeared to visit Sinai and interact with locals soon after ISIS's regional defeat, his only public appearance in Sinai in 2016 and 2017. The five-image post begins with two shots of Colonel al-Rifai standing among his officers and soldiers as they all pose. A subsequent image features al-Rifai sharing a friendly conversation with two armed soldiers in the trenches. He then appears on the street greeting a local elderly woman with a kiss to her forehead. Al-Rifai also poses for a picture with the old woman, ten kids from the same Sinai neighborhood, and military personnel in front of a house that has an Egyptian flag raised on the front patio. At the same time, the scenes showing destruction and no human beings involved in the operations peaked in February, with destroyed tunnels, confiscated vehicles, and burned hideouts as indicators of the Egyptian state's success. Upon ISIS's regional defeat, the military's visual narrative stressed solidarity between civilians and the state's security personnel, perhaps as a justification for its destructive battle against Wilayat Sinai.

WEST MOSUL OPERATION

The onset of the west Mosul operation coincided with a temporary increase in Wilayat Sinai's photographic output. For one week after the operation had started on February 19, 2017, Wilayat Sinai disseminated more than 40 percent of its photographic output that month. The images showed a diverse set of military activities, including a rocket attack on an Israeli settlement, the sniping of an Egyptian soldier on a surveillance tower, IED attacks against two armored personnel carriers, and a battle against Egyptian forces. Yet the group's output subsequently dropped by half in March, before another major drop in April. Wilayat Sinai's failure to sustain its online visual resistance as Iraqi forces continued to advance into west Mosul likely resulted from ISIS's disrupted centralized media outfit.

After the launch of the west Mosul operation, Wilayat Sinai presented itself as a devout force still committed to the defense of Islam. One photograph distributed on March 5, for example, features an armed, masked militant raising both hands to his ears as he calls for prayer in an open battlefield. A subsequent image released the same day displays another armed militant sitting on the ground and reading the Qur'an, with the caption describing the activity as typical during the fighters' leisure time. Concurrently, the group reduced its displays of deaths, impending deaths, and destruction. With ISIS facing setbacks in Mosul, Wilayat Sinai's photographs stressed the common religious identity that united militants and stimulated their perseverance in times of hardship.

Simultaneously, the west Mosul operation coincided with a shift in the Egyptian military's photographic output. The state was at its highest level of visual presence, with February and March 2017 being the most productive months in 2016–17. The images not only displayed the outcome of counterterrorism operations but also showed security officials in North Sinai, school openings, aid distribution, and public figures visiting injured soldiers. The Egyptian military's high levels of photographic activity during the battles in west Mosul emphasized that Sinai was strongly protected.

During west Mosul operations, the military also used visual imagery to define itself as a provider of social services. A twenty-one-image post on March 9, 2017, shows military personnel distributing food packages to civilians in North Sinai for the first time in 2016–17. Egyptian flags appear on each of the packages, in the hands of pictured civilians, and on the outfits of military personnel. Moreover, a five-image post on March 17 shows the minister of defense walking in the streets of North Sinai alongside the minister of the interior and other top security officials, shaking hands with officers and soldiers, and speaking to civilians. This was the first time the military distributed images of both ministers in North Sinai in seven months. Together, the images portrayed Sinai as a safe place due to the presence of authorities who cared about the welfare of the civilian populations.

At the completion of the west Mosul operation, another disruption in Wilayat Sinai's photographic output occurred. When Iraqi prime minister Abadi declared victory over ISIS in Mosul on July 10, 2017, Wilayat Sinai ceased to disseminate any photographs for thirty-one days. Then, after releasing an image on August 11, Wilayat Sinai's photographic campaign sat dormant for another twenty-two days. The group's lowest productivity point between July 10 and the end of August did not coincide with a lack of local attacks in Sinai, as Wilayat Sinai claimed responsibility for a total of thirty-five attacks in July and August 2017, at least twelve of which came after the liberation of west Mosul. The fall of a key ISIS media center coupled with local military pressure in Sinai appeared to severely hinder Wilayat Sinai's ability to produce and disseminate images.

As Wilayat Sinai struggled to continue releasing images after the liberation of west Mosul in July, the Egyptian military disseminated about two images daily the same month. The military increased its output by half, focusing mainly on the security operations in Sinai, ranging from scenes of confiscated materials to airstrikes on militant targets. The military mostly displayed ongoing destruction and excluded pictures of humans engaged in the operations. In a Facebook post on July 21, for example, five photographs depict the destruction of IEDs and the airstrikes targeting militants' hideouts with no humans appearing at the scene. The Egyptian military's decision to reinforce its image as a destructive war machine, however, corresponded both to the west Mosul liberation and to the launch of a new phase of the Martyr's Right Operation in Sinai.

RAQQA OPERATION

Wilayat Sinai increased its monthly photographic output following the launch of the Raqqa operation by the Syrian Democratic Forces in early November 2016. The surge echoed the general increase that occurred during the east Mosul operation around the same time. A closer look, however, reveals that

Wilayat Sinai did not disseminate any images for about two weeks after the November 6 start of the Raqqa operation. Further, the uptick in the November output was mainly due to a twenty-one-image photo report that the group disseminated in late November to visually display a major attack on the al-Sabil military checkpoint. Taken as a whole, the onset of the Raqqa operation may have actually disrupted Wilayat Sinai's media operations temporarily, before the photographic campaign rebounded through their strategy of focused visualization on a single major attack on the local front.

During the Raqqa operation, Wilayat Sinai presented itself as a deadly force not only against security forces but also against civilians. The group's death images peaked in November, the month when the Raqqa campaign began. In fact, a nine-image photo report distributed around mid-November showing the execution of two civilians was the first thing Wilayat Sinai distributed after the Raqqa operation commenced. It begins with the display of a militant reading publicly from a sheet of paper. The caption identifies the reader as delivering a verdict, as over a dozen fellow militants surround him in the desert. The subsequent shots depict two similar punishment scenes where an old blindfolded clergyman kneeling in an orange jumpsuit with hands tied behind his back submissively leans his head on a big wooden log. A masked militant dressed in black stands by the clergyman's side and swings down a sword until it severs the old man's head. The final image further amplifies the horror with a close-up shot of one of the severed heads. As ISIS faced regional pressure, Wilayat Sinai delivered a clear warning to locals not to cross its group.

The completion of the Raqqa operation hampered Wilayat Sinai's media productivity. The month of October constituted the peak of the group's output in eighteen months. After the fall of Raqqa on October 20, Wilayat Sinai disseminated over two dozen images in just eleven days. But then the group failed to release any images for a week, the longest silence in October. The remaining images came in two generic photo reports showing green fields and destruction in Sinai. The output then faltered in November with a 92 percent drop. As in the aftermath of west Mosul's liberation, ISIS's defeat in Raqqa severely disrupted Wilayat Sinai's media operations despite the ongoing local attacks.

The fall of Raqqa also corresponded to a shift in the provincial group's visual messaging strategy. After coalition forces liberated the Syrian city, Wilayat Sinai failed to maintain its image as a deadly and destructive fighting force. Instead, it emphasized the suffering of residents at the hands of the Egyptian military and the beautiful landscape of North Sinai. A thirteen-image photo report on October 28 shows fruit hanging from trees in a field, which constituted the first display of Sinai green fields in twenty months. The other seventeen-image photo report on October 29 shows purported scenes of destruction in Rafah and residents moving out of their homes as a result of the military's actions. This second report was also the first to depict such scenes of destruction in about a year. Wilayat Sinai's photographs emphasized the grievances of Sinai locals upon the loss of Raqqa.

On the other hand, the fall of Raqqa boosted the Egyptian military's output. In the days following the liberation, the military disseminated numerous images showing the aftermath of its local operations. In the next month, the military's output reached its highest point in five months. The official images mostly depicted counterterrorism operations, the destruction of drugs, and the military's newly appointed chief of staff, Major General Mohamed Fareed, visiting the security forces in North Sinai. The increasing Sinai photographs after ISIS's regional defeat may have been a tactical choice by the military to suggest a near victory against the militants in Sinai.

After the liberation of Raqqa, the Egyptian military further depicted itself as a deadly and destructive war machine against militants. Upon the fall of Raqqa, the military showed the corpses of armed militants at a rate higher than in most months. Subsequently, images displaying ongoing destruction peaked in November, showing explosions from airstrikes and vehicles, hideouts, and drugs ablaze. Meanwhile, the military documented Major General Fareed's visit in four of the images, the first of a senior security official in North Sinai since March 2017. Together, the images presented a more secure, safer Sinai.

Loss of Leaders at the Local Level

The loss of key Wilayat Sinai leaders had a varied relationship with the Sinai battlefield of online visual contestation. The killing of two local Wilayat Sinai leaders and dozens of militants coincided with major drops in photographic output. In this period Wilayat Sinai's photographs featured warning messages to local residents and displayed retaliations against collaborators with the military, perhaps in an effort to avoid such group losses in the future. Meanwhile, the loss of the two leaders corresponded with a boost, or at least similar levels of the military's photographic output. In the aftermath of these operations, the increasing displays of military martyrs, top security officials, and tours in central Sinai served to reinforce the military's narrative of victory.

In his Facebook statements, the Egyptian military spokesman clearly treated Wilayat Sinai's senior leaders differently from the hundreds of dead militants in 2016 and 2017. The spokesman rarely cited names of any of the more than eight hundred Wilayat Sinai members whom the military claimed responsibility for killing over the two-year period. But he made an exception to publicize the death of two senior leaders of the group: Abu Duaa al-Ansari and Abu Anas al-Ansari. A closer look at the photographic aftermath of the two deaths helps explain the relationship between loss of leaders and the visual contestation.

Abu Duaa Al-Ansari's Death

The killing of Wilayat Sinai's leader Abu Duaa al-Ansari played a role in disrupting the militant group's photographic campaign. On August 4, 2016, the Egyptian military spokesman announced the killing of al-Ansari and over forty-five other militants in a series of airstrikes. The statement specified neither the exact date of the operation nor al-Ansari's real name. About ten days before the announcement though, Wilayat Sinai's photographic output stopped, ceasing altogether between July 25 and August 24, 2016. For the entire month of August, the group chose not to display photos of any of its claimed attacks with a single exception. It released five images on August 25, showing the execution of a guard working for the Ministry of the Interior in al-Arish. Three of the images display the guard's impending death, with the accompanying textual content verifying his death. The remaining two images show the front and back of the guard's national ID as evidence of his involvement with the police. The killing of al-Ansari and his associated group members corresponded to the lowest point of Wilayat Sinai's 2016 photographic campaign.

The killing of al-Ansari also marked a shift in the Egyptian military's visual messaging strategy. Raising its image output after al-Ansari's death, the military focused on its own leaders as well as on the outcomes of its counterterrorism operations. Eight images on August 17, for example, featured then–minister of defense Sedki Sobhi and then–minister of the interior Magdy Abdelghaffar in North Sinai checking on the security forces, handing out gifts to soldiers and officers, and posing for group pictures. These images were the first to portray leaders visiting the peninsula since the two ministers met with the security forces in North Sinai in mid-May 2016. The military reportedly released cockpit images of the airstrikes, but quickly removed them.[8] The military thus used its imagery to present itself as an effective force against militants and to identify Sinai as a safe place for top security officials to visit, rather than run the risk of elevating the martyr status of al-Ansari for the Sinai civilian population.

Abu Anas Al-Ansari's Death

The killing of senior leader Abu Anas al-Ansari also disrupted Wilayat Sinai's output. On April 2, 2017, the Egyptian military spokesman announced their March 18 airstrikes had killed Abu Anas al-Ansari and seventeen other militants. The released announcement provided al-Ansari's real name and described him as one of the founders of the group. For nine days after the fatal airstrikes, the militant group released no images whatsoever. It then distributed two images visualizing the confiscated belongings of a policeman, followed by another image eulogizing one of the group members in late March.

The group further saw an additional drop in photographic output in the following month.

After the leader's loss of life, Wilayat Sinai presented itself as a strict, deadly fighting force. One photo report issued a clear warning for Sinai residents siding with the Egyptian military. Several images of the report showed militants distributing written warnings on the streets and accepting individuals who had repented from collaborating with the Egyptian military in Sinai. The remaining photographs highlighted the fate of those who did not repent, such as four images of collaborators with the Egyptian military photographed right before their executions according to accompanying text. Wilayat Sinai emphasized the harsh consequences that await locals who prove to be disloyal to the group.

The killing of Abu Anas simultaneously corresponded to a boost in the Egyptian military's output. The military distributed dozens of images in the three weeks following the airstrikes of March 18, 2017. Although the airstrikes that killed Abu Anas did not appear in the photographic campaign, the military did release a video on the same day showing eight different airstrikes in Sinai. A sizable portion of the photographs between March 18 and 31 showed underground tunnels, confiscated vehicles, burning drugs, militants' corpses, officials visiting injured soldiers, school openings, and the military's martyrs. Subsequently in the first week of April, the military put out numerous images displaying both First Lieutenant General Sobhi visiting injured soldiers and the immediate aftermath of the counterterrorism operations in Sinai. The photographs thus presented the killing of the Wilayat Sinai leader as just one component of an intensified military campaign in Sinai.

The military used the images to bolster its standing as an effective force. The spokesman distributed over a dozen images early April 2017 to show a recorded tour in Halal Mountain for journalists and TV reporters, where the Egyptian military had recently regained full control. More importantly, the only three certain death images of martyred officers that the military disseminated in 2016–17 came in the week after the March 18 airstrikes. In addition, the military stressed the compassion of its leaders by featuring the minister of defense, minister of the interior, the chief of staff, and politicians visiting injured soldiers as well as the minister of education opening a school in Sinai. Hence, the military complemented its power displays with images that portray its personnel as heroic and its leaders as caring, despite their killing of Wilayat Sinai's founder.

Loss of Leaders at the Regional Level

Unlike media shifts corresponding to the deaths of local Wilayat Sinai leaders, the loss of regional ISIS leaders, in most cases, did not relate to changes in the online visual contestation space of Sinai. Although the loss of two regional media leaders, Abu Sulayman al-Iraqi and Yusuf Demir, did align with shifts in output, the majority of the other killings did not. The differences between the loss of al-Iraqi and Demir, as compared with the other regional leaders, is not explainable by the nature, location, or target of the attacks. Notable changes in the two competing media campaigns associated with the senior status of al-Iraqi and Demir, for example, did not apply to the deaths of other senior media officials. The only difference consistently emergent from the aggregated leader loss was the date of death. The loss of the two media leaders that did correspond to shifts in photographic output and strategy occurred in early July and late November 2017, respectively. The two periods coincided with other factors occurring on both the local and regional fronts, such as the launch of the fourth phase of the Martyr's Right Operation in Sinai and the full liberation of Mosul and Raqqa. Hence, shifts in output corresponding to the loss of al-Iraqi and Demir may have more to do with the disruption of Wilayat Sinai's local media infrastructure and ISIS's regional media hubs responsible for disseminating provincial images online.

For al-Iraqi, Demir, and other leaders, the Pentagon was the source announcing their deaths in Iraq and Syria throughout 2016 and 2017. The Pentagon statements identified the coalition airstrikes as the main cause of death for almost all leaders during that period. The leaders targeted for death included those in ISIS's military, financial, religious, and media sectors.

In 2016, Wilayat Sinai's photographic productivity continued despite the group's losses of senior commander Abu Omar al-Shishani, spokesman Abu Muhammad al-Adnani, head of media Abu Muhammad al-Furqan, and media facilitator Mahmoud al-Isawi in Syria. In fact, the group's output increased in line with its typical distribution patterns in the months corresponding to the deaths. Similarly, the loss of ISIS leaders did not appear to prompt changes in the Egyptian military's output. The shifts were more in line with the downward trend in place during the first three-quarters of 2016 and the regular monthly ebbs and flows in the fourth quarter.

In 2017, most of the killings of media, clerical, and financial leaders in Iraq and Syria also did not hamper Wilayat Sinai's photographic campaign. For example, the provincial group disseminated more images in May despite the April and May deaths of ISIS media leaders Abu Ali al-Janubi, Abu Sayf al-Isawi, and Abu Khattab al-Rawi. The death of the head of Amaq media wing Rayan Meshaal, cleric Turki al-Bin Ali, and the top financier Fawaz al-Rawi be-

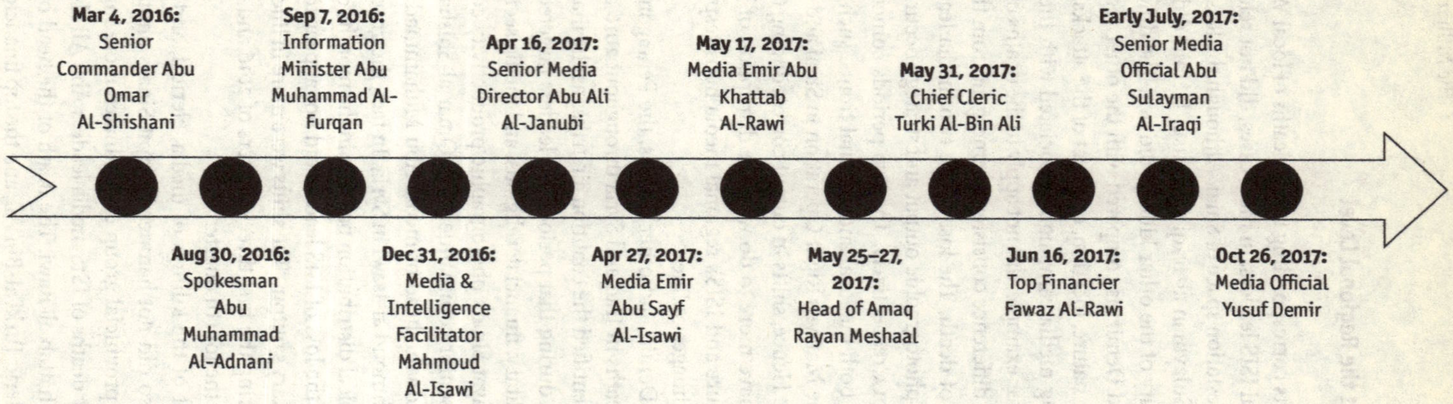

Mar 4, 2016: Senior Commander Abu Omar Al-Shishani

Aug 30, 2016: Spokesman Abu Muhammad Al-Adnani

Sep 7, 2016: Information Minister Abu Muhammad Al-Furqan

Dec 31, 2016: Media & Intelligence Facilitator Mahmoud Al-Isawi

Apr 16, 2017: Senior Media Director Abu Ali Al-Janubi

Apr 27, 2017: Media Emir Abu Sayf Al-Isawi

May 17, 2017: Media Emir Abu Khattab Al-Rawi

May 25–27, 2017: Head of Amaq Rayan Meshaal

May 31, 2017: Chief Cleric Turki Al-Bin Ali

Jun 16, 2017: Top Financier Fawaz Al-Rawi

Early July, 2017: Senior Media Official Abu Sulayman Al-Iraqi

Oct 26, 2017: Media Official Yusuf Demir

FIGURE 11. Timeline of reported ISIS leaders killed in Iraq and Syria, 2016–17. Source: U.S. Department of Defense's Statements on Operation Inherent Resolve.

tween late May and mid-June did not correspond with any major declines in Wilayat Sinai and the Egyptian military's outputs either. Further, none of the images distributed by both sides addressed, mourned, or celebrated the death of ISIS leaders in Iraq and Syria. Although the loss of ISIS leaders in 2017 did not generally correspond with substantial shifts in the photographic output or messaging strategies in the online space of Sinai visual contestation, al-Iraqi's and Demir's deaths served as exceptions. An examination of those two incidents helps provide a more nuanced understanding of how leader loss corresponds to competing state and non-state media campaigns.

Abu Sulayman Al-Iraqi's Death

The killing of media leader Abu Sulayman al-Iraqi coincided with a drop in Wilayat Sinai's photographic output. On July 27, 2017, the Pentagon announced the early July killing of al-Iraqi in an airstrike near Mosul without specifying the exact date. The same statement described him as a senior media official who oversaw the production of ISIS media products. Perhaps unsurprisingly, then, Wilayat Sinai did not release any images between June 30 and July 8. For the next eight weeks, the group distributed a single news brief on July 9 that shows the attack on a military checkpoint south of Rafah and only one other image in August eulogizing one of its militants.

In contrast the Egyptian military dramatically increased its output following the ISIS's leader loss at the regional level. While the timing implies that the regional leader's death may have influenced image output levels, the content of the images suggests otherwise. The bulk of the images showed death and ongoing destruction that captured conditions on the ground in Sinai. Consequently, local conditions rather than regional loss of leaders in the ISIS group appear to have motivated the shift in visual messaging strategy.

Yusuf Demir's Death

The killing of media leader Yusuf Demir corresponded with another drop in Wilayat Sinai's output. On November 14, 2017, the Pentagon announced the October 26 killing of Demir near al-Qaim, Iraq, describing him as a media official who had links to ISIS's networks in the Middle East. For about two weeks between October 29 and November 13, Wilayat Sinai did not disseminate any images. Having distributed dozens of images in October before Demir's death, the group released barely six images in November following his passing.

In contrast, the Egyptian military sharply increased its photographic output after the ISIS media leader's death. The military reached one of its highest output peaks in the two-year period in November, the month following his death. None of these images, however, addressed the loss of Demir or any other leader outside Egypt. The November shifts in the display of ongoing destruction and top security officials in North Sinai in the military's images instead reflected local conditions on the ground.

Introduction of Groups to the Local Battlefield

The introduction of local Bedouin tribes participating in the on-the-ground battles played an important role in the online visual contestation related to Sinai. Despite the surge in both Wilayat Sinai and the Egyptian military's outputs, the two sides in the conflict communicated different messages. Wilayat Sinai's photographic campaign sent a warning, stressing that retaliatory acts would happen against tribal members who had collaborated with the Egyptian security forces. Meanwhile, the military's photographic campaign communicated a message of victory and dominance by emphasizing the positive outcomes of its counterterrorism operations. The changing dynamics of local battles appeared to influence the Sinai photographic warfare, with both sides using the engagement of tribal fighters as a pretext to frame their conflicting messages.

Al-Tarabin Bedouin tribe, for example, spearheaded an initiative to join the Egyptian military in the fight against Wilayat Sinai militants in the North. In mid-April 2017, militants reportedly shot at a truck that was smuggling cigarettes into North Sinai, which spurred clashes between Wilayat Sinai and local tribal members. The local Bedouins then reportedly kidnapped three of Wilayat Sinai's members, after which the militants kidnapped tribal leaders in response. Tensions further escalated when a Wilayat Sinai suicide attacker detonated a car bomb at al-Tarabin tribal checkpoint in Rafah, killing at least four. In turn, al-Tarabin tribe declared war on Wilayat Sinai after releasing a statement late April stressing its ability to forcefully respond to "terrorists" and calling on other North Sinai Bedouin tribes to stand up and join the fight. For a timeline of the escalating tensions between al-Tarabin and Wilayat Sinai, see Figure 12.

The introduction of al-Tarabin tribe into the ongoing fight against Wilayat Sinai coincided with a boost in the group's photographic output. With the assistance of al-Tarabin tribesmen, the Egyptian military's counterterrorism operations peaked in May 2017. In response, Wilayat Sinai's photographic output in May almost doubled, with the majority of the images showcasing the fight against al-Tarabin members and its outcome. A four-image news brief on May 13, for example, begins with a shot of four Toyota pickups lined up next to one another. The caption describes the vehicles as spoils of Wilayat Sinai's victory against the tribal fighters. The two subsequent shots display a large number of confiscated AK47s, rifles, pistols, ammunitions, rockets, and two-way radios

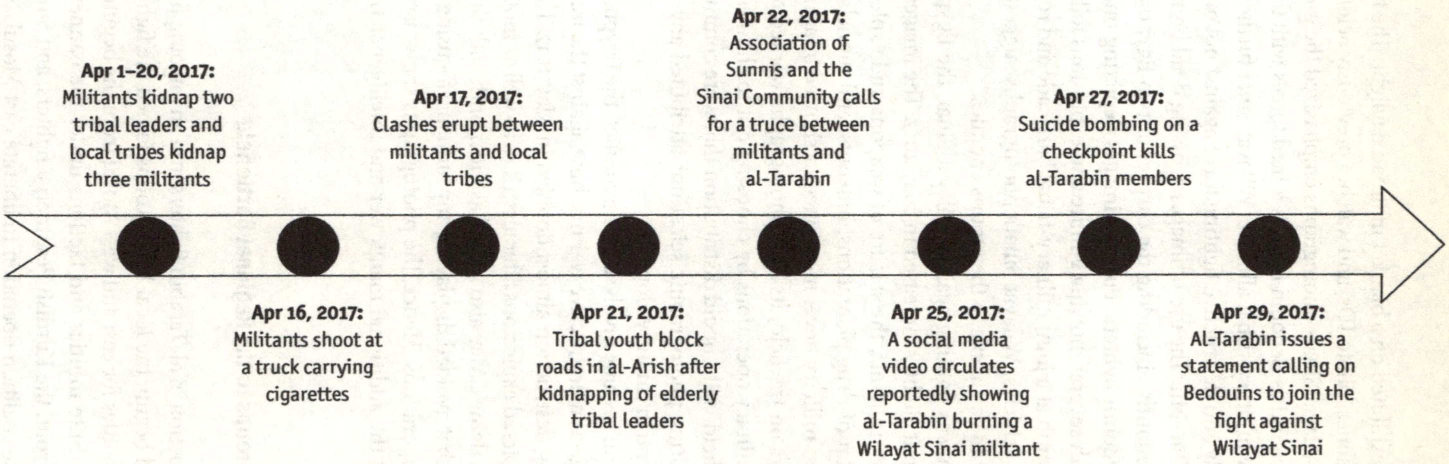

Apr 1-20, 2017: Militants kidnap two tribal leaders and local tribes kidnap three militants

Apr 16, 2017: Militants shoot at a truck carrying cigarettes

Apr 17, 2017: Clashes erupt between militants and local tribes

Apr 21, 2017: Tribal youth block roads in al-Arish after kidnapping of elderly tribal leaders

Apr 22, 2017: Association of Sunnis and the Sinai Community calls for a truce between militants and al-Tarabin

Apr 25, 2017: A social media video circulates reportedly showing al-Tarabin burning a Wilayat Sinai militant

Apr 27, 2017: Suicide bombing on a checkpoint kills al-Tarabin members

Apr 29, 2017: Al-Tarabin issues a statement calling on Bedouins to join the fight against Wilayat Sinai

FIGURE 12. Timeline of key tensions between Wilayat Sinai and local tribes, April 2017.

that the militants exhibited on a blanket in broad daylight. The final images focus on multiple phones, photo IDs, and watches previously belonging to the al-Tarabin fighters. Wilayat Sinai's photographs emphasized the group's increased presence on the ground as Bedouin fighters joined forces with the military.

After the new military-tribal alliance, Wilayat Sinai further reinforced its identity as a deadly and destructive fighting force against not only the security forces but also al-Tarabin. The use of images showing dead bodies in May was the highest in six months, including the corpses of two Egyptian soldiers and five al-Tarabin Bedouin fighters. Further, images depicting ongoing destruction increased, with several showing gunfire and explosions following the detonation of a car bomb at a joint military-tribal barricade and roadside IED attacks on military vehicles. Wilayat Sinai's photographs suggested that defeat was the only outcome available to the group's enemies.

As al-Tarabin was fighting against Wilayat Sinai, the Egyptian military's photographic output slightly increased in May 2017. The images displayed the arrest of suspected militants, the seizure of weapons and explosive materials, and the destruction of drug plantations, hideouts, and tunnels at the border. While the Egyptian military never mentioned or showed images of collaborating tribal members on the field, its May photographs worked to focus viewer attention on its military operations by choosing not to show other images of school openings, field visits, or aid distribution that were common in previous months. The resulting photographic selections attributed any success on the ground to the Egyptian military alone.

After al-Tarabin became involved in the conflict, the Egyptian military underscored its image as a destructive war machine against the militants. Images displaying ongoing destruction almost doubled in May 2017. The destruction-related images depicted explosions after airstrikes as well as motorcycles, hideouts, and drugs in flames. May also served as the month with the second highest use of images that avoided displaying any humans, focusing instead on the outcomes of the operations. Hence, the photographs showcased the victories that accompanied the additional manpower and intelligence the military enjoyed at that time.

Introduction of Groups to the Regional Battlefield

Unlike the introduction of al-Tarabin fighters into an ongoing fight in Sinai after operations had begun, the local Iraqi groups joined the fight alongside the Iraqi army in the battles for east and west Mosul from the beginning of the operations. Armed Shiite militias and factions under the banner of the Popular Mobilization Front, the Kurdish Peshmerga fighters, and Sunni tribal units were all part of the coalition operation to liberate east Mosul. Nonetheless, to avoid civil and sectarian strife, a political agreement prior to the onset of the east Mosul operation dictated that only the Iraqi army would enter the city. The other local groups encircled the city to cut off supply and escape routes. As a result, between the beginning of November 2016 and late January 2017, the Iraqi army fought ISIS militants on the front lines inside east Mosul. The west Mosul operation followed a similar plan except that the Peshmerga fighters did not take part. By late February 2017, the Iraqi army and security forces entered west Mosul and fought ISIS until they liberated the city in July. The complicated on-the-ground context prevents examination of particular groups from an evolutionary perspective, as the individual contribution of any one group could not be disaggregated from the broader collective.

The Raqqa operation, by contrast, did not involve a leading state military force like the operations in Mosul or Sinai. The U.S.-backed Syrian Democratic Forces was an alliance of different local groups, including Arab, Kurdish, and Turkman fighters prior to the onset of the battle for Raqqa. The anti-ISIS alliance launched the operation to encircle the city and eventually liberate Raqqa. With support from the broader international coalition, the Syrian Democratic Forces successfully liberated the city after almost one year. Here, the local groups were already the initiators of the military operation rather than newcomers joining the fight at some midpoint. Again, this context does not allow for a comparable examination of the interaction between the introduction of particular groups to the regional battlefield or Sinai's two competing media campaigns.

Concluding Thoughts

This chapter has demonstrated that the competing sides battling online with photographs to control the Sinai narrative in 2016–17 were not simply altering their productivity to respond to each other's media campaigns. In fact, no consistent, identifiable patterns existed between Wilayat Sinai and the Egyptian military's photographic outputs when considered exclusively within the media context.

Instead, the Sinai photographic warfare closely interacted with military conditions happening on the ground. Five key battlefield factors corresponded with shifts in the competing photographic campaigns: attacks by militant groups, onset of counterterrorism military operations, successful completion of counterterrorism military operations, loss of militant group leaders, and battlefield alliances carried out between local tribes and groups with state-based military forces. The introduction of each military condition coincided with shifts in both the level of the photographic output and the visual messaging strategies. Such interactions reveal that while the military context influences the output of and messaging strategies in the competing campaigns, the photographs also can shape viewers' perceptions of what is taking place on the ground.

As both state and non-state actors now pledge allegiance to broader collectives to enhance their security interests, consideration of both the local and broader regional/global contexts is necessary to avoid distorted understandings of how militant groups conduct photographic warfare. At the local level in Sinai, the onset of the Egyptian military's counterterrorism operations and the loss of militant leaders coincided with disruptions of Wilayat Sinai's photographic campaign, while major attacks by the militant group helped maintain its online presence. The introduction of a participating tribal group into the battlefield activities prompted a surge in Wilayat Sinai's photographic campaign. At the regional level, the completion of counterterrorism operations in Mosul and Raqqa and the loss of two media leaders in Iraq corresponded with major drops in Wilayat Sinai's online visual presence.

Local and regional/global military contexts are also critical for understanding how state actors deploy photographic warfare in the contemporary environment of global communications. At the local level, the Egyptian security operations, the targeting of Wilayat Sinai's leaders, and the involvement of the al-Tarabin tribe in the Sinai battlefield all corresponded to an expanded use of the Egyptian military's photographic campaign. At the regional level, the fall of Mosul and Raqqa also coincided with major surges in the Egyptian military's output.

Consideration of the visual messaging strategies that state and non-state actors employ is key to further contextualize the shifts in photographic warfare. Wilayat Sinai's depiction of ongoing fires and explosions, for example, dropped as the group's attacks declined in Sinai, the weapon of choice shifted, and the local and regional military pressure increased. The provincial group started to circulate more death images after select major local attacks at times of mounting pressure on Mosul and Raqqa. In the meantime, all the spikes in the Egyptian military's display of death were directly addressing and/or responding to Wilayat Sinai's major deadly attacks in North Sinai. After the fall of east Mosul and Raqqa, the Egyptian military chose to disseminate images of top security officials safely visiting North Sinai. A quantitative approach that only counts the images would treat all output as equal. Thus, examining the content using a set of relevant visual elements and tropes helps identify the shifting visual strategies in the photographic campaigns in relation to military conditions.

This chapter has further revealed that an exclusive focus on a single military factor can eclipse other elements of the military-photography nexus. For example, when Wilayat Sinai disseminated only one image in almost two months in the summer of 2017, the drop corresponded to a conflation of factors: the killing of a senior ISIS media leader near Mosul in early July, a deadly military checkpoint attack by Wilayat Sinai on July 7 that sparked retaliation from the military, the full liberation of Mosul on July 10, and the onset of the Egyptian military's fourth phase of the Martyr's Right Operation on July 17. Similarly, the surge in the military's output in November 2017 and the heightened displays of destruction and dead militants also corresponded to several factors: a couple of deadly attacks by Wilayat Sinai in mid-October, an uptick in the number of counterterrorism operations in Sinai, and the full liberation of Raqqa. Hence, a collective approach to analyzing on-the-ground events allows state actors and researchers to identify the changing military dynamics and their corresponding shifts in the photographic warfare.

Accounting for the photographic template is also necessary in today's online media battlefield. Print media restrictions on the quantity of printed photographs no longer apply to state and non-state actors competing in digital photographic warfare. Both sides engaging in a visual contestation can easily disseminate an entire photo album in one post on Telegram, Facebook, and other platforms. Wilayat Sinai's output of twenty-two images in July 2017, for example, was higher than the group's total photographic output in eleven other months included in the two-year period. However, this previous statement would be misguiding without knowing they all made up one photo report focusing on a single incident. Similarly, the Egyptian military often disseminated multiple images per Facebook post, sometimes exceeding twenty. Simply counting the monthly visual output can misrepresent the intensity of an actor's photographic production in relation to on-the-ground military conditions. Insights on the template can thus clarify the magnitude of online photographic campaigns more accurately.

Meanwhile, available data limitations complicate understandings of how on-the-ground military conditions intersect with the photographic warfare operations of state and non-state actors. Counting ISIS's attacks in Iraq and Syria, for example, posed a challenge because the available online data sets exhibit stark methodological differences. START's GTD draws on open-source materials—news articles, journals, books, and legal documents—to provide longitudinal data on terrorism incidents by group, country, and month from 1970. Jane's Terrorism and Insurgency Centre (JTIC) also draws from open-source materials to provide an annual global attack index of attacks per group and country since 2009. But unlike GTD, JTIC's publicly available data do not provide a breakdown of attacks per month. Other organizations employ a less reliable methodology than GTD and JTIC. The PeaceTech Lab NGO, for example, uses crowdsourced data from Wikipedia to map terrorism incidents by both group and country since 2016. The controversial Religion of Peace website uses public news sources to provide a list of attacks since 2002, but the list neither specifies the perpetrator group nor includes incidents related to combat. This chapter relied on the GTD data set to extract ISIS's attacks in Iraq and Syria in 2016 and 2017. However, GTD includes counts of attacks that security officials believe ISIS perpetrated even if the group does not claim responsibility. Such a methodology can skew the data away from Wilayat Sinai's claimed attacks. With the precise error rate from these data sources unknowable, the data collection process nonetheless suggests variables that deserve consideration in debates about the military-photography nexus.

Moreover, some aspects of the Egyptian military operations were difficult to ascertain. This chapter used the Egyptian military's statements as the main source of information on counterterrorism operations and loss of leaders. But the military may have also conducted covert counterterrorism operations in Sinai that they did not publicly report. The military may have also killed other influential leaders in Wilayat Sinai, but for strategic reasons may not have publicized those results. Further, unlike ISIS in Iraq and Syria, Wilayat Sinai did not govern cities in Sinai for the Egyptian military to liberate. Accordingly, the second, third, and fourth phases of the Martyr's Right Operation did not have clear end dates to mark liberation. These factors made it difficult to definitively investigate shifts in the visual contestation relating to the completion of local operations or other unpublicized developments on the ground.

This chapter has taken a first step in examining the relationship between competing photographic campaigns and a range of local and regional military factors in times of conflict. Future work can apply this approach to other conflicts to understand visual contestation beyond the Sinai Peninsula. In addition, this chapter has used a case study of two main players: the state and a militant group. Other conflicts, however, may involve more than two competitors on the military and media battlefields. Researchers can build on this approach to examine the visual contestations among multiple actors and utilize time series analysis as an indicator of shifts over time.

CHAPTER 3

The Visual Framing Battle

The online media structures and products of non-state militant actors today contest and complicate conventional visual wartime campaigns of nation-states. Key Islamist militant groups, like al-Qaeda, which encompasses branches in North Africa, Somalia, Yemen, Syria, and south Asia, have evolved into transnational organizations, each with its own designated media operations. ISIS's network of provincial media offices further projects militant operations as well as semblances of state-building efforts in numerous African, Asian, and European countries.

However, considering various non-state actors as composite members of one high-profile, collective organization at war with state opponents can be misleading. Localized strategies and exchanges render each context unique. Robert Entman's conception of framing is helpful, as his framework can unveil the interactions between frames put out by a local branch, province, or state. It can also highlight how visual messages cohere into a synergistic campaign.[1] Nonetheless, his approach stops short of providing an evaluative framework for gauging competing content of oppositional actors.

To address the need to better understand contested online media campaigns in wartime, this chapter assesses the visual field constructed by ISIS's Wilayat Sinai and the Egyptian military at the peak of the Sinai insurgency in 2016 and 2017. The two sides of the conflict use photographers and online platforms to not only create, emphasize, and ignore different messages about Sinai but also converse with one another in their efforts to dominate the frames. The chapter begins by showing how Entman's four framing associations—problem definition, causal interpretation, moral evaluation, and treatment recommendation—work together to present a unique picture for each side of the Sinai conflict. It dissects the most recurring frames on each side, describes the reinforcing roles of visual and text messaging in the frame construction process, compares select visual exemplars to standard practices, and emphasizes the significance of key frames to each side's corresponding narratives. It then lays out how the opposing visual frames interact with each other through competition, negation, and expansion. The chapter concludes with a discussion of how these interactive strategies can guide better understandings of photographic warfare between state and non-state actors in times of conflict.

Wilayat Sinai's Photographic Campaign

Wilayat Sinai presented eight hundred online images in 2016 and 2017. At the bottom of each image, a superimposed caption described and highlighted various aspects of both the displayed scene and the conflict at large. The Wilayat Sinai logo on the bottom right of each image consistently identified the source of the images. The full array of posted images fell into two main categories: military and nonmilitary activities. The military images made up the majority of the group's photographic campaign.

Wilayat Sinai's use of force is what the military images focused on. They comprised four visual frames: combat, battlefield aftermath, martyrdom, and military training. The combat visual frame simply involved the actions on the battlefront. The battle aftermath visual frame focused on the fighting outcomes. The martyrdom and military training visual frames highlighted the militants' physical and spiritual preparations before the actual battles.

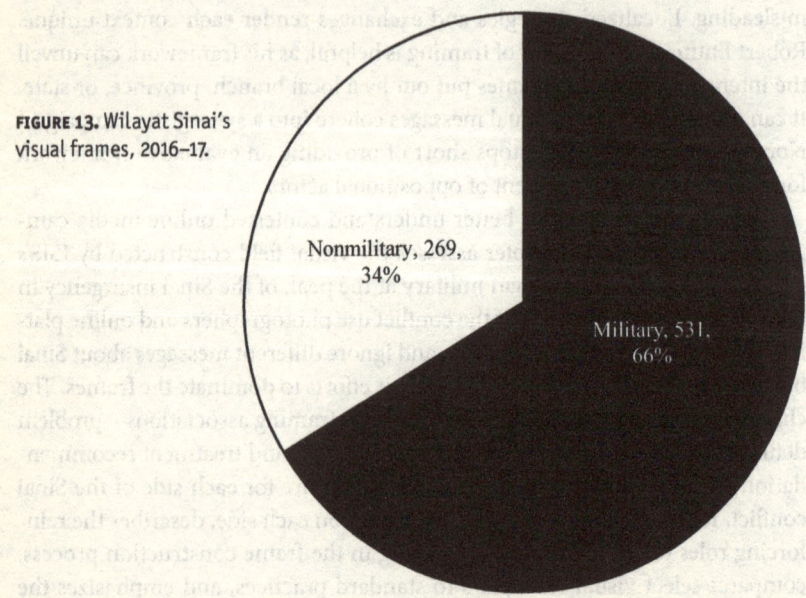

FIGURE 13. Wilayat Sinai's visual frames, 2016–17.

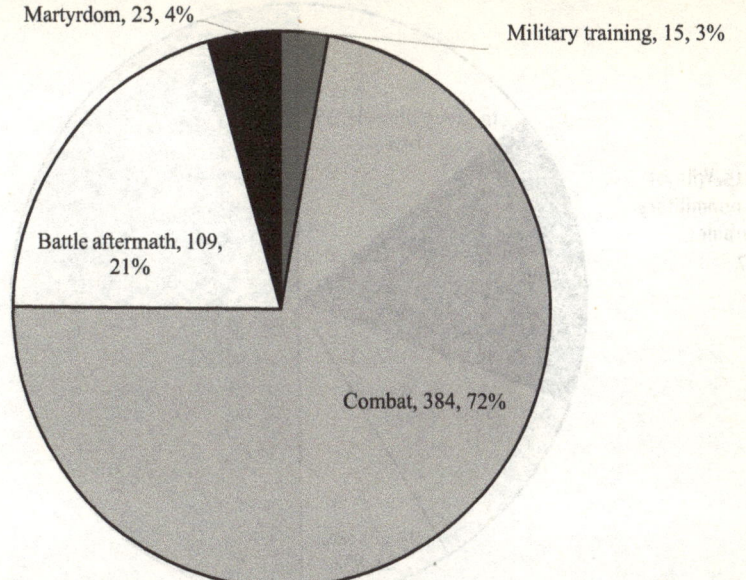

FIGURE 14. Wilayat Sinai's military visual frames, 2016–17.

Meanwhile, the nonmilitary photographs foregrounded life in Sinai away from the battlefield. They revealed five visual frames: law enforcement, victimhood of Sinai Muslims, in-group lifestyle, Sinai landscape, and healthcare. The law enforcement visual frame focused on the maintenance of order in the peninsula. The victimhood of Sinai Muslims visual frame highlighted the consequences of the Egyptian military actions on the Sinai citizenry. The in-group lifestyle frame involved the activities members chose to perform in their spare time. The Sinai landscape frame depicted nature and the proximate fields, while the healthcare provision frame featured an independent social service available to care for the sick and injured in the province.

Together, Wilayat Sinai's military and nonmilitary visual frames cohered into an overarching narrative that exhibited all of Entman's four categories (see Table 3). Through photographs and captions, the group identified the presence of apostates, spies, polytheists, and Jews as a problem. The oppression of Sinai Muslims and collusion with security forces constituted the underlying cause for the apostasy of ISIS's opponents. Wilayat Sinai's photographic campaign foregrounded training, fighting apostates, spies, and Jews, conducting suicide operations, confiscating the opponents' belongings, executing spies and polytheists, and providing healthcare as the treatment recommendations needed to end the Sinai conflict. Morally, the group juxtaposed its own notions of piety, camaraderie, and protection of the community with their enemies' airstrikes

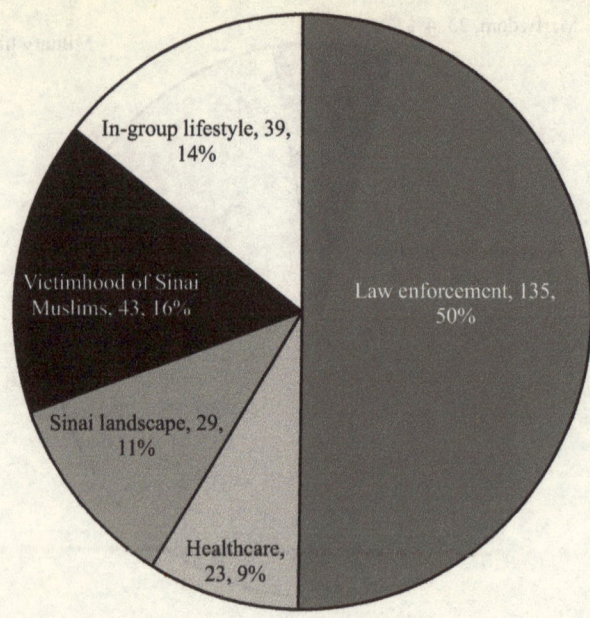

FIGURE 15. Wilayat Sinai's nonmilitary visual frames, 2016–17.

TABLE 3. Wilayat Sinai's framing categories in 2016–17

Framing category	Visual frame	Message
Problem definition	Combat	Apostates and Jews are in and around Sinai
	Battle aftermath	Spies operate in Sinai
	Law enforcement	Vice and polytheism exist in Sinai
Causal interpretation	Victimhood of Sinai Muslims	Evicting Sinai Muslims and destroying their homes make the Egyptian security forces apostates
	Law enforcement	Collaborating with the Egyptian security forces makes individual Muslims spies and apostates
		Practicing Sufi Islam makes individual Muslims polytheists
Treatment recommendation	Combat	Fight and destroy the apostates and spies
	Battle aftermath	Confiscate enemy artillery and belongings
	Martyrdom	Conduct suicide operations
		Fight in the media battlefield
	Military training	Work together and prepare for battle
	Law enforcement	Execute spies and polytheists
		Destroy forbidden materials
	Healthcare	Provide healthcare services

Framing category	Visual frame	Message
Moral evaluation	Martyrdom	Wilayat Sinai members are pious and willing to sacrifice their lives for their cause
	In-group lifestyle	Group members are brothers who share one mission
	Sinai landscape	The group is morally obligated to protect the sacred land of Sinai
	Law enforcement	The group will apply shari'a law to protect Sinai from vice and treason
	Victimhood of Sinai Muslims	The Egyptian military lacks morality because it oppresses Sinai Muslims

Results emerged from an analysis of both the photos and the captions.

and evictions of Muslims in Sinai. All categories together presented Wilayat Sinai as the only side in the conflict that could preserve the Islamic faith and fight state oppression.

Key Military Frames
COMBAT

Combat was the most recurring visual frame in Wilayat Sinai's photographic campaign. Making up 70 percent of the group's distributed military-related photographs in 2016 and 2017, the combat images depicted ISIS's ability to use various means to attack the Egyptian security forces in Sinai and, to a lesser extent, to target Israel across the border. The types of military actions in the combat frame included IED attacks, suicide bombings, group-based militant assaults, sniper shots, rocket attacks, and assassinations. Wilayat Sinai generally portrayed the armed militants engaged in both individual and group actions, the Egyptian soldiers and vehicles as targets of the attacks, and the ongoing destruction and impending death of those targets as recurring battlefield features. The image captions in the combat frame offered a theological justification for the attacks by labeling the militants as caliphate soldiers, the Egyptian security forces as apostates, and Israelis as the Jewish enemy.

Roadside IED attacks constituted the most frequent form of violence that Wilayat Sinai displayed in its combat visual frame. Frequently, the images depicted the group's ability to target the security forces without engaging in direct confrontation. Over one-third of combat images showed the detonation of IEDs targeting Egyptian armored vehicles, tanks, personnel carriers, minesweepers, Humvees, and foot soldiers. The images often appeared in news briefs and photo reports solely focused on this type of attack. However, each image did not always constitute a unique incident. Instead, Wilayat Sinai covered every IED attack with a visual sequence of at least two images. A news brief displaying three images posted on March 4, 2016, for example, details an IED attack against

PHOTO 11. ISIS's detonation of an IED against a military vehicle in central Sinai, disseminated March 4, 2016. Source: ISIS.

a vehicle that the group described as belonging to "the apostate military."[2] The brief starts with an image of the military vehicle carrying several soldiers on an empty highway against a background of Sinai mountains. Subsequently, two shots show a sudden explosion that engulfs the vehicle and then rapidly intensifies as the military target burns in flames (see Photo 11).

Images of IED attacks emphasized impending death and destruction of the enemy. Wilayat Sinai implied that its explosions were particularly causing the deaths of the Egyptian soldiers. In fact, the IED-related combat images composed the majority of all possible death images where neither the textual nor visual context confirmed the fate of these soldiers in the group's photographic campaign. Fires and explosions added to the spectacle, as roughly half of the ongoing destruction images in the group's photographic campaign showed an IED attack in progress. Wilayat Sinai militants were always missing from the displayed scene of the IED attacks, suggesting that fighters could safely watch the targets from a distance as the explosive devices detonated. The visual frame juxtaposed the vulnerability of the military in Sinai with the militants' ability to covertly and safely attack their enemies.

Aside from IED attacks, the remaining types of combat actions often appeared in tandem. The non-IED attack images diversified the means through which Wilayat Sinai attacked its adversaries: suicide bombings, group attacks, sniper shots, and rocket launches. Many news briefs and photo reports combined these actions to characterize Wilayat Sinai's offensive and defensive operations. A twenty-two-image photo report posted on July 9, 2017, for example, combines group assaults and suicide attacks at a military checkpoint south of Rafah. Such combinations appeared throughout the two-year period. An-

PHOTO 12. ISIS militants attacking al-Matafi checkpoint in North Sinai, disseminated January 11, 2017. Source: ISIS.

other twenty-nine-image news brief posted on January 14, 2016, further illustrates the point. It mixes group actions with sniper and rocket attacks to block what ISIS labels as an offensive operation by "the Egyptian apostate military." The brief starts with ten different shots of armed militants holding rifles, RPGs, shotguns, and snipers in prone, sitting, kneeling, and standing positions as they work together to repel an invisible opponent. The battle dynamics then shift toward the end, as five consecutive photographs show a masked militant in clean fatigues with a watch on his right hand kneeling behind a rocket launcher, aiming, and taking a shot at an Egyptian M60 tank, which subsequently bursts into flames.

The non-IED attack images often added a human element to the displayed spectacle. Militants often appeared on the front lines as they confronted Egyptian security forces (see Photo 12). Other non-IED attack images emphasized death as a likely outcome for adversaries, composing over one-third of the entirety of the photographic campaign's cache of possible death images. One image in a fourteen-image photo report posted on May 22, 2016, for example, shows gunfire and an Egyptian soldier in the crosshairs of a hidden Wilayat Sinai sniper to imply his death without confirming it in the caption. The images also stressed destruction as another fateful outcome awaiting Wilayat Sinai's opponents. By way of illustration, two images posted on February 22, 2017, show two flaming Katyusha rockets as they launch and then fly midair in the direction of what the group labeled "the settlements of the Jews," in reference to Israeli targets across the border. The collective fusion of these different types of attacks reinforced ISIS's strength in the Sinai conflict.

In sum, the photographs appearing in Wilayat Sinai's combat frame projected a religious war against enemies of Islam in and around Sinai. The superimposed captions emphasized the deviance of ISIS's Muslim opponents, by consistently characterizing them as apostates who had left the folds of Islam altogether. They also tapped into anti-Jewish and anti-Israeli sentiments by implying Jewish targets on the other side of the border were within the reach of Wilayat Sinai's rockets. The visuals portrayed a select group of Muslim men selflessly fighting with IEDs, rockets, firearms, snipers, and suicide attacks against Egyptian security forces and Israel. The accompanying text reiterated that an Islamic caliphate in Sinai was the ultimate goal. The combat visual frame thus utilized religion as a subtext to reinforce ISIS's polarizing rhetoric, which could further enflame the Sinai conflict.

BATTLE AFTERMATH

The battle aftermath visual frame was also prominent in Wilayat Sinai's photographic campaign. Making up over one-fifth of the group's military images in 2016 and 2017, the aftermath images presented ISIS as victorious militarily against the Egyptian security forces and their collaborators. The group exhibited confiscated military belongings, armored vehicles in flames, and soldiers and tribal fighters' casualties across the Sinai Peninsula. As with the combat visual frame, the captions highlighted a theological justification for the attacks, attributing the losses of the apostates to victories of the mujahidin and soldiers of the caliphate.

The battle aftermath images suggested that Wilayat Sinai's combative action had already succeeded and would continue to result in a standard costly outcome for the group's opponents. Almost half of these photographs highlighted the group's war spoils, displaying the acquisition of the opponents' weaponry, vehicles, and personal belongings. Four images posted on May 13, 2017, for example, depict five pickup trucks, rifles, pistols, identification cards, and cell phones that the group claimed to have confiscated from "apostate," progovernment al-Tarabin fighters (see Photo 13). Presuming death through the exhibition of implements of violence and destruction recurred in the majority of the battle aftermath images. One of the images in a photo report posted on November 27, 2016, shows a military tank on fire as it reportedly flees the battlefield. In other images Wilayat Sinai presented death as the definitive outcome awaiting its enemies, with numerous battle aftermath shots showing corpses. Three of the images in a photo report posted on September 13, 2017, combine the destructive and fatal outcomes of the group's attacks by showing dead policemen on the road covered in blood as flames engulf the police armored vehicles in the background and armed, masked militants assume control of the checkpoint. The war booty and death images in the aftermath frame combined to emphasize the superiority of Wilayat Sinai in battle.

PHOTO 13. ISIS showcasing tribal fighters' confiscated weaponry and personal belongings in Sinai, disseminated May 13, 2017. Source: ISIS.

The battle aftermath photographs suggested ISIS was winning the religious war against its opponents. The text expanded the pool of apostates in Sinai to include Bedouin militants and informants who align themselves with the Egyptian state against ISIS. The visuals standardized the outcome that awaited ISIS enemies: death and impending death. The militant group insinuated that the technological competitive advantage held by conventional police and military forces was a curse rather than a blessing. Hence, the battle aftermath visual frame served as a psychological weapon that could fracture the image of a potent Egyptian state, while spreading fear among those battling or considering joining the local fight against ISIS in Sinai.

MARTYRDOM

The martyrdom visual frame, which appeared in only twenty-three of the military images, eulogized the group's fighters, suicide attackers, and media operatives who died while defending the so-called caliphate. Wilayat Sinai portrayed its martyrs holding weapons, carrying media equipment, and displaying religious symbols. The captions stressed the spirit of camaraderie among members by labeling every individual a brother, often hailing the individual as part of broader movement labeled the Martyrs' Caravan. The captions also rendered martyrdom a goal and a way of pleasing God by always including the standard prayer "May Allah Accept Him."

Wilayat Sinai elevated the status of its group members who appeared in its martyrdom images. In the vast majority of those photographs, the group valorized its martyrs by highlighting only one individual per image. In sharp contrast to its depictions of Egyptian soldiers and al-Tarabin fighters' casualties, the group always presented its martyrs as alive and in a position of strength. The one exception to that pattern was an image showing the clean face of a bearded young man laying down in peaceful repose; its caption clarified his death and hailed him as "the martyr of the raid." But even then, the staged display of the dead militant diverted from photographs of bloody, dusty, and/or burnt corpses of opponents who almost always lay on the ground in restless postures. Additionally, Wilayat Sinai frequently showed the martyrs with rifles in their hands or next to them and often displayed religious identity symbols at the scene. When eulogizing a suicide bomber who attacked a church, for example, Wilayat Sinai showed a masked individual in military fatigues facing the camera, holding a rifle in his left hand, and pointing his right index finger to the heavens as a monotheism gesture. Other martyr displays showed young men reading the Qur'an. Martyrdom images stressed the individuals' strength, sacrifice, religiosity, and moral superiority.

ISIS and the Revolutionizing of Martyrdom Visuals

ISIS builds on a long tradition of visualizing revolutionary martyrs in Muslim societies and deviates from standard commemorations in other faiths. The dramatic displays of saints, nuns, rabbis, and laymen suffering in pain, facing torture, or lying dead and mutil1ated are common in Christian, Jewish, and Sikh art.[1] They serve as testaments to strong faith and sacrifice in times of affliction, often appearing in spectacular execution scenes. ISIS intentionally veers away from the "non-violent and unintentional martyrs" trope,[2] opting instead for a more revolutionary fervor. Most notably, the group's martyr displays resemble Iranian paintings of a strong Imam Hussein (Prophet Muhammad's grandson) carrying his sword on the battlefield in Karbala, modern-day portraits and murals celebrating Iranian fighters who lost their lives in the Iran-Iraq War, and Palestinian posters and graffiti idolizing fallen individuals who fought for liberation.[3] While the commonalities are most evident when compared to martyrdom visuals in Muslim cultures as they often invoke similar religious symbols, ISIS's projection of arms, power, and masculinity also mimics revolutionary art in other secular contexts, such as Italian independence and the U.S. Black Power movement.[4] In doing so, ISIS uses martyrdom visuals to venerate and promote heroic violence rather than nonviolence.

ISIS also projects a unique framing of who can qualify as a martyr. It does not reserve its praise for its fighters only. The group displays its "media martyrs" in Sinai and other provinces, holding their production gear as equivalent to rifles. A Wilayat Sinai photograph captures that distinctive fram-

PHOTO 14. Two martyred ISIS media operatives in Sinai, disseminated February 8, 2017. Source: ISIS.

ing strategy (see Photo 14). Unlike typical revolutionary martyrdom visuals, the image shows two young men holding a DSLR camera with a mounted lens and three tripods at the center of the frame as they face the photographer. With weapons absent from the scene altogether, the camera gear features as a weapon-like figure and symbolic artillery that together pictures ISIS's words to its field crews and online supporters when describing "media shells" as deadlier than airstrikes.[5] The camouflage pants on the media worker on the right and the shoulder strap on the other further reinforce the metaphor.

Yet ISIS here somehow manages to fracture the stereotypical image of the heroic, muscular warrior on the battlefront. The two men seem to be around twenty years of age, are slim, and have weak eyesight in the case of the one carrying the camera. Despite all that, the superimposed text to their left presents the slogan, "Oh You Media Operative, You Are a Mujahid," while the caption elevates them to martyrdom status by including a prayer that God accepts them. The interplay between the visual and text also invokes migration in the path of God, a master narrative in Islamic tradition dating back to Prophet Muhammad's time. The aliases in the caption refer to the man with the eyeglasses as "al-Masry" (the Egyptian) and the other one on the left as "al-Ansari" (the Supporter), which is a label used to refer to people of Medina who welcomed Prophet Muhammad and early Muslims after they fled Mecca in the seventh century. These names suggest that an ordinary young man left his home in mainland Egypt to move to Sinai, where locals supported him in the fight for Islam, albeit the struggles shared by Bedouins in the peninsula.

In fact, al-Ansari's posture with his left shoulder behind al-Masry's right arm echoes the message of backing, while his staring eyes leave the viewer wondering about what he and his family may have endured throughout their lives in North Sinai. Al-Masry's smile, the serene background, and the sunflowers surrounding them insinuate the two not only are united in their cause of fighting behind the camera but also have achieved martyrdom and found their way to the heavens. This unique trope expands beyond the concept of "citizen camera-witnessing," which involves ordinary citizens using phones as a vehicle for activism and public testimony in times of dissent and repression.[6] ISIS's framing of media martyrs expands the entry point to martyrdom and calls on ordinary young Muslim men to engage in citizen camera-fighting as official appointees in the group's ranks instead.

NOTES

1. See Terry, "Donatello's Decapitations and the Rhetoric of Beheading"; Quash, "'If We Be Dead with Christ'"; Axel, "Digital Figurings of the Unimaginable"; High, "Victims and Martyrs"; Walker, "'Hangd for the True Faith'"; Mackintosh and Quance, "Speaking/Seeing Saints"; Hadjittofi and Sivan, "Staging Rachel"; Friedlaender and Friedlaender, "Saints Cosmas and Damian"; Milwright, "Martyred Sultan"; Van Duijnen, "'Only the Strangest and Most Horrible Cases'"; Ahern, "Visual and Verbal Sites"; Raheja, "Warriors of Goja"; Chao, "Representations of Female Sainthood."

2. Lewis, "Digitally Mediated Martyrdom," 172.

3. See Vanzan, "Holy Defense Museum in Tehran"; Flaskerud, "Redemptive Memories"; Allen, "Getting by the Occupation"; Abu Hashash, "On the Visual Representation of Martyrdom in Palestine"; Verkaaik, "Notes on the Sublime"; Khosronejad, "Introduction"; Saramifar, "South Side of Heaven."

4. Doss, "'Revolutionary Art Is a Tool for Liberation'"; Romani, "Fashioning the Italian Nation."

5. "Oh, You Media Operative." ISIS released this online booklet to praise the work of media crews in its ranks and deem them as necessary warriors who spread Islam and protect Muslims from the corrupt media work of enemies.

6. Andén-Papadopoulos, "Citizen Camera-Witnessing," 766.

The martyrdom visual frame added humanity to ISIS's framing in Sinai. The visual emphasis and celebration of individual martyrs, who departed from the standard practice of wearing a facial covering, positioned them to hold a higher status within the group's ranks. The invocation of religious symbols further suggested their higher standing in the afterlife as well. Meanwhile, the captions informed the reader about the nature of "jihad" that the photo subjects had pursued to reach that point. This idealization created a romanticized superhero image that could prompt ordinary supporters wanting to partake in a pursuit bigger than themselves to follow a similar path.

Key Nonmilitary Frames

LAW ENFORCEMENT

The law enforcement visual frame was the most common type Wilayat Sinai used in its nonmilitary images, making up about half. These images depicted the provincial group's ability to maintain order and implement punishments in Sinai through shari'a law. To display its law enforcement capabilities, Wilayat Sinai showed the death or impending death of soldiers and collaborators as well as the destruction of outlawed materials, such as drugs and cigarettes. The captions utilized in the law enforcement frame laid out the crimes (e.g., espionage, sorcery, and advocating Sufism), described the acts of punishment as implementations of the rulings of Allah, and presented ISIS's representatives on the streets as the Islamic police and men of *hisba* (moral policing).

In many of the law enforcement images, Wilayat Sinai stressed that capital punishments awaited individuals working with the Egyptian security forces, spying for the Israeli Mossad, or practicing Sufi Islam in Sinai. Such executions appeared in over half of the law enforcement visual frame images. As in the group's strategy of presenting IED attacks in visual image sequence, the group displayed most executions in at least two consecutive images. A three-image news brief posted on January 4, 2016, for example, shows the execution of two blindfolded individuals whom the group labeled "spies for the Egyptian apostate military." The news brief starts with an image of the two individuals in orange jumpsuits kneeling on one side of the road with two armed militants behind them. The second image in the sequence shows the two militants lifting their rifles up toward the back heads of the two individuals. The final image displays both hostages lying dead in their own blood.

The execution images emphasized death as the unescapable consequence for crossing ISIS's normative behavioral expectations. Unlike the favorable image of the group's own fallen fighters in the martyrdom visual frame, Wilayat Sinai depicted all of the photographed hostages as helpless, whether they were about to die or lay breathless in their own blood. In dozens of images with accompanying textual confirmations of the deaths of the photo subjects, the group displayed civilians who had collaborated with the military, police guards, al-Tarabin tribal members, and Sufi clerics with a militant ready to shoot or sever their heads. Corpses often appeared as well to reinforce the fate of Wilayat Sinai's enemies.

Further, the group stressed the weakness of its foes by displaying the hostages in orange and red prison jumpsuits in many law enforcement displays. For example, a nine-image photo report posted on November 18, 2016, depicts the beheading of two clerics, a punishment that ISIS described as "the implementation of the shari'a ruling on two soothsayers." Twenty militants initially appear in the desert with one of them reading aloud from a docu-

PHOTO 15. ISIS hisba man overseeing the burning of cigarettes in Sinai, disseminated June 14, 2017. Source: ISIS.

ment the caption identified as the shari'a ruling. The remaining images break down the beheading of the clerics into two paired three-shot sequences. First, a masked militant dressed in black holds up a sword next to the blindfolded cleric kneeling in an orange jumpsuit with his chin fixed on a wooden log. In the following shot, blood spills as the head flies in midair on its way to falling to the ground. The final shot displays the corpse of the cleric lying on the ground. The gore and ultraviolence in the execution images presented the group as the unwavering dispenser of the most severe punishments available under shari'a law.

Beyond the display of execution images, Wilayat Sinai focused its law enforcement frame on moral policing efforts. The images depicted preventive actions designed to protect the community from vice and punishment. The photographs mostly appeared in photo reports displaying a wide range of moral enforcement efforts. A ten-image report posted on June 14, 2017, for example, shows *hisba* men in their standard brown uniforms standing at checkpoints confiscating "sorcery-related" objects, burning packs of cigarettes, advising an old man to repent from "polytheistic Sufi thought," destroying tombstones to prevent the worship of graves, and monitoring a shop's food products to ensure freshness.

The moral policing images also emphasized Wilayat Sinai's action plan for dealing with threats to the community. The group depicted confiscation and burning of contraband as the consequence for drug and cigarette possession in numerous law enforcement images. Wilayat Sinai showed its militants handling security threats by checking identification papers and arresting suspects

PHOTO 16. A group of so-called spies who repented to ISIS in Sinai, disseminated September 26, 2017. Source: ISIS.

at checkpoints in dozens of other images. Perhaps most importantly, Wilayat Sinai often emphasized the group's willingness to spare citizens from executions if they repented. A twenty-one-image photo report posted on September 26, 2017, for example, displays both execution and moral policing shots. The report begins with multiple images of masked militants distributing by hand a document calling on pedestrians and drivers to stay away from security forces. The following photographs show individuals who the captions claim were spies who had repented sitting in a half circle and listening to the militants. The report ends with ten execution shots of individuals who apparently had not repented. Taken together, the moral policing images served as a counterbalance to the gore of executions by showing other law enforcement actions aimed at protecting rather than punishing the community.

In short, the law enforcement photographs implied that an emerging actor was now capable of implementing divine law in Sinai. The text stressed apostasy as the theological byproduct of collaborating with the state. Following the change in Wilayat Sinai's leadership in 2017, the captions further expanded the scope of deviance and moral threats to include the contraband trade and practice of Sufi Islam. At the same time, the visuals conveyed the group's on-the-ground efforts to safeguard the community from vice and treason through means of execution and destruction. The law enforcement visual frame not only complemented battle aftermath photographs as a fear tactic to deter future transgressions but also assured supporters that an Islamic Caliphate project was well under way in Sinai to replace the Egyptian state rule over the peninsula that had enraged many locals for decades.

VICTIMHOOD OF SINAI MUSLIMS

Victimhood of Sinai Muslims constituted the second most recurring visual frame in Wilayat Sinai's nonmilitary images. It simply focused on the misery of civilians resulting from the Egyptian military's airstrikes and the Rafah eviction policy that had started in summer 2013. To emphasize citizen grievances, ISIS exhibited the destruction of houses and religious shrines. The captions attributed these damaging acts to the Egyptian military, while labeling the actions' victims as Muslims.

The victimhood images emphasized human rights abuses as consequences of the state's actions in North Sinai. Wilayat Sinai implied the death or eviction of residents by excluding humans from almost all of the victimhood images. Instead, the images displayed the aftermath of military airstrikes and house demolitions. An eleven-image photo report posted on October 24, 2016, for example, shows only destroyed houses and plantations with no residents in the vicinities. The group describes the scenes as the outcome of "the Egyptian apostate military's airstrikes on the properties and houses of Muslims."

ISIS further used children and sacred places to bring human rights abuses in full view. A photo report posted on October 29, 2017, involves kids at the scene to further emphasize the tragic loss of residents due to Rafah evictions near the border. One photograph shows a man and a boy searching through the rubble of a destroyed building as a woman and a little girl watch from a distance (see Photo 17). Others show children watching their families as they pack up belongings in anticipation of leaving their homes. Further, all five pictures

PHOTO 17. A house in Rafah reportedly destroyed by the Egyptian military, disseminated October 29, 2017. Source: ISIS.

of mosques anywhere in Wilayat Sinai's photographic campaign are related to the victimhood frame, as each appeared in a state of destruction. The victimhood photographs presented Muslim civilians and their sacred places as the military's main target.

The victimhood of Sinai Muslims visual frame projected a sacrilegious image of the Egyptian state. The captions foregrounded the religious identity of those whom state policies and actions in Sinai had impacted, while maintaining that ISIS's enemies in the Egyptian security forces were not even Muslims even if they identified as such. The photographs further exacerbated local grievances by emphasizing the tragic consequences of Egyptian security force actions on Muslim homes, lands, and houses of worship. By vilifying the state, Wilayat Sinai's victimhood narrative visually positioned disgruntled individuals and those against the Egyptian military as members of the ISIS collective as well as promised a better future to North Sinai residents who had long suffered from alienation.

IN-GROUP LIFESTYLE

The in-group lifestyle frame encompassed 14 percent of Wilayat Sinai's nonmilitary images. The photographs depicted the daily lives of ISIS members in their spare time after they had finished fighting or training for the day. To display their habits, the group showed the militants cooking, eating, reading, practicing their religion, and holding their weapons. The captions described the photo subjects as soldiers of the caliphate striving in the path of God.

The lifestyle images emphasized the spirit of camaraderie present among ISIS members in Sinai. The militants shared different activities, ranging from eating and praying to watching videos. Two images posted in September 2016, for example, show the group members as they hug one another and prepare food as part of their feast celebration. Yet even in the more relaxed lifestyle images, Wilayat Sinai underscored the preparedness of its group members by displaying their weapons in over half of the lifestyle photographs. Highlighting their lifestyle as Islamic, numerous images also depict the group members making the monotheism gesture, praying, or reading the Qur'an (see Photo 18).

Moreover, the lifestyle visual frame highlighted alternative media sources that the group members consumed. Over a dozen of the lifestyle images show individuals reading ISIS's *al-Naba'* newsletter or watching its provincial video releases. A two-image news brief posted in September 2017 depicts several group members watching a new video on a laptop that al-Barqa province in Libya had released earlier. Wilayat Sinai further reinforced the connectedness to ISIS by showing group members raising ISIS's black flag in a few images. Together, the visual frame depicted the life of Wilayat Sinai members as one that involved sharing with and caring for others.

PHOTO 18. An ISIS militant reading the Qur'an during his break in Sinai, disseminated March 5, 2017. Source: ISIS.

The in-group lifestyle photographs thus personified ISIS militants operating in Sinai. Departing from battlefield portrayals, the visuals in this frame projected an ascetic, utopian life that would bring together Muslims wanting to revolt against and change the oppressive status quo. The text simultaneously reiterated the photo subjects' mission to establish and uphold an Islamic caliphate. Complementing the martyrdom portraits, the in-group lifestyle frame added a more mundane, humane angle to ISIS's presence in Sinai that broadened identification appeals to those who might want to join the militants.

The Egyptian Military's Photographic Campaign

The Egyptian military presented 1,105 images in 2016 and 2017. Superimposed captions appeared on only twenty of the images to describe the scene. The images also carried no logos or identifiers of the source. Instead, the military relied on longer Facebook posts, with an average of 166 words per post, to contextualize the scene, the military's role, and the broader conflict. Similar to Wilayat Sinai's campaign, the pool of images encompassed two main categories: military and nonmilitary. The military images made up a little over half of the photographic campaign, with nonmilitary images constituting the remainder.

The photographs showing the Egyptian military's use of force comprised three visual frames: combat, battle aftermath, and martyrdom. The combat visual frame displayed military actions on the Sinai battlefront. The battle aftermath visual frame focused on the outcomes of the military's combative action. The martyrdom visual frames eulogized fallen soldiers who gave their lives fighting the militants of Wilayat Sinai.

Nonmilitary images, on the other hand, focused on the Egyptian military's efforts beyond the battlefield. They comprised three visual frames: law enforcement, public figure visits, and service provision. The law enforcement visual

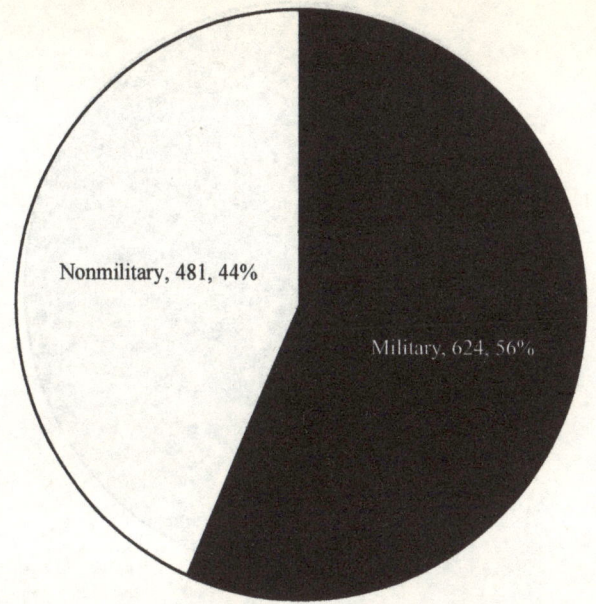

FIGURE 16. The Egyptian military's visual frames, 2016–17.

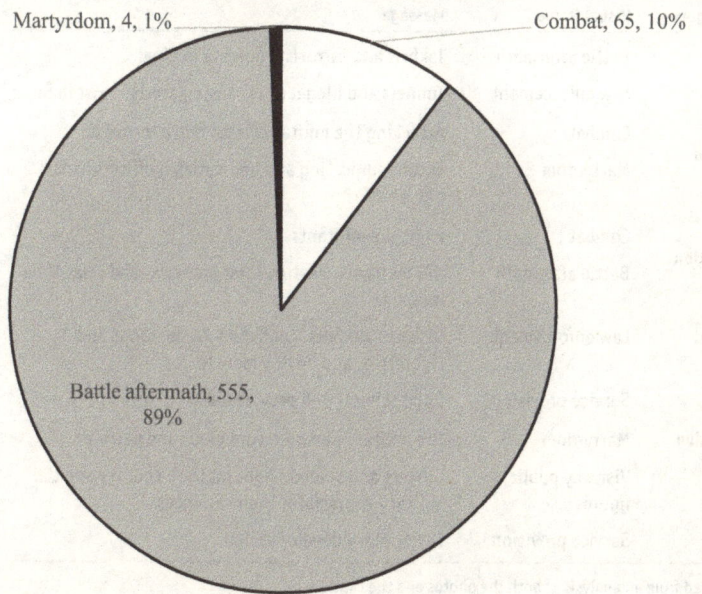

FIGURE 17. The Egyptian military's military visual frames, 2016–17.

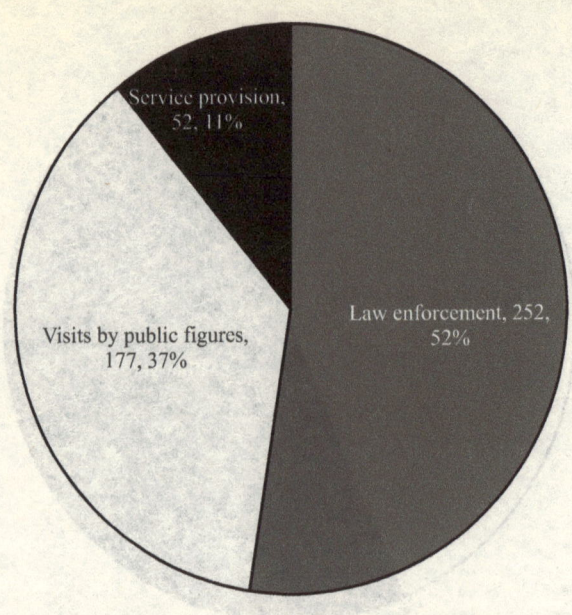

FIGURE 18. The Egyptian military's nonmilitary visual frames, 2016–17.

TABLE 4. The Egyptian military's framing categories in 2016–17

Framing category	Visual frame	Message
Problem definition	Battle aftermath	Takfiris and terrorists operate in Sinai
	Law enforcement	Tunnels and illegal drugs and cigarettes exist in Sinai
Causal interpretation	Combat	Attacking the military makes one a terrorist
	Martyrdom	Excommunicating and apostatizing officers makes one a takfiri
Treatment recommendation	Combat	Fight the militants
	Battle aftermath	Kill militants, destroy their property, and seize their weapons
	Law enforcement	Discover tunnels, confiscate illegal drugs and cigarettes, and deploy more forces
	Service provision	Open schools and provide aid
Moral evaluation	Martyrdom	The military personnel are pious and patriotic
	Visits by public figures	Officers and soldiers fight for their country and the military appreciates their sacrifices
	Service provision	The military develops Sinai

Results emerged from an analysis of both the photos and the captions.

frame showcased the activities intended to maintain order in Sinai. The public figure visits frame focused on the appreciation of soldiers taking part in the counterterrorism operations. The service provision frame highlighted Wilayat Sinai's aid and development initiatives.

Overall, the Egyptian state's photographic campaign projected a coherent narrative that incorporates Entman's four framing categories (see Table 4). The military identified the presence of "*takfiri* terrorists," weaponry, contraband tunnels, and illegal drugs and cigarettes in Sinai as a problem. It highlighted the attacks against the military and the killing of officers as evidence for the spread of takfiri ideology, which tends to excommunicate opponents and deem them as disbelievers. Hence, the appropriate treatment recommendations for the Sinai conflict included fighting and killing the militants, destroying their property, confiscating their weapons, discovering tunnels, burning drugs and cigarettes, opening schools, and providing food to civilians. The Egyptian military emphasized its moral superiority by underscoring the sacrifices of its patriotic, pious troops, exhibiting appreciation for such acts, and manifesting the leadership's efforts to help the Sinai residents. Together, the four framing associations in the Sinai context presented the Egyptian military as the sole protector of the nation against terrorism and extremist ideologies and a willing participant in the development of the territory's citizenry.

Key Military Frames
BATTLE AFTERMATH

The battle aftermath visual frame was the most recurring in the Egyptian military's photographic campaign, making up almost 90 percent. Overshadowing the images of fighting and combative action, the aftermath visual frame focused instead on the success of the counterterrorism operations in Sinai. The military exhibited Wilayat Sinai's burned vehicles and hideouts, confiscated weapons and flags, and dead or arrested militants. Only three aftermath images had captions, and each of these labeled the militants as takfiris (excommunicators or those who declare others disbelievers), while the Facebook posts focused on the military's efforts to combat terrorism in Sinai.

The aftermath images emphasized various positive outcomes of the military's operations in Sinai. Unlike the combat images, the Egyptian military mostly excluded the human element from the scene, with the majority of aftermath photographs focusing solely on property damage or military gains. Highlighting its destructive power, the military frequently showed the obliteration of militants' hideouts, caves, and vehicles. Out of eight images posted on April 26, 2017, for example, five show hideouts in flames and explosions after the Egyptian military "[destroyed] a large amount of explosive materials used by the tak-

PHOTO 19. The military destroying hideouts in Sinai, disseminated April 26, 2017. Source: Egyptian Army Spokesman.

firi elements" in North Sinai (see Photo 19).[3] Two hundred images also stressed the military's ability to seize the militants' weapons, IEDs, explosive materials, computers, cameras, vehicles, clothes, and money. Black ISIS flags, which appeared only in the battle aftermath visual frame, indicated the identity of the owners of these lost belongings. Generally, the images presented the military as an unseen war machine whose destructive power was manifest.

The military also focused on the capture and death of militants in aftermath images. The photographs depicted the captured militants as helpless, with their hands tied behind the backs. One of the images uploaded on September 8, 2017, shows two blindfolded individuals on their knees in the desert, with the Facebook post describing them as "two very dangerous takfiris" whom the military captured in central Sinai.[4] Further, the military highlighted the fatal outcome of the counterterrorism operations by often showing the militants' corpses, which is averse to the standard practices of Western media and states in twenty-first-century war photojournalism, but somewhat in tune with some Arab news networks.[5] Collectively, the images presented arrest and death as the fates awaiting the militants.

The images in the battle aftermath visual frame asserted the Egyptian military's dominance over enemies of the state in Sinai. Countering ISIS's own labeling of its militants as mujahidin, soldiers of the caliphate, and martyrs, the text characterized the very same people as terrorists and excommunicators who threaten Egypt's stability. Meanwhile, the visuals portrayed the military's brute power as the optimal solution whereby Egypt could defeat and humiliate the terrorists. The aftermath photographs emphasized a sense of security arguably to elicit more public support for the use of force rather than other counterterrorism strategies.

COMBAT

One out of every ten military images depicted the Egyptian military as the powerful adversary in the Sinai conflict. To emphasize the scope of war, the Egyptian military showed its soldiers taking part in counterterrorism operations on the ground and jets bombing the militants from the air. Only one combat image had a caption, which labeled the militants again as takfiris, while the Facebook posts identified the military's mission as combatting terroristic activity in Sinai.

The combat images emphasized the military's full-scale engagement in Sinai. They often depicted Egyptian soldiers riding in tanks and Humvees, holding their weapons, walking together, and checking caves. A two-image post on May 30, 2016, for example, shows Egyptian soldiers riding in armored vehicles and aiming at some distant objects. According to the accompanying Facebook post, the soldiers killed sixteen of the "dangerous terrorist elements" in North Sinai (see Photo 20).[6] In contrast, the military generally excluded displays of the militants in the battlefield altogether. In the meantime, the Egyptian Air Force was a major player in the combat images, with the military displaying its airstrikes in over half of its combat photographs. Those images showed Egyptian jets flying over Sinai and targeting specific buildings and vehicles. With the focus on soldiers, weapons, tanks, jets, and missiles, the visuals worked in tandem to imply that militants faced a presumption of death from the omnipresent and invincible Egyptian military forces.

The combat visual frame suggested the Sinai conflict was much more than a battle against a small number of insurgents. The visuals emphasized the need for all military units in Sinai to encircle terrorists on the ground to position them for destruction from the air. The text often included the enemy's large death toll and arrest numbers in Sinai, while simultaneously identifying them as proponents of the takfiri ideology in an effort to link them to a wider community threat present in the region. The images in this frame can serve a dual purpose, aiming to inspire confidence in the military's efforts while also preparing the audience for a prolonged war in Sinai.

PHOTO 20. Egyptian soldiers on the front lines in a counterterrorism operation in Sinai, disseminated May 30, 2016. Source: Egyptian Army Spokesman.

Key Nonmilitary Frames

LAW ENFORCEMENT

Law enforcement was the most recurring visual frame appearing among the nonmilitary images, making up over half. To emphasize the effectiveness of its crackdown on illegal activities in Sinai, the military showed drugs and underground tunnels. A total of sixteen images had captions that laid out the features of the tunnels in Rafah, while the Facebook posts reiterated the military's mission to eradicate terrorism, disrupt the illegal trade with Gaza, and secure Sinai.

Three types of law enforcement activities appeared in the photographs. First, most of the law enforcement photographs showed the underground tunnels the military had discovered in Rafah. Five images posted on February 6, 2016, for example, depict the discovery steps involved in finding the tunnels, starting with the detection of its ceiling, the digging of an opening, and the eventual unveiling of the parameters of the underground facilities (see Photo 21). Second, the military released many images that showcase its crackdown on drugs and the illegal smuggling of cigarettes. In an eight-image Facebook post on November 5, 2017, five photographs show the confiscation of drugs at checkpoints and the destruction of drug plantations in central Sinai. Like the battle aftermath visual frame, the military's law enforcement photographs mainly excluded humans from the scenes of drugs and tunnels. Third, the remaining law enforcement images showed the military providing security for international events in South Sinai, including the African Trade Investment Forum and high-level meetings of the African Ministers of Defense in Sharm El Sheikh. The law enforcement images thus juxtaposed the pervasiveness of illegal activities in North Sinai with the safety of the South.

PHOTO 21. The military discovering an illegal tunnel in Rafah, disseminated February 6, 2016. Source: Egyptian Army Spokesman.

Taken together, the law enforcement visual frame expanded the pool of threats in North Sinai to include underground tunnels at the border. Similar to the combat visual frame's emphasis on the large number of militants, the text here informed the audience about an enormous network of tunnels that could destabilize the peninsula. The visuals simultaneously suggested that the military could uncover and eliminate that lifeline for illegal contraband trade. The frame thus provided visual evidence that could garner support for the state's eviction policy and plan to create a buffer zone in North Sinai.

VISITS BY PUBLIC FIGURES

Another recurring visual frame among the nonmilitary images was public figure visits. The 177 public figure visit photographs made up over one-third of the nonmilitary images. These shots focused on visits by top security officials and other public figures to the soldiers in hospitals or in the field in Sinai. None of the images had captions, but the Facebook posts named the visitors and praised the soldiers, labeling them as the heroes of the armed forces for fighting terrorism in Sinai.

The Egyptian military emphasized the country's appreciation for the soldiers and their sacrifices in Sinai. Praising those who had suffered injuries in Sinai, the military dedicated the vast majority of its public visit images to showing top security officials as well as politicians, actors, media persons, and clerics visiting, talking with, and exchanging smiles with Egyptian soldiers in hospitals. A ten-image Facebook post on April 30, 2016, for example, displays Minister of Defense Sedki Sobhi next to the hospital beds of ten soldiers, shaking their hands, patting them on their shoulders, and kissing their foreheads. White sheets of paper hanging behind the soldiers' beds indicated the nature, date, and exact location of their injuries sustained in Sinai battles against ISIS.

The remaining photographs also showed top security officials but on battlefield visits interacting with soldiers and honoring their efforts. For instance, a six-image Facebook post on February 12, 2016, shows Minister of Defense Sedki Sobhi and Minister of the Interior Magdi Abdelghaffar with soldiers in North Sinai, shaking their hands and handing them gifts, while the corresponding Facebook post describes the soldiers as "Egypt's heroes."[7] In both the hospital and field visit photographs, Sobhi and the Egyptian flag were the most recurring symbols, appearing in over half of the images. The photographs stressed the military's patriotism and the leaders' constant interaction with both injured and healthy soldiers serving in combat.

The visit visual frame humanized the military and its soldiers. Unlike ISIS's photographs that avoided leader portrayals altogether, the military's images foregrounded the Egyptian minister of defense as the vanguard of the state's war on terrorism in Sinai. Also, departing from ISIS's constant displays of soldiers as victors, the military's photographs showed the soldiers in a state of physical weakness in hospitals. But the accompanying text emphasized that their setbacks were only temporary, pointing out their sacrifices and their adamance to return to the battlefield. The visits frame projected an emotional narrative of individual patriots willing to defeat the odds and protect their motherland.

Egypt's Hyperemotional Visual Treatment of Military Leaders

The recurring Egyptian military visuals in hospitals embody the affective shift in twenty-first-century war photography. Communication scholar Lilie Chouliaraki argues the "hyper-emotionalisation" of military troops in recent decades has disrupted the soldier-hero narrative that dominated the visual sphere since the early 1900s.[1] Soldier displays are no longer limited to combat scenes where male warriors act as mighty war machines. They too can now appear in vulnerable states, struggling with trauma and injury or even dead in caskets draped with their countries' flags. While the Egyptian military tends to avoid images of dead soldiers in Sinai battles altogether, physical injury is the prevalent mode of vulnerability in its photographic warfare against ISIS. A prototypical photograph shows a young soldier in his early twenties sitting on a bed and wearing military hospital pajamas as he receives his senior commanders in the room (see Photo 22). The only apparent injury is under the bandage on his left arm, yet the written words on the paper hanging behind his bed reveal the gravity of the situation. A mine explosion in Rafah seven months earlier fractured al-Said Mohamed's skull, broke his right femur and two legs, and injured his brain and eyelid. The date of the accident suggests prolonged treatment. Despite all that, Mohamed's styled hair and smile project heroism of a different kind, as evidenced by his positivity as he recovers from such a tragedy. Those emotional, visual narratives tend to justify the war in Sinai and draw public support for the leadership's decisions and retaliatory actions.

What the Egyptian state does differently, however, is extending the hyperemotional visual treatment to military leaders on a regular basis. For decades, states have been keen on glamorizing their top leaders and portraying them as untouchable, physical embodiments of strength. Think of U.S. Civil War–era stoic portraits of military generals in full fatigues, Cecil Beaton's iconic photographs of Churchill and British commanders holding cigars, the 1940s portrayals of China's president with his sword, and contemporary displays of Serbian warlords carrying tigers in the battlefield or Donald Rumsfeld in the situation room giving orders and overseeing opera-

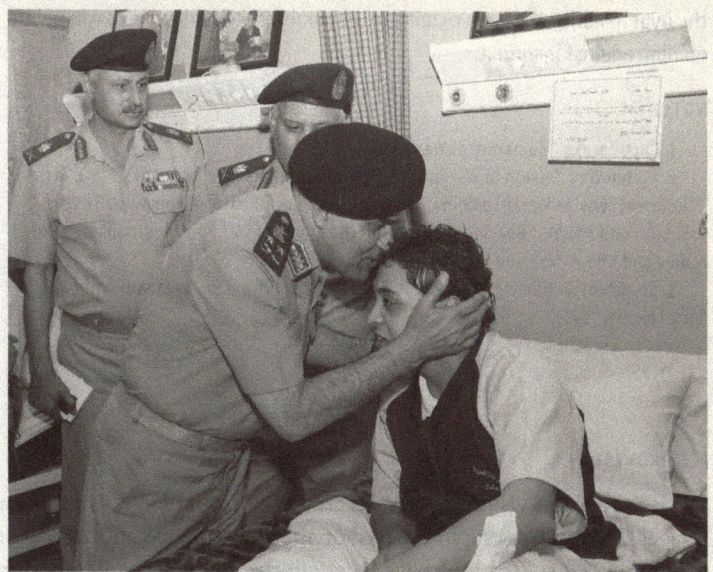

PHOTO 22. Egypt's then-minister of defense Sedki Sobhi in a hospital visit to soldiers who were injured in Sinai counterterrorism operations, disseminated April 30, 2016. Source: Egyptian Army Spokesman.

tions in Iraq.[2] Even when vilifying enemy leaders, a common visual tactic has been to overemphasize their might and hostility.[3] The Egyptian minister of defense, Sedki Sobhi, by contrast, appears as a sympathetic father figure in the recurring hospital images.

Going back to the prototypical image mentioned above, Sobhi is no longer the mighty leader standing straight as he gives orders or speaks to hundreds of his men. Instead, he is giving his undivided attention to one as he kindly holds Mohamed's face and leans forward to kiss his injured head. The framed photographs of prior visits on the wall suggest Sobhi is not there simply for a publicity stunt but is a caring father for all Egyptian soldiers. In the meantime, the scene exemplifies the strength of leadership as the lieutenant general remains in full military fatigues with two commanders behind him, while the injured soldier appears to be in awe. Similar emotional displays often involve state leaders who serve as civilian heads of the military, including Obama and Bush when they visited Walter Reed or Sisi as he wept listening to speeches by injured officers. But official state sources and social media accounts rarely, if ever, show top military generals in that situation. The recent internal conflicts in Arab countries thus seem to be prompting the hyperemotionalization of military generals as a visual trope to win public opinion against insurgents.

NOTES

1. Chouliaraki, "Humanity of War," 330.
2. Perlmutter, "Vision of War in High School Social Science Textbooks," 150; Taylor, "'Occupied Lens' in Wartime China," 303; Francis, "Cecil Beaton's Romantic Toryism," 108; Lukk and Doubt, "Bearing Witness and the Limits of War Photojournalism," 630; Fahmy and Kim, "Picturing the Iraq War," 454.
3. Goldstein, *Capturing the German Eye*, 113; Seo, "Visual Propaganda in the Age of Social Media," 157.

SERVICE PROVISION

The service provision visual frame appeared in one out of every ten nonmilitary images. These photographs focused on the government's efforts to develop Sinai and its citizenry. To emphasize these efforts, the military mainly showed its soldiers giving out food and leaders opening schools. None of the images had captions, but the Facebook posts provided the location, identified the participating officials, and labeled all activities as part of an ongoing project to develop the Sinai Peninsula.

The service provision images highlighted two main military-sponsored initiatives in Sinai. First, half of the photographs depicted military personnel distributing food packages to the people of Sinai. The images of aid distribution often displayed elderly men and women and children waiting for or holding their packages of food. Two images posted on December 5, 2017, for example, show a military officer handing packages to civilians in al-Rawda village, where militants had bombed a mosque two weeks earlier (see Photo 23). Such scenes juxtaposed the state's care for Sinai locals with ISIS's strategy of targeting mosques in the peninsula. Second, the military used many of its service provision images to highlight the construction of new schools and religious centers. A three-image Facebook post on March 31, 2017, starts with soldiers and civilians in a playground surrounding Minister of Education Tarek Shawky, the military commander of the unified leadership east of the canal Mohamed Abdel Illah, and the governors of North and South Sinai as they cut the red ribbon to open a school in Sinai. The subsequent photographs show the minister of education and military commanders cutting another red ribbon at a new social unit, about a dozen mostly veiled, fully covered women in a room using sewing machines to tailor clothes, and an empty school playground with an Egyptian flag on a pole flying high at the center of the frame. Images of the minis-

PHOTO 23. Food distribution by the military in Al-Rawda village in North Sinai, disseminated December 5, 2017. Source: Egyptian Army Spokesman.

ter of international cooperation's visits to a development project and of military personnel donating money to a Sinai public bank in support of the development projects also appeared in other posts, but less frequently. Throughout the photographs displaying these initiatives, the military used the Egyptian flag as a prominent symbol. The flag appeared on school building walls, military fatigue patches, and food packages as well as in the hands of those civilians receiving aid. The images reinforced the military's engagement in Sinai's humanitarian and developmental initiatives.

The service provision frame thus emphasized the state's eagerness to address underlying grievances in Sinai. The visuals underscored education and the economy as two prongs of an ongoing state-building effort to salvage local communities. The text reiterated that the pictured scenes made up only a small part of a comprehensive development plan targeted at the entire Sinai population. Some of the photographic taglines focused particularly on the North, where Bedouins had suffered for decades since the peninsula's liberation in 1982. Taken together, the problem-solution format of the service provision frame presents Sinai locals as victims of poverty, while positioning Egyptian military personnel as their saviors.

Photographic Warfare: Contestation of Visual Frames

Moving beyond the construction of a coherent narrative on each side, Wilayat Sinai and the Egyptian military's visual frames implemented three interaction strategies: competition, negation, and expansion. At times, the two sides directly competed over the same visual frames to claim superiority and power. At others, they negated the messaging in the opposing visual frames by presenting different ones that claim to undermine the credibility of the opponent. Each side also expanded beyond the scope of the opponent's visual frames by constructing unique scenes presenting their perspectives.

One key area where Wilayat Sinai and the Egyptian military competed was in the display of combat. Wilayat Sinai mainly defined battle through sequential scenes of combat that implied motion on the ground. They showed IED attacks, suicide missions, group operations, and assassinations that the militants carried out on the battlefront as they fought security forces. The military instead defined the battle mostly by displaying scenes of the destructive aftermath of precision airstrikes and counterterrorism operations. The images rarely exhibited ground actions in progress or the soldiers' involvement on the front lines. By doing so, the military presented static pictures of battle in Sinai that, when compared to dynamic scenes, are less likely to stimulate brain activity or influence attitudes.[8] Showing the fight in process and highlighting the fighters' actions on the battlefield are likely to engage viewers and trump the focus on destroyed objects in the aftermath.

ISIS and the Egyptian state also competed over the portrayal of martyrs. The militant group treated its fallen soldiers in Sinai as religious actors by showing the militants reading the Qur'an and making the monotheism gesture as they posed for the camera. The superimposed captions reinforced the message, describing them as martyrs who had died striving in the path of God. The very few times the military depicted its own martyrs, it instead relied on national symbols to identify those who died fighting for its side of the cause, such as the Egyptian flag and the military uniform. Facebook texts bolstered the message by hailing the fallen officers as defenders of the nation, while also describing them as practicing Muslims. With no depictions of religious symbols, however, patriotism visually dominated the military's portrayal of martyrs as expected in state media campaigns. This competition drew a sharp contrast between the motivational goals of the fighters. Wilayat Sinai attempted to appeal to those wanting to fight in support of their faith against the state; the Egyptian military reached out to a much wider audience supporting or willing to protect the country against terrorism while upholding their religious ties.

Wilayat Sinai and the Egyptian military also competed over the appropriate framework for law enforcement. Both sides displayed crackdowns on drugs and cigarettes. The militant group used the captions to describe the contraband items as impurities forbidden under shari'a law. The military instead used text on Facebook to describe drug plantations and smuggled substances in Sinai as illegal. It further highlighted the threat emanating from breaches to the Rafah-Gaza border through the recurring displays of underground tunnels. The competition here drew again a sharp contrast between the different motives for law enforcement. Wilayat Sinai presented its actions as moral; the Egyptian military highlighted its activities as legal. In short, the displayed motivations reinforced the conflict as one between Islamic shari'a and state laws.

Additionally, the two sides competed over perceived capacity to offer social services to the Sinai populations. The militant group limited its depicted services to healthcare for its fighters displayed in several scenes of a clinic and a first aid workshop. The military, by contrast, presented a wide array of services the Egyptian state provided to its residents—food distribution, schools, religious centers, and other development projects. The Egyptian military highlighted the state's comparatively higher level of competence over ISIS as a provider of social services for those in need of food, education, and jobs.

Beyond directly competing over visual frames, ISIS and the Egyptian state negated each other's frames too. Wilayat Sinai, for example, negated the Egyptian military's depiction of the outcomes of its Sinai operations. The military presented visual frames emphasizing how its precision airstrikes effectively targeted terrorists, its school projects helped Sinai residents, and its crackdown on underground tunnels secured the border. The militant group negated such claims by simply presenting the airstrikes as having turned civilian houses, mosques, plantations, and schools into devastating piles of rubble. It further displayed that outcome of the military's plan of action to destroy the underground tunnels and create a buffer zone between Rafah and Gaza as children fleeing with their families from homes near the border. Wilayat Sinai's alternative outcomes attempted to discredit the state and undermine its credibility using images of innocence and destruction that are likely to personify injustice and prompt support for a forceful response.[9]

The Egyptian military, by contrast, negated the presentation of ISIS's fighting power featured in the militant group's combat images. In response to Wilayat Sinai's emphasis on scenes of militants' engagement in attacks that it deemed successful, the Egyptian military used part of its battle aftermath images to redefine the power dynamics in the Sinai conflict. It presented scenes of arrest, death, and destruction of militants as the actual outcomes of militants' attacks. The humiliating appearances of militants in shackles or in their own blood further magnified the punishment that the military implemented for lawbreakers. The Egyptian military's alternative picture attempted to debunk ISIS's claims of success on the Sinai battlefield using negative and often disturbing images that are more likely to grab attention and enhance recall.[10]

Having directly engaged the Egyptian military's framing of the conflict through competition and negation, Wilayat Sinai went further to expand beyond the scope of the military's visual frames. The focus of the group's effort was on displaying life in Sinai. The militant group utilized the in-group lifestyle photographs to emphasize the camaraderie and piety present among the Sinai militants. The images showed militants praying, eating, and living together.

The Sinai landscape also highlighted the beauty of the sacred land through a small number of images of green fields, water streams, and fruit trees. Such images of a spiritual, moral, and egalitarian lifestyle close to nature occurred only in the militant group's photographic campaign as a way of magnifying a utopian dream.

The Egyptian military likewise expanded beyond the scope of the militant group's visual frames to display interactions between leadership and troops. The military utilized its visits frame to emphasize a father-son relationship between military leaders and their soldiers. The images mostly showed top security officials, such as the minister of defense, the minister of the interior, and the army chief of staff, standing by the soldiers' beds in hospitals and next to them in the field in Sinai. Such images displaying a morally responsible leadership who honored, directed, and worked together with its subordinates occurred only in the military's photographic campaign.

The three interactive strategies revealed the nature of state and non-state actors' messaging approaches in conflict. Competition was the main strategy evident in Wilayat Sinai and the Egyptian military's counter-messages. Each side used the military, law enforcement, and social service frames in the vast majority of the images. Negation was another strategy manifest in the two groups' counter-messages. The militant group highlighted the victimhood of Sinai locals; the state emphasized the humiliation of militants whom ISIS valorizes. Meanwhile, expansion was the only strategy present in the construction of alternative messages on both sides. The militant group exclusively endorsed the militant lifestyle in and the serene nature of the peninsula; the state instead promoted leadership as caring and society as united. The incorporation of counter- and alternative messaging reveals that neither approach is unique to antiextremism or counterterrorism media campaigns. Instead, militant groups like Wilayat Sinai rely on the two approaches as much as state actors for competition, negation, and expansion. In short, counter- and alternative narratives can operate in tandem within state and non-state actors' media campaigns.

Concluding Thoughts

This chapter has demonstrated how militant groups and state actors frame their photographic campaigns differently during times of conflict. Focusing on the Sinai conflict in 2016–17, an inductive, grounded theory approach highlighted context-specific visual frames that ISIS and the Egyptian military had constructed. The militant group and the state were generally more reliant on the visual frames pertaining to military action, such as combat and battle aftermath. However, other nonmilitary activities such as law enforcement, social service provision, and visits to soldiers made their way into the photographic campaigns.

The formats of surrounding text in the Sinai conflict presented an additional function of captions in digital photographic warfare. Wilayat Sinai used superimposed captions as framing devices and the provincial logo as its visual identifier on each of its eight hundred images. The militant group used captions to tell a story, contextualize the scene, and reinforce the visual frames. But the superimposed captions further allowed the visual frames to retain meaning as the images digitally circulate as individual media products across platforms. The Egyptian military, on the other hand, relied on the Facebook posts as static framing devices to perform the typical functions of captions. With no superimposed caption or logo on almost all of the 1,105 images, however, the association was not as immediate for the viewer and the meaning was more difficult to decipher. The meaning would be less clear as the images themselves circulated with no surrounding text. In visual contestations, superimposing the caption on the image allows the visual frame to transcend its initial context, and the lack thereof can result in a loss of meaning in the cluttered digital space.

The contesting visual frames in Sinai exhibited similarities and differences with image distribution in previous conflicts. Wilayat Sinai's visual frames mostly aligned with previous analyses of ISIS images.[11] Like these earlier studies, the militant group emphasized its attacks in combat and battle aftermaths, highlighted state-building efforts with a particular focus on law enforcement, the Sinai landscape, and healthcare, displayed religious symbols and bonding icons in relation to martyrs and the everyday life of its communities, and utilized the about-to-die visual trope in almost all its military images. Nonetheless, Wilayat Sinai's photographic campaign strategies also diverged from those of other militant groups. For example, Sinai's provincial militant group omitted the display of leaders and civilian casualties, which serve as key features in images of al-Qaeda, Hamas, and the Syrian opposition. Instead, the group stressed the victimhood of Sinai residents through images of house demolitions and residents fleeing their homes. Wilayat Sinai's avoidance of leader depictions along with the incorporation of victimhood may well be a means to demonstrate stark differences from the Egyptian military's recurrent displays of top security officials.

The Egyptian military's visual frames mostly align with the strategies of many state actors in photographic warfare over the past three decades.[12] As others before it, the Egyptian military used images to focus on the war machine in scenes of artillery and airstrikes rather than soldiers on the battlefield, the state's humanitarian aid and social services, and the unified community as exemplified by visits from security officials, members of parliament, journalists, actors, and clerics to wounded soldiers. Two main exceptions, however, were in the portrayal of military leaders and in death displays. Egypt introduced a hyperemotional visual treatment of the minister of defense on hospital visits, which departs from the typical appearances of mighty military generals yet also constructs a narrative of fatherhood and patriotism in the face of insurgency. In Sinai, the military also did not censor death like other states, but rather frequently incorporated graphic images of enemy corpses on the battlefield. The Egyptian military's incorporation of death may well be a reflection of ISIS's humiliating depictions of soldiers and civilians in Sinai as well as a response to the deadly attacks during that period.

Most importantly, this chapter has demonstrated that understanding photographic warfare requires an examination of contested visual frames. Entman's four framing associations serve as recurrent areas of stasis that allow for insightful comparisons of the visual frames of militant groups and state actors. This chapter has shown that Wilayat Sinai's visual frames work in tandem to communicate a coherent localized story that identifies the apostasy of the Egyptian security apparatus as a problem, oppressing Sinai residents as the problem's primary cause, protecting the community as a moral responsibility, and fighting the Egyptian state and its collaborators as the main treatment. Meanwhile, the Egyptian military's visual frames created a much broader story that presents terrorism as a problem, attacking and excommunicating the military forces as the problem's cause, defending the country as a moral responsibility, and fighting terrorists as the main treatment. Comparing the similarities and differences between the visual frames of militant groups and state actors helps one understand the messages operating within the conflict.

The second level of analysis important to a full understanding of how the visual frames function in the contested online environment involves a close examination of the interactions between state and non-state actors. This analysis of ISIS and the Egyptian state revealed that the visual interactions involved competition, negation, and expansion strategies. The militant group and the state competed over the framing of similar messages, such as the nature of combative action, martyrdom, and the ability to provide services. Each side used its own images to negate the other's framing of messages. Wilayat Sinai negated the military's framing of precision airstrikes by emphasizing civilian targets. The military negated Wilayat Sinai's framing of combative action by highlighting the death and arrest of militants. They also expanded beyond the direct visual confrontation by leveraging their relative moral positions through unique messages like camaraderie, beauty, and responsible, sympathetic leadership. Examining the three interaction strategies helps further explicate how the state and non-state actors utilize counter-messages and alternative narratives in photographic warfare.

Future studies can apply the same visual framing approach to both photographs and videos in other conflicts. Visual messaging strategies may very well differ from one case study to another. Hence, studies should extract the applicable visual elements they need to examine from the surrounding context and the relevant existing literature. Finally, other conflicts may generate additional or different modes of interaction between the opponents' visual frames. Researchers can build on competition, negation, and expansion to develop a broader framework for context-specific visual framing interactions in photographic warfare.

CHAPTER 4

The Visual Semiotic Battle

Internationally recognized, militant, non-state groups mainly operate across Africa and Asia. Terrorist and corresponding sanctions lists of the United Nations, the European Union, and the United States include about four hundred such groups in total, with fewer than 10 percent of those functional in Europe and the Americas.[1] Similar lists that Arab countries have constructed contain, for the most part, groups from the Middle East, the Indian subcontinent, and Southeast Asia.[2]

The cultural context of non-state militant actors shapes the implications of their visual semiotic choices on their followers. As chapter 1 mentioned, Geert Hofstede and Edward Hall's works identify ample cultural differences that exist across regions and countries. Those notably highlight differences between the individualistic, low-context West and the collectivist, high-context, and masculine East bent on large power distance (see Table 5).[3] Yet despite these differences, American and Western European frameworks tend to set the standards and implication assumptions of visual semiotics. While useful as starting points, however, the Western frameworks may lack full explanatory power when applied in non-Western conflicts.

This chapter dissects the visual semiotic practices in the Arab photographic warfare between ISIS and the Egyptian state to pinpoint semiotic similarities and differences across Western and non-Western cultures. The sophisticated media operations on both sides of the Sinai conflict suggest strategic factors govern the visual semiotic choices of the competing media campaigns even during combative action. ISIS's internal documents reveal that a central media office provides the local provinces with a semiotic guidebook on how to purposefully use camera framing, positioning, and lighting to compose photographs and generate meaning.[4] In fact, the instruction booklet differentiates between random snapshots that do not require much preparation

TABLE 5. Characteristics of Arab and Egyptian societies based on Edward Hall and Geert Hofstede's cultural frameworks

Cultural dimension	Description
High context	Cohesive, family-oriented societies in which most of the information is implicitly communicated in the context or through symbols rather than in the explicit message
Masculine	Associates toughness, assertiveness, and success with males and shows admiration for strong figures
Large power distance	Unequal, hierarchical, and more respectful of elderly figures
Polychronic	Involves more multitasking and needs greater centralization and absolute control over individuals
Short-term oriented	Possesses universal guidelines about good and evil and considers the most important life events as either in the past or taking place now
Restrained	More morally disciplined, does not perceive leisure as important, and tends to have more police officers

and aesthetic photographs that depend on meticulous creative and technical processes. ISIS calls on its media workers to opt for the aesthetic choices that project the group's strength and the enemy's weakness in the ongoing warfare. Meanwhile, the Egyptian military has had a full Department of Morale Affairs in charge of psychological operations and media production for years. The department not only documents the military's efforts in Sinai but also amplifies its narratives in mainstream media. Although battlefield conditions can hinder photographers' ability to fully control photo production, digital photography allows them to capture tens or even hundreds of shots of the same action and select the best visuals later. ISIS and the Egyptian state can now control their battlefield semiotic choices more than ever before.

To assess how the media operations on both sides of the conflict strategically utilize visual semiotics, the chapter begins by providing a quantitative overview of the human subjects displayed in the photographic media campaigns of the militant group and the Egyptian military. Then, it focuses on five semiotic categories, mining previous research for the potential effects of those devices on Western viewers, examining how the media apparatuses of ISIS and the Egyptian state employ them in their respective campaigns, and integrating cultural dimensions to help explain unique semiotic choices. The chapter further analyzes how competing semiotic approaches interact with one another through competition, alignment, and expansion. Finally, it concludes with a discussion of how the Sinai conflict introduces context-specific visual semiotic applications that align with and diverge from Western approaches and of how future studies should direct their efforts moving forward.

Human Subjects in the Sinai Photographic Warfare

Wilayat Sinai portrayed human characters in almost two-thirds of its total photographic output in 2016–17. The displayed character types included militants (identified ISIS members), Egyptian soldiers (military conscripts, officers, and police guards), state collaborators (civilians and other tribal members who interacted, assisted, and worked with the Egyptian security forces), and ordinary civilians (those standing in, passing by, and driving through Sinai streets). The vast majority of the images portraying humans displayed only one character type, while the remaining photographs mixed human representatives of more than one group in the same scene. ISIS militants were the most visible in Wilayat Sinai's campaign, followed by Egyptian soldiers, state collaborators, and other civilians.

The Egyptian military portrayed human characters in half of its total output in 2016–17. The character types included Egyptian soldiers (military conscripts and officers from first lieutenants to brigadier generals), leaders (the army chief of staff and ministers of defense and the interior), Wilayat Sinai militants (all identified members of ISIS), and civilians. Various characters appeared together in numerous images, while almost 60 percent focused on one type. The Egyptian soldiers were more likely to be the solo character type in the human photographs, followed by militants, and civilians (i.e., government officials, members of parliament, journalists, religious clergy, and Sinai residents). Leaders were visible throughout the campaign as they interacted with other people in the scene rather than appearing on their own.

In short, ISIS and the Egyptian state's photographic campaigns exhibited different levels of emphasis based on displayed character types. Each group emphasized its own members as the most frequent human photo subjects. Yet leaders, for example, constituted a unique, recurrent character type that appeared only in the military images. The two groups also differed in their relative emphasis on opponents and supporters in the Sinai conflict. In ISIS's human photographs, Egyptian soldiers and state collaborators were prominent, while supporters were hardly present. In the Egyptian state's human photographs, on the other hand, militants were the least visible character type with civilian supporters appearing more frequently. Hence, ISIS depicted the Sinai conflict as one involving a large group of militants fighting security forces and the civilians helping them; Egypt presented a large pool of soldiers backed by their leaders and the public as they fought a small group of militants. The full import of the differences becomes more understandable with an examination of how each visual semiotic device intersected with the character types. For an overview of Wilayat Sinai and the Egyptian military's levels of dependence on semiotic strategies, see Table 6.

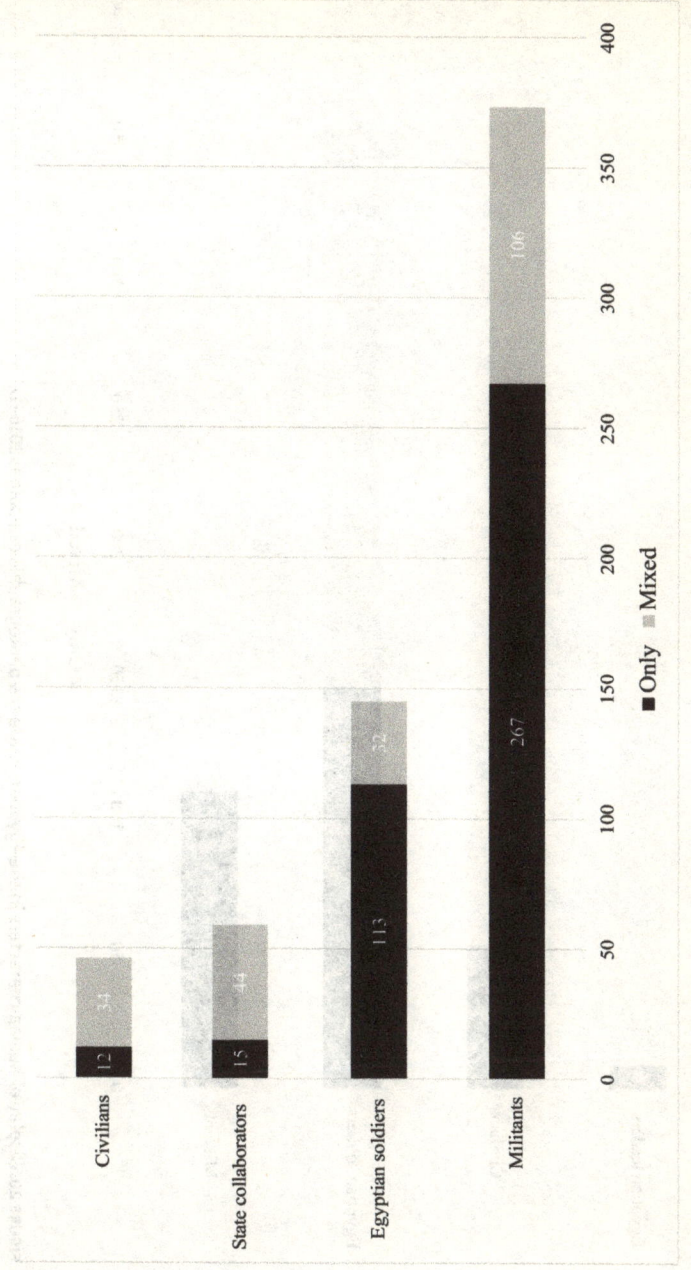

FIGURE 19. Display of human characters in Wilayat Sinai's photographic campaign, 2016–17.

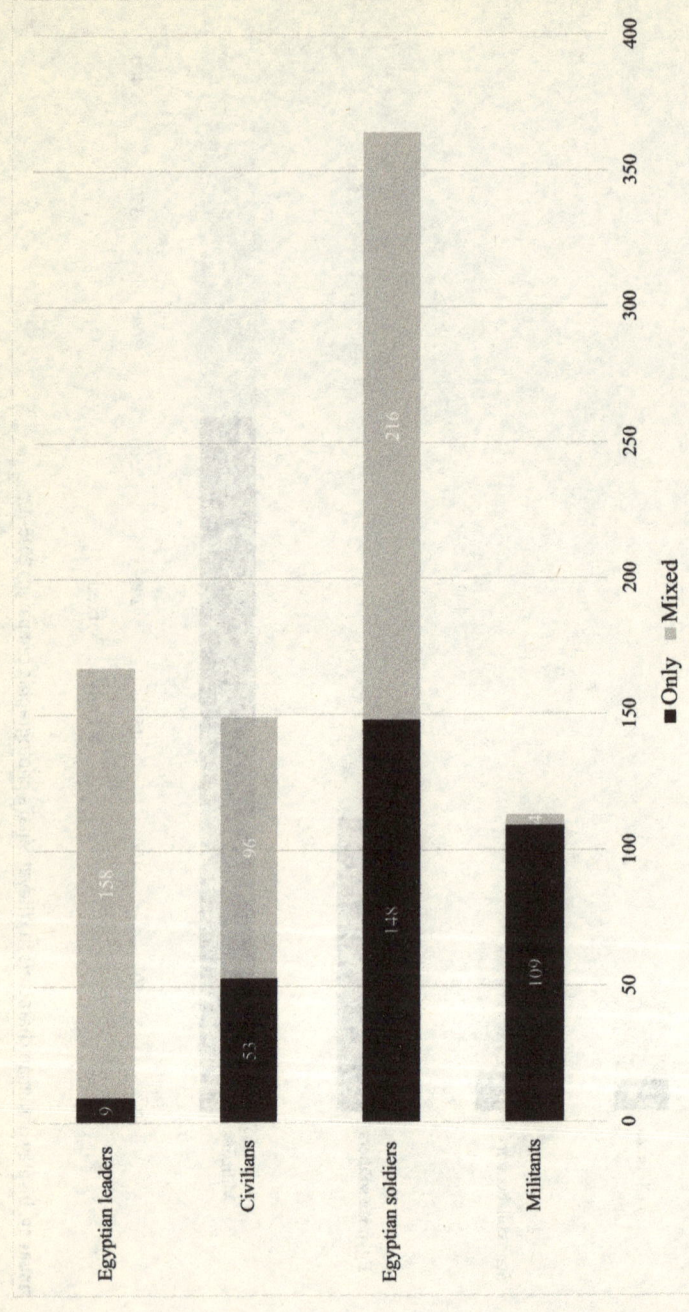

FIGURE 20. Display of human characters in the Egyptian military's photographic campaign, 2016–17.

TABLE 6. Statistical overview of the levels of dependence on visual semiotic devices in the Sinai photographic warfare

	Wilayat Sinai photographic campaign (percentage)	Egyptian military photographic campaign (percentage)	Chi-square test	
			x^2 value	Sig.
Social/public distance	46 percent	42 percent	$x^2(1, N = 1,071) = 1.53$	$p > .05$
Intimate/personal distance	34 percent	21 percent	$x^2(1, N = 1,071) = 22.66$	$p < .001***$
High camera angle	21 percent	26 percent	$x^2(1, N = 1,071) = 3.53$	$p > .05$
Low camera angle	10 percent	4 percent	$x^2(1, N = 1,071) = 18.01$	$p < .001***$
Negative facial expression	2 percent	0.2 percent	$x^2(1, N = 1,071) = 10.31$	$p < .01***$
Positive facial expression	3 percent	26 percent	$x^2(1, N = 1,071) = 119.14$	$p < .001***$
Direct eye contact	8 percent	2 percent	$x^2(1, N = 1,071) = 20.66$	$p < .001***$
Point-of-view shot	5 percent	1 percent	$x^2(1, N = 1,071) = 20.63$	$p < .001***$
Over-the-shoulder shot	8 percent	0.2 percent	$x^2(1, N = 1,071) = 44.13$	$p < .001***$

***Very significant, $p < .01$.

Viewer Distance

Studies of visual semiotics in the Western context typically utilize viewer distance to suggest a perceived relationship between the photo subject and the viewer. In *The Hidden Dimension*, Edward Hall coins the concept of proxemics, or the use and perception of personal space. In line with his framework, empirical research has found that at a social/public distance, the viewer has more difficulty recognizing the face of the photo subject, is more likely to perceive the character as a stranger or the other, and is less threatened by the subject's hostile actions.[5] But at an intimate/personal distance, the viewer can identify the photo subject's face, recognize their emotions in some cases, and foster a perceived closer relationship with them.[6] American political leaders, for example, are more likely to appear at a close to medium distance on the covers of American magazines than their foreign leader counterparts.[7] Immigrants, on the other hand, are more likely to appear at a long distance in some national newspapers compared to local citizens.[8]

Social/Public Distance

Wilayat Sinai and the Egyptian military both used social/public distance to portray human subjects in their respective media campaigns. The human characters appeared more than four feet away from the viewer in almost half of the militant group's and the military's images. Both groups shared an interest in providing a wide view of Sinai that positioned human photo subjects as recurrent part of the scenes. Disaggregation of the photographs by character types, however, revealed important differences between the two campaigns.

Wilayat Sinai often used social/public distance to depict its militants, particularly those engaged in combat or law enforcement activities. The battlefield images showed the militants at a distance, shooting, firing rockets, and attacking security checkpoints. Picturing an attack on al-Safa checkpoint in March 2016, for example, five images show several militants at a public distance jumping out of a pickup, running, and firing at the checkpoint (see Photo 24). The campaign photographs also displayed militants from afar distributing warning documents to civilians, confiscating drugs and cigarettes, burning the forbidden materials in public, and getting ready to execute state collaborators and Sufi clerics. The social/public distance emphasized that the group was serving as a trustworthy guardian of the community, in its handling of both the internal and the external threats facing those living in Sinai.

ISIS also used social/public distance to depict Egyptian soldiers displayed in images of combat and its aftermath. Wilayat Sinai's photographs showed distant Egyptian soldiers only as targets and nonthreatening opponents, rather

PHOTO 24. A social/public distance shot of ISIS militants attacking al-Safa checkpoint, disseminated March 20, 2016. Source: ISIS.

than as agents of action like their militant counterparts. The Egyptian soldiers stood passively unaware of snipers targeting them, walked or drove onto explosives unknowingly, fell on the ground or ran in response to militia attacks, and rushed to carry away their injured. Dozens of images snapped from a social/public distance, for example, show IED attacks and their destructive aftermath for Egyptian soldiers. Taken as a whole, ISIS's use of social/public distance emphasized the impotence of the Egyptian soldiers when they faced Wilayat Sinai militants on the battlefield.

By contrast, the Egyptian military used social/public distance to depict its soldiers competing successfully in photographs of combat, battlefield aftermath, and law enforcement activities. The battlefield photographs showed distant Egyptian soldiers lining up before operations, riding armored vehicles, entering caves, posing alongside confiscated belongings, and standing next to burning vehicles and hideouts. Picturing the aftermath of a counterterrorism operation on April 2, 2017, for example, four images show masked soldiers in long shots after they had confiscated explosive materials, computers, and vehicles in North Sinai (see Photo 25). The Egyptian soldiers also appeared at a distance destroying drug plantations, confiscating contraband cigarettes, and filling the streets to secure international events in the southern part of the peninsula. The social/public distance emphasized the strength of the Egyptian soldiers by showing both the broad scope and positive outcomes of the state's Sinai operations.

The Egyptian state further used social/public distance to depict ISIS militants along with local civilians in photographs of the battle aftermath and in law enforcement scenes. Unlike Egyptian military campaign photographs of

PHOTO 25. A social/public distance shot of Egyptian soldiers next to a confiscated vehicle, disseminated April 2, 2017. Source: Egyptian Army Spokesman.

PHOTO 26. A social/public distance shot of two ISIS militants under arrest in Sinai, disseminated September 8, 2017. Source: ISIS.

soldiers who always appeared powerful and victorious, the same group's shots of militants showed them under arrest on a distant battlefield. A long shot posted on September 8, 2017, shows two individuals kneeling in the desert with their hands tied behind them and faces blurred after their arrest in central Sinai (see Photo 26). The Facebook post identifies both men as "very dangerous takfiris."[9] Meanwhile, distant shots of dead militants showed them in humiliating conditions with their blood spilling, their weapons next to their bodies, and/or their vehicles burning in the nearby surroundings. Some law enforcement images also displayed civilians under arrest for engaging in smuggling activity from a long distance. For instance, two long shots posted on November 12, 2017, show two blindfolded individuals in a very similar position to ISIS militants, with blurry faces and hands tied upon arrest as they stand in front of their confiscated vehicles and materials at checkpoints. The Facebook post describes them as drug and cigarette smugglers.[10] Together, the social/public distance shots emphasized the eventual fate of separation from the rest of the Sinai community that awaited both captured militants and smugglers.

Intimate/Personal Distance

Wilayat Sinai was more likely than the Egyptian military to use photographs shot at an intimate/personal distance. The human characters appeared less than four feet away from the viewer in over one-third of the militant group's images, but in about one-fifth of the military's images. Based on Western conceptions of the element's impact on viewers, the differential level of dependence suggests the militant, non-state actor placed more emphasis on creating a closer and more personal relationship with the viewer. Considering the context of the media blackout in Sinai, however, the strategy could also relate to the militant group's desire to bring the on-the-ground conditions closer to its viewers in Sinai and beyond.

Wilayat Sinai used intimate/personal distance mainly to depict its own militants in combat and pre-battle scenes. The images focusing on the battlefield showed engaged militants as they assembled rockets and fired gunshots at distant, invisible enemies. Photographs snapped away from the battlefield showed militants standing or sitting at a close to medium distance holding weapons, cameras, or the Qur'an (see Photo 27). In these eulogy photographs, the immediate textual context always identified the militants as "martyrs" who had died subsequently in attacks or suicide operations. Out of all eulogy images in the group's campaign, nearly 80 percent depicted the ISIS martyrs in close-up. The patterned use of intimate/personal distance to show depicted militants and martyrs suggested the viewer should feel a close, personal relationship to those willing to fight and die for the group's cause.

PHOTO 27. An intimate/personal distance shot of a martyred ISIS militant in Sinai, disseminated January 28, 2017. Source: ISIS.

ISIS also used intimate/personal distance to depict Egyptian soldiers and state collaborators, but to send very different messages. The use of close distance in photographed post-battle scenes showed Egyptian soldiers and tribal fighters only as corpses or as images shown on confiscated photo identification cards with accompanying visual and textual contexts confirming their death and defeat. Visualizing the aftermath of an attack on a security convoy in Beer al-Abd in September 2017, for example, two images show dead Egyptian soldiers on the ground at a close distance with burned skin, torn clothes, and bloody bodies. Images displaying law enforcement scenes, on the other hand, utilized close shots to show Egyptian soldiers, tribal fighters, and other state collaborators immediately before, during, and after their executions. The image sequences presented AK47s, pistols, and knives as the weapons of choice in these graphic scenes. In total, two-thirds of all death images in the group's photographic campaign depicted the militants' enemies at a close distance. This patterned use of intimate/personal distance highlighted the gruesome fates that awaited Egyptian soldiers and collaborators working to combat ISIS forces in Sinai.

The Egyptian military, by contrast, used intimate/personal distance to depict ISIS militants in the aftermath of the Sinai combat operations. The bulk of images with close views showed militants lying dead in stained fatigues with shattered heads and severed body parts. The only close-up shots of militants alive displayed subjects kneeling upon their arrests. To illustrate, a total of sixteen close to medium shots posted on October 16, 2017, show disfigured corpses of over a dozen militants on the ground, each with burns on their skin and blood covering their body. In those graphic scenes, the immediate textual

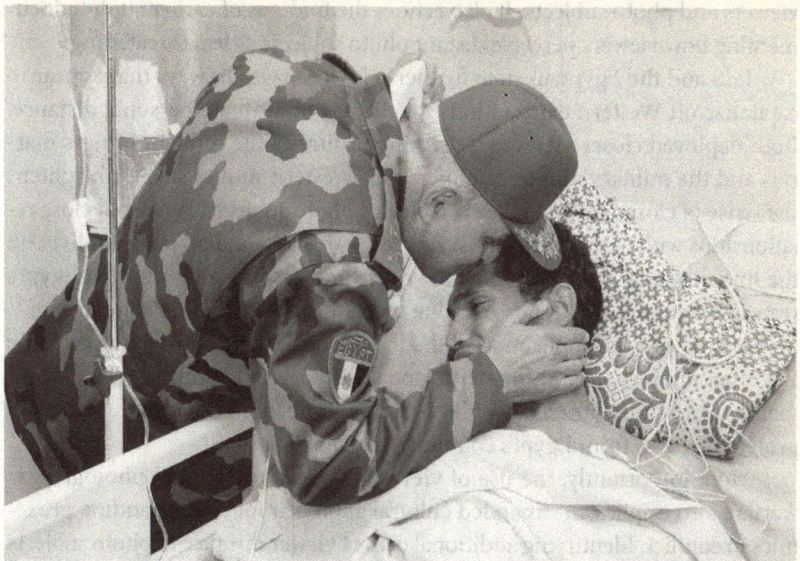

PHOTO 28. An intimate/personal distance shot of Egypt's then–minister of defense Sedki Sobhi visiting injured soldiers, disseminated January 26, 2016. Source: Egyptian Army Spokesman.

context identifies the dead individuals as terrorists and takfiris who had attempted to carry out attacks in Sinai. Quite like Wilayat Sinai, the military depicted militants at a close distance in almost two-thirds of all death images. The intimate/personal distance emphasized the consequences that enemies of the state can expect in Sinai by bringing graphic details of their death and arrest to closer view.

The Egyptian military also used intimate/personal distance to depict top security officials interacting with the injured soldiers lying in hospital beds or with conscripts in the Sinai barracks. Four close to medium shots posted on January 26, 2016, show Minister of Defense Sedki Sobhi shaking hands, patting shoulders, and kissing injured soldiers (see Photo 28). The intimate/personal distance worked to humanize the two characters by positioning the Egyptian soldier as vulnerable in some respects and the top generals as leaders who genuinely care and have concern for the men under their commands.

To some extent, Wilayat Sinai and the Egyptian military's use of viewer distance in the Sinai conflict aligns with existing Western frameworks of expected visual semiotic outcomes. Each side utilized social/public distance to push its enemies away from the viewer and depict them as the nonthreatening other, just like we would expect using Hall's proxemics framework. The Sinai conflict's approach appears somewhat consistent with previous studies conducted in Western cultures showing that social/public distance disconnects viewers and photo subjects. It also echoes the findings of earlier studies documenting how viewers perceive distant photo subjects as less threatening.

ISIS and the Egyptian state further rely on images in ways that appear to capitalize on Western expectations for the use of intimate/personal distance. Both deployed closer views as a defining feature of the militant group's martyrs and the military's injured soldiers that Western studies suggest heightens the sense of closeness that viewers feel with photo subjects. Perceived close relationships with each group's most revered warriors who had put their lives on the line may also help legitimize the cause and inspire supporters in Egypt's restrained culture that tends to value moral discipline and devalue leisure.[11] Moving beyond the application of the technique to rank-and-file soldiers, the Egyptian military used intimate/personal distance to legitimize its top commanders, a feature absent in Wilayat Sinai's campaign perhaps as a means of protecting them from Egypt's counterterrorism efforts.

More importantly, the use of viewer distance in the Sinai photographic warfare also implies an expanded cultural approach for understanding proxemics in conflict. Identifying additional uses of viewer distance to photo subjects in non-Western contexts suggests differential cross-cultural interpretations of the same visual semiotic element that warrant experimental investigation. Neither Wilayat Sinai nor the Egyptian military limited their application of social/public distance to image depictions of the other in the media campaigns. The Arab culture where those photographs circulate can help explain the lack of adherence to standard Western semiotic expectations. When featuring their fighters at a social/public distance, for example, ISIS and the Egyptian state almost always portrayed their forces as tough collectives capable of safeguarding the Sinai community. Displaying their protagonists farther away from the viewer here emphasized strength on the ground and a sense of belonging to the in-group, which reinforce key values in collectivist, masculine cultures. At least in the Egyptian context, long-distance shots in the photographic campaigns broaden the scope of the fighting group's own efforts and suggest their omnipresent strength in combatting current or future enemies.

Moreover, ISIS and the Egyptian state expanded the implied messaging incorporated in the non-Western use of intimate/personal distance. Dozens of these shots in ISIS and the Egyptian state's campaigns brought the photo subject closer to the viewer when lying dead, facing execution, or kneeling upon arrest. Neither the militant group nor the military appeared to be suggesting intimacy and friendship between the viewer and the enemy characters per se. Instead, they singled out individual enemies, restricting their viewer proximity to humiliating and dire situations to send a warning message to those who would oppose them. Using the same semiotic device across different character types, the two sides in the photographic warfare drew a sharp contrast between morally disciplined, unified protagonists and helpless, isolated opponents. They simply stripped any semblance of power or belonging to a collective from antagonists, while bringing them closer to the viewer in ways that emphasize an outlier status in a collectivist, masculine, and restrained culture. In the Egyptian context, close to medium shots can serve as warning signs that magnify the imminent, swift retaliation that awaits the other in times of conflict.

Camera Angle

The visual semiotics literature in the Western context typically utilizes camera angles to convey relative levels of symbolic power. A high camera angle pointing downward can present photo subjects as weak, passive, and less significant.[12] At extreme height, the bird's-eye view can even depersonalize the human bodies underneath, while offering the viewer "god-like powers of surveillance."[13] By contrast, a low camera angle pointing upward can prompt positive assessments of the photo subject's authority, dominance, boldness, and influence.[14] The Associated Press, for example, was more likely to use a high camera angle in its portrayals of Afghani women under the Taliban regime until its initial defeat at the hands of the U.S.-led coalition in late 2001, after which their depiction shifted to more favorable angles.[15] In the meantime, when showing objects (rather than human subjects) in a scene, high or low camera angles do not usually carry the same connotations, however, as viewers tend to prefer looking down at them for practical reasons, such as checking out their most salient parts.[16]

High Camera Angle

The level of reliance on high camera angles to portray human subjects in Wilayat Sinai and the Egyptian military's media campaigns was pretty similar. The high camera angle featured human characters from elevated positions in over one-fifth of the militant group and the military's images. The two sides shared the same approach by providing the viewer a chance to perceptually demean selected character types in their images.

As expected, ISIS used high camera angles to depict Egyptian soldiers and state collaborators. The post-battle images used high camera angles to depict the soldiers lying dead in their own blood, under attack, or with their images on display in confiscated identification card photographs. Three high-angle photographs posted on November 4, 2016, look down at headshots of a military brigadier general on three different identification cards, with accompanying captions confirming his assassination in al-Arish. Similarly, shots of public executions used high camera angles to show dead Egyptian soldiers and state collaborators lying on the ground or the same character types kneeling or lying on their stomach as they face impending death. In fact, the vast majority of death images in the militant group's campaign depicted the enemies from a high angle. Positioning the viewer to look down emphasized the humiliation of the dead Egyptian soldiers and collaborators.

But Wilayat Sinai also used high camera angles to depict its own militants at times. In images of the barracks and the battlefield, the camera positioned the viewer to look down at the militants' hands as they held food, the Qur'an, copies of the ISIS's *al-Naba'* newsletter, and confiscated weapons or belongings. Three high-angle shots on February 7, 2017, for instance, display ISIS's newsletter in the hands of militants as they held, read, and distributed it within Sinai. Other photographs used high-angle shots of clinics and medical workshops to show viewers the hands of militants as they held medical equipment and medicine or as they conducted first aid training workshops on prone fellow militants. The high-angle shots here shared details of ISIS militants' lifestyle by offering a top view of the most salient parts of objects they use in daily activities.

As in the case of Wilayat Sinai's media campaign, the Egyptian military also used high camera angles to depict its enemies. The militants were, by far, the main character type displayed in high-angle shots, predominantly those to do with the aftermath of battles. The camera positioned viewers to look down at the militants as they lay dead on the ground in the aftermath of military operations or as they knelt blindfolded after their arrests. Two high-angle images posted on March 23, 2017, for example, display the bloody corpses of six militants with their faces either facing the ground or covered by their own clothes. The Facebook post describes the context of the displayed scene as the outcome of a counterterrorism operation against takfiri terrorists in central Sinai.[17] Almost all death images in the military's campaign positioned the viewer to look down at the enemies who served as photo subjects. The high-angle shots emphasized the humiliation that defeated militants suffered in battles against the Egyptian state.

To a much lesser extent, the military also used high camera angles to depict its own soldiers engaged in particular tasks. In post-battle images, photographs utilizing high camera angles showed Egyptian soldiers confiscating weapons from caves, standing next to explosive materials, or clearing hideouts. To illustrate, four high-angle shots posted on February 11, 2017, show soldiers inside an underground weapon storage facility retrieving rifles, rockets, ammo, and explosive materials. Other photographs deploying high camera angles showed Egyptian soldiers as they confiscated drugs and contraband or as they destroyed underground tunnels. The high-angle shots shared details of the security threats that Egyptian soldiers were handling in Sinai by positioning the viewer to look down at and scrutinize illegal objects.

PHOTO 29. A high-angle shot of ISIS militants distributing *al-Naba'* newsletter in Sinai, disseminated February 7, 2017. Source: ISIS.

PHOTO 30. A high-angle shot of Egyptian soldiers discovering a weaponry storage unit in Sinai, disseminated February 11, 2017. Source: Egyptian Army Spokesman.

Low Camera Angle

Wilayat Sinai was more likely than the Egyptian military to use low-angle shots in its photographs of human subjects. One out of every ten militant group images featured low camera angles pointing upward, while the military rarely used such technique. The differential level of emphasis suggests ISIS's heightened interest in exaggerating the power of the photographed human subjects in its campaign, perhaps in an attempt to bridge the wide strength gap it faced on the ground as compared to Egypt's armed forces in Sinai.

Wilayat Sinai relied exclusively on low-angle shots to depict its own militants. Photographs of pre-battle preparations and battlefield operations utilized low camera angles to look up at the militants as they mounted antiaircraft guns, fired gunshots, launched rockets, surveilled Egyptian security forces, engaged in military exercises, marched to battle, posed with their gear on top of pickup trucks, and called for prayer. Five low-angle shots on February 11, 2017, for example, feature militants, in what the group describes as an antiaircraft brigade that targets enemy jets in the Sinai airspace (see Photo 31). In photographs of executions, the low camera angles also situated the viewer to look up at the militants as they shot and beheaded state collaborators and Egyptian soldiers. The low-angle shots emphasized the militants' dominance by positioning them above all other photo subjects and the viewer.

Similarly, the Egyptian military used low-angle shots to depict its own personnel. Photographs of the counterterrorism operations used low camera angles to position the viewer to look up at the Egyptian soldiers burning hideouts on the ground, firing missiles from jets, and searching mountain caves. For instance, two low-angle shots posted on February 17, 2017, display soldiers on Halal Mountain in central Sinai clearing hideouts of weapons, explosive devices, and motorcycles. In other images not related to counterterrorism operations, the low camera angles situated the viewer to look up to top security leaders as they visited soldiers in the barracks or in hospitals (see Photo 32). Low-angle shots emphasized the strength of the Egyptian military personnel and leaders by always positioning the viewer to look up at them.

The application of camera angles in the Sinai conflict closely aligned with visual semiotic study findings documented in Western contexts. Each side utilized photographs shot with high camera angles to imply the weakness and insignificance of dead enemies it had killed in combat operations and opponents it had arrested. In fact, the use of high camera angles was a defining feature associated with death images of the enemy on both sides of the Sinai conflict. In contrast, the two groups used low camera angles to signify boldness, authority, and power by situating viewers to look up at their own fighters and leaders. Even in the rare cases when ISIS and the Egyptian state showed their own fighters in some of the high-angle shots, the images did not suggest their weakness but rather exhibited a choice to emphasize and focus viewer attention on select objects in their hands (e.g., Qur'an, food, and enemy belongings, etc.).

Applied in the polychronic Egyptian culture that involves absolute control over individuals reinforced through the hierarchical society, camera angles in Wilayat Sinai's campaign disrupted expected power dynamics. The upward positioning used to picture militants projected power in the face of what

PHOTO 31. A low-angle shot of ISIS militants targeting jets in the Sinai airspace, disseminated February 11, 2017. Source: ISIS.

PHOTO 32. A low-angle shot of Egypt's then–army field of staff visiting soldiers in Sinai, disseminated February 23, 2017. Source: Egyptian Army Spokesman.

ISIS considers a weak state. The Egyptian military's photographs, by contrast, maintained the image of the existing social hierarchy by bolstering the credibility of the Egyptian forces and demeaning that of the insurgents.

Facial Expressions

Studies of visual semiotics in the Western context typically explore facial expressions as a signifier of human emotions. Images displaying photo subjects' negative facial expressions have prompted viewer assumptions that the displayed characters are afraid, skeptical, and unaffiliated with the viewer and lack the ability to dominate their situational contexts.[18] By contrast, the display of photo subjects' positive facial expressions generally implies good intentions, familiarity, genuineness, high affiliation, and dominance.[19] Some British tabloid newspapers with conservative political leanings, for example, used photo subjects' positive facial expressions to depict joyous coalition soldiers with local civilians in Iraq after the fall of Saddam Hussein to help frame the 2003 invasion as a liberation rather than an invasion.[20] Meanwhile, old images showing former president Mubarak sad or in shock began to appear in the Egyptian media only shortly after his ouster in the Arab Spring uprisings.

Negative Facial Expressions

Despite the small number of images, Wilayat Sinai was more likely than the Egyptian military to use negative facial expressions with its photographed human subjects. Negative facial expressions were almost nonexistent in the military's campaign, as only one image showed the burned face of a dead militant staring with his mouth wide open. The militant group used negative facial expressions a bit more frequently, yet only in twelve of its distributed images. The different level of emphasis suggests the militant group's interest in showing the emotional distress of some human photo subjects and instilling fear by presenting individuals' allegiance to the Egyptian government as a precursor to their negative emotional states.

Wilayat Sinai used negative facial expressions only to depict Egyptian soldiers and state collaborators. The negative facial expressions conveyed feelings of devastation and anguish on the faces of hostages in their final moments prior to their executions. Take, for example, a three-image post on September 26, 2017, that displays sadness and bewilderment on the faces of three civilian hostages of different ages whom the captions describe as apostates and collaborators with security forces. The subsequent images in the same photo report show the militants carrying out their brutal shooting and beheading punishments.

The Visual Semiotic Battle **135**

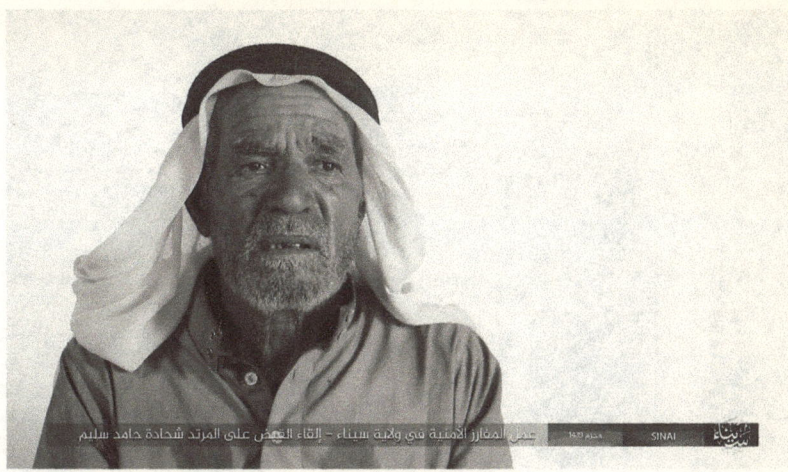

PHOTO 33. An old man exhibiting a negative facial expression before being shot in the head by ISIS for collaborating with the Egyptian security forces, disseminated September 26, 2017. Source: ISIS.

Negative facial expressions emphasized the emotional breakdowns of the enemies as they neared death due to their opposition of ISIS.

Positive Facial Expressions

On the other hand, the Egyptian military was much more likely to use positive facial expressions than Wilayat Sinai in photographs incorporating human subjects. Smiling faces appeared in over a quarter of the military's images, but rarely in the militant group's campaign. The different level of emphasis indicates the Egyptian military had a higher interest in showing the positive emotions of select human subjects in its campaign.

Wilayat Sinai reserved positive facial expressions for a special group of militants from among its ranks. In such photographs, smiling militants stood at the ready to conduct operations for the group in Sinai. The accompanying text confirmed their subsequent martyrdom. To illustrate, an image posted on September 13, 2017, displays a smiling suicide attacker as he stands by his concealed car bomb. He points his index finger to the heavens before setting out to attack a security convoy in Beer al-Abd (see Photo 34). The following images in the same photo report depict the destructive aftermath of his attack and the human losses that the police suffered as a result of his martyrdom. Positive facial expressions recorded the happiness that accompanied individuals' selection for martyrdom operations and validated their choice to sacrifice their lives in attacks against the Egyptian state.

PHOTO 34. A martyred ISIS militant exhibiting a positive facial expression before carrying out a suicide bomb attack, disseminated September 13, 2017. Source: ISIS.

Likewise, the Egyptian military used positive facial expressions to depict its own personnel. The Egyptian soldiers and leaders were, by far, the main characters displayed with positive facial expressions. Photographs of hospital visits showed the joyous faces of injured soldiers and their leaders as they met and talked with one another. Eight images posted on April 30, 2016, for instance, show Lieutenant General Sedki Sobhi exchanging smiles with soldiers lying on hospital beds who suffered burns and broken limbs in defense of Sinai. In images of the soldiers' barracks, the minister of defense, the minister of the interior, and the army chief of staff also appeared positive as they shook hands with the soldiers, handed them gifts, and posed for group pictures. The positive facial expressions emphasized the unity and pure intentions of the Egyptian military personnel to protect Sinai despite any setbacks.

But the Egyptian military also used positive facial expressions to depict its civilian supporters and beneficiaries. Photographs shot in hospitals showed actors, journalists, and religious clerics visiting and exchanging smiles with the injured soldiers. An image posted on October 6, 2017, illustrates the pattern as it shows a smiling journalist handing a gift to a soldier in a wheelchair after he had lost both of his legs in Sinai battlefield operations. Images of Sinai's streets displayed residents happily shaking hands with military leaders and cheerfully receiving aid from soldiers. Among those, six images posted on March 9, 2017, show smiling men and children posing happily for the camera after receiving food packages from the military. The positive facial expressions emphasized the affiliation of Egyptian civilians with their state by presenting favorable emotional outcomes of solidarity with the soldiers and the military's humanitarian operations.

PHOTO 35. A man happily holding a food package he received from the Egyptian military, disseminated March 9, 2017. Source: Egyptian Army Spokesman.

The displayed facial expressions in the Sinai photographic warfare closely aligned with previous visual semiotics research findings conducted in Western contexts. ISIS used negative facial expressions to stimulate skepticism and suggest its dominance over its enemies. The group displayed the agony of individual Egyptian soldiers and local state collaborators, regardless of their age, as a tool to instill fear in viewers. The military, instead, depicted many of the militants as dead or under arrest without displaying photo subjects with negative facial expressions, perhaps to further detach them from the viewer by stripping away any emotional cues. Operating in a high-context, high-power-distance, and short-term-oriented culture, ISIS weaponized visual cues to further disrupt the power dynamics. They projected an image of an egalitarian society governed by divine law that punishes the old and young, the rich and poor, and the Egyptian military soldier and the Sinai Bedouin if and when they transgress.

In the competing media campaigns, both sides also used smiling faces to emphasize the genuineness and positive intentions of their own fighters. In Wilayat Sinai's photographs, martyrs were the happiest of all for suppressing their worldly desires, supporting a higher cause, and eventually sacrificing their lives for their faith. Each represented a valued trait of Egypt's restrained culture. The military displayed positive facial expressions to suggest familiarity and a high degree of affiliation among its top leaders, soldiers, and loyal civilians, thus tapping into the values of a cohesive, collectivist culture in the nation-state. In sum, nuanced, culture-specific, visual approaches to photographic warfare can utilize facial expressions to bolster portrayals of competing forces that bifurcate dichotomous emotional states and exclusively limit happiness to the in-group.

Eye Contact

Studies of visual semiotics in the Western context typically utilize various types of eye contact to connect with viewers and to bolster positive character traits of photo subjects. In Kress and van Leeuwen's grammar of visual design, the direct gaze establishes an imaginary relationship with and conveys a demand to the viewer that is dependent on the surrounding context.[21] Further, images displaying an individual looking directly at the camera tend to attract heightened levels of viewer attention and present the subject as credible, attractive/favorable, competent, and potent.[22] Avoidance of eye contact, on the other hand, can emphasize otherness, withdrawal, and social anxiety.[23] Many al-Qaeda videos, for example, show leaders looking directly at the camera as they call supporters to action, while some European newspapers show comparatively more immigrants looking away from the camera in shots of them in their new host countries.[24]

Wilayat Sinai was four times more likely than the military to incorporate human subjects with direct eye contact in the Sinai photographic warfare. Human photo subjects looked directly at the camera in about one in every ten of the militant group's images; they rarely did so in the military's campaign. The differential usage of the direct gaze demonstrates the militant group's heightened interest in establishing a higher level of interaction with viewers and a stronger sense of nonverbal dialogue between the selected human subjects and viewers.

ISIS used photographs incorporating direct eye contact when it depicted its own men. Mainly, the pictured militants appeared prior to their own operations targeting the Egyptian state. Texts accompanying the images with direct eye contact characterized the militant photo subjects as "martyrs" who had conducted suicide attacks and operations. Two images posted on October 14, 2017, for example, display two muscular militants dressed in fatigues holding rifles and wearing masks that covered their faces completely except for their eyes looking directly at the viewer. The two accompanying captions identify the individuals as suicide attackers undertaking a martyrdom operation designed to strike a military battalion in al-Arish. The direct gaze was recurring across the eulogy images, invoking an imaginary relation between the viewer and those sacrificing their lives in the field. The direct eye contact thus emphasized the powerful status of militants vowing to martyr themselves for the group's cause.

Surprisingly, Wilayat Sinai used direct eye contact also when depicting the enemies at times. The battlefield images displayed Egyptian soldiers appearing on the front of confiscated identification cards looking directly at the viewer. Although the soldiers were not physically present, the captured photographs in the militants' hands cued their defeat on the battlefield. Two images posted on

PHOTO 36. A middle-aged man looking straight to the camera before being shot by ISIS for collaborating with the Egyptian security forces, disseminated September 13, 2016. Source: ISIS.

PHOTO 37. A martyred Egyptian officer looking straight to the camera in an old personal photograph, disseminated March 24, 2017. Source: Egyptian Army Spokesman.

June 17, 2016, for instance, display the face of one soldier on his identification card looking straight at the viewer. The card appears next to the soldier's pistol, credit card, and portable power bank, while the accompanying caption indicates his assassination in al-Arish. Almost all shots of confiscated identification cards in the militant group's campaign showed the Egyptian soldiers and officers looking directly into the camera. In the militant group's public execution photographs, the camera also positioned the viewer to look state collaborators in the eyes as they awaited their severe punishments (see Photo 36). The subsequent images in such photo reports always revealed the gruesome details of the executions, with accompanying captions charging the individuals with espionage and apostasy. The direct eye contact here emphasized the vulnerability of the captured enemies and prophesized a similar fate for others choosing to oppose ISIS.

The Egyptian military used direct eye contact almost exclusively when depicting its leaders and personnel. These images positioned the viewer to look directly into the eyes of officers before they died in battle, soldiers who distributed food packages to Sinai residents, injured soldiers on their hospital beds surrounded by visitors, and soldiers posing for the camera with their leaders in the field. To illustrate, three direct eye contact images posted in March 2017 display martyred officers with Facebook posts describing them as heroes.[25] The three photographs were the only instances where the military portrayed its martyred officers in the campaign. The direct eye contact emphasized the competence and favorability of the military personnel who sacrificed their lives to secure Sinai and help its residents.

Therefore, each side in the Sinai conflict used direct eye contact to emphasize the high status of its fighters and create a connection with the viewer in ways that align with the grammar of visual design in Western culture. Direct eye contact functioned as a defining feature in the martyrs' photographs that both sides distributed. The militant group portrayed its martyrs as selfless, potent, and credible, typically before they headed off to the battlefield to die. The direct gaze highlighted intentionality that demanded praise for the martyrdom act. Although the Egyptian military showed its three martyrs looking to the viewer, the images lacked a similar pre-martyrdom visual context. Instead, the military shared personal photographs from the soldiers' past that emphasized its martyrs as favorable photo subjects who justify retaliation for the ISIS's killings.

Nonetheless, the militant group and the military's patterned usage of eye contact in the Sinai photographic warfare did suggest additional uses of the semiotic tool in Arab cultures. Similar to the two groups' appropriation of intimate/personal distance, ISIS and the Egyptian state alike utilized direct eye contact to depict enemies and smugglers looking directly at the viewer as they faced punishment. Featuring the other alone and humiliated starkly differs from the potent, revered martyrs. The gaze of the enemy conveys guilt and sadness in ways that reinforce weakness, disgrace, and isolation. Rather than transmit only the positive traits consistent with earlier findings of studies conducted in the Western context, direct eye contact in high-context cultures can carry alternative meanings. The nonverbal strategy can serve as a warning sign for viewers considering connecting with the humiliated other.

Furthermore, the Sinai conflict presented a setting where Western findings related to eye contact avoidance may not even apply. Both Wilayat Sinai and the Egyptian military avoided deploying the display of direct eye contact in the vast majority of their images. This avoidance, however, did not necessarily present the human photo subjects as socially anxious or as an exemplar of the other. In fact, both campaigns displayed this visual semiotic element across all character types, including fighters, supporters, and enemies. The military, for example, blurred or covered the faces of many soldiers, militants, and smugglers in the field, which can limit the viewer interaction with all the different characters, including its own personnel. Protecting and avoiding the distraction of fighters on the battlefield may also explain the lacking eye contact in the recurring combat images on both sides. In the Sinai photographic warfare, avoidance of eye contact functioned as the norm to suggest the photo subjects' full engagement in the conflict and to conceal their identities for security purposes.

Subjective Shots

Studies of visual semiotics in the Western context typically associate subjective shots with attempts to identify with the viewer. Branigan's theory of subjectivity defines the point-of-view (POV) shot as a cinematic technique that narrates the scene from the perspective of the main character.[26] It serves to merge the viewer with the character in action, increase presence, and stimulate more enjoyment.[27] Take, for example, first-person shooter games that incorporate the POV technique to attract and entertain young gamers by immersing them in the protagonist's action. The over-the-shoulder (OTS) shot is yet another subjective camera technique that positions the viewer to look over the shoulder of the character in the scene.[28] Despite less reliance on subjectivity than POV shots, OTS shots can provide a more stable view of "the direct spatial relation" between the subject and other objects in the scene.[29] The OTS shot is also common in video games to allow the player to follow the main avatar, see what it is doing, and know where it is heading. The existing literature shows that complementing POV and OTS shots with added character reaction shots can further promote viewer identification.[30]

Point-of-View and Over-the-Shoulder Shots in Human Photographs

ISIS and the Egyptian state used subjective shots differently in human photographs during the Sinai conflict. Wilayat Sinai was much more likely than the military to use POV and OTS shots. In fact, the Egyptian state barely used any of the two subjective shots in its photographic campaign. For example, the military's one and only OTS shot showed the destruction of a hideout from over the shoulder of a soldier as he stood in a field talking into a handheld transceiver. The comparative emphasis that the two sides placed on subjective shots is suggestive of ISIS's focused interest in highly engaging viewers in its photographed scenes.

Wilayat Sinai used POV shots only when depicting its own militants. The battlefield photographs positioned the viewer to take on the militant's role of attacking security forces, conducting checkpoint shootings, sniping targets, killing soldiers, and burning vehicles. Picturing an attack on al-Matafi checkpoint in January 2017, for instance, seven POV shots present the assault from the militants' visual perspectives as they hold their rifles, shoot a soldier in the back, take over a checkpoint, and stand victoriously over the rubble (see Photo 38). Other images in the same photo report serve as reaction shots that confirm the identity of ISIS militants. The POV shots in Wilayat Sinai's media campaign virtually engaged the viewer in belligerent action against state forces using a semiotic element that can create a viewer's presence in the scene to act on behalf of the militants.

Wilayat Sinai also used OTS shots when depicting its own fighters. With the exception of one OTS shot from behind a man repenting to ISIS for collaborating with security forces, militants were the only character type displayed in all OTS shots. The battlefield images placed the viewer over the shoulder of a militant shooting at distant targets, launching rockets, and pointing antiaircraft guns at jets in the sky. Images away from the battlefield positioned viewers to imagine themselves peering over the shoulders of militants standing in the desert at sunset, distributing ISIS publications, watching videos, cooking food, boiling water, or reading the Qur'an. Two OTS shots posted on February 7, 2017, illustrate the point as they place the viewer in a position to join a sitting militant in the process of reading ISIS's flagship *al-Naba'* newsletter while having tea (see Photo 39). The OTS shots engaged the viewer in both the fighting and the leisure activities by visually embedding them with ISIS militants.

Meanwhile, the Egyptian military's POV shots depicted only soldiers in the field. The photographs visually placed the viewer in a position to assume the Egyptian soldier's role of holding a rifle or a torch to clear underground tunnels or of standing over the opening of a storage unit housing contraband explosives discovered in North Sinai (see Photo 40). The POV shots encouraged the viewers to imagine themselves involved in the military counterterrorism operations by giving them rare access to sites associated with security threats in Sinai.

PHOTO 38. A point-of-view shot of an ISIS militant firing inside a Sinai checkpoint, disseminated January 11, 2017. Source: ISIS.

PHOTO 39. An over-the-shoulder shot of an ISIS militant reading *al-Naba'* newsletter in Sinai, disseminated February 7, 2017. Source: ISIS.

PHOTO 40. A point-of-view shot of an Egyptian soldier checking an underground tunnel in Sinai, disseminated February 21, 2017. Source: Egyptian Army Spokesman.

Beyond Human Photographs

The two groups' photographic campaigns also utilized subjective shots in images that showed no human characters. Although the images omitted the visual presence of human photo subjects or body parts altogether, the POV technique nevertheless implied the presence of human characters at the scene closely monitoring an impending destructive act against hidden human targets. Across all nonhuman photographs, Wilayat Sinai and the Egyptian military's reliance on POV shots was relatively minimal, but around the same level. The two sides thus shared a common tactic, allowing viewers to fill in the missing details regarding the unseen human characters.

Wilayat Sinai used POV shots to depict many of its IED attacks. Neither the militant nor any other character type appeared in these combat scenes. The images, however, positioned viewers to imagine themselves taking on the role of an ISIS militant conducting surveillance, marking the target, or waiting for Egyptian military vehicles to progress toward roadside IEDs. The subsequent, associated shots always displayed explosions and fire surrounding the targeted vehicles. Three POV shots posted on May 22, 2017, for example, present a moving military armored vehicle and a personnel carrier at the center of red target markers before the detonation of IEDs in North Sinai. These POV shots posi-

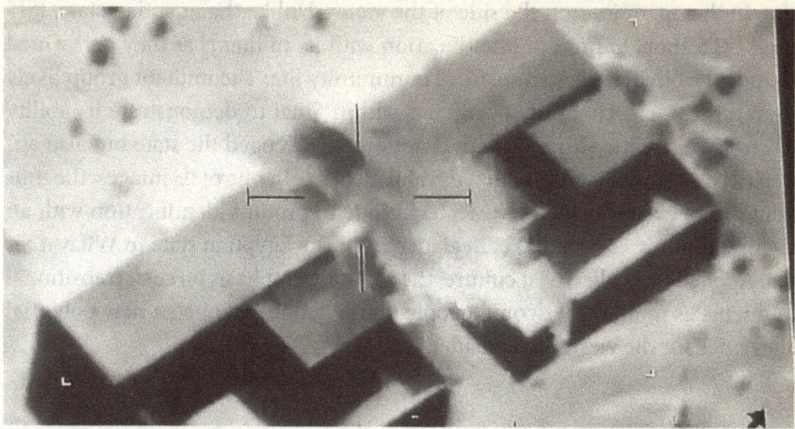

PHOTO 41. A point-of-view shot showing Egyptian airstrikes in North Sinai, disseminated November 16, 2017. Source: Egyptian Army Spokesman.

tioned the viewer to safely witness the hidden strength of ISIS in Sinai, to recognize the vulnerability of the group's enemies, and to understand the ways of contributing safely to the fighting effort.

The Egyptian military, by contrast, used POV shots to depict the airstrikes it conducted within the boundaries of Sinai. No Egyptian soldiers or any other character type appeared in these combat scenes either. The aerial photographs, however, did position the viewer to imagine their participation as a fighter pilot in the military's air force. Collectively, the POV shots placed the viewer in the position to adjust the scope's crosshairs, strike the targets, and watch the immediate aftermath from the cockpit. Two POV shots posted on November 16, 2017, for instance, record airstrikes on weapon storehouses and four-wheel-drive vehicles in North Sinai without including human photo subjects in the photographic frame. The majority of airstrike photographs in the Egyptian military's campaign used this type of smart bomb and drone visions, "granting the viewer god-like powers" through the bomber's view that objectifies, takes revenge on, and obliterates the target.[31] The POV shots invited viewers to imagine participating in the acts of destruction against ISIS in Sinai by offering a rare view from inside the military's fighter jets in action.

The application of subjective shots in the Sinai conflict closely aligned with the theory of subjectivity and its implications in Western contexts. Both the state and the militant group used POV shots to create a perceptual alliance between the group and viewers, fostering the sense of belonging to the collective, while pushing the out-group away from the viewer. Each placed the viewer within battlefield scenes of a masculine Egyptian culture where a victorious outcome seemed assured. Photographs of military airstrikes, in particular, used POV shots as a defining visual strategy to encourage viewer participation in the operations on the side of the victor. Unlike the Egyptian state, ISIS used OTS shots to prompt identification with its militants as they performed mundane activities characteristic of community life. The militant group likely shared these aspects of life occurring within Sinai to demonstrate its ability to create an ascetic social code that not only challenged the state but also appealed to a retrained culture that devalues leisure. In one of its images, the militant group even utilized the OTS technique to prompt identification with an enemy, but only as he shifted allegiance from the Egyptian state to Wilayat Sinai. Applied in a collectivist culture, the semiotic emphasis on such transitional moments as militants welcome people on their side can open a new potential allegiance for the viewer to consider.

Photographic Warfare: Contestation of Visual Semiotics

While both sides in the Sinai conflict deployed similar semiotic tools to convey their intended messages, each side applied them differently to create unique visions of militants, soldiers, collaborators, leaders, and civilians. The visual semiotic contestation between Wilayat Sinai and the Egyptian military revealed three interactive strategies for portraying human characters: competition, alignment, and expansion. At times, the two sides competed over the use of visual semiotics to depict a differential protagonist and antagonist. At others, they used the visual semiotics in ways that aligned with one another to similarly treat a given character type. Each side also expanded their use of visual semiotics beyond the depiction of human subjects to heighten engagement of the viewer's imagination.

Competitive Approaches to the Sinai Conflict

Wilayat Sinai and the Egyptian military competed over the depiction of the antagonist. The militant group defined the Egyptian soldiers and their collaborators as the opposing characters facing defeat in the Sinai conflict. It used intimate/personal distance, high camera angles, negative facial expressions, and direct eye contact to emphasize the humiliation of the out-group. This visual semiotic constellation encouraged viewers to watch the dead opponent or the one who was about to die up close, look down at his body as he laid or knelt on the ground, recognize his anguish, and look directly into his eyes before death. ISIS's approach conveyed the emotional breakdown of the antagonist, identified the militants as the superior force in the Sinai conflict, and prompted fear in viewers considering opposing the group.

The Egyptian military, instead, identified the militants as the antagonist that would meet defeat in Sinai. It featured the humiliation of the dead and arrested militants using intimate/personal distance and high camera angles. This visual semiotic constellation positioned viewers to look down at the dead and captured militants lying or kneeling on the ground at a close distance. The semiotic approach encouraged viewers to evaluate the militants' power negatively and reinforced such a conclusion by utilizing proximity to focus viewers' attention on the military's warning against thinking otherwise. Applied in the context of arrest photographs, however, the military's semiotic constellation omitted the use of negative facial expressions and direct eye contact, cues that could further intensify group warnings in high-context cultures through heightened viewer connection and emotional recognition.

ISIS and the Egyptian state also competed over the depiction of the protagonist. The militant group presented members of the in-group as the heroes of the Sinai conflict. It used intimate/personal distance, positive facial expressions, and direct eye contact to humanize the protagonist. The constellation of semiotic elements positioned viewers to have a seemingly close relationship with the militant and empathize with him before he undertook his martyrdom operation. Wilayat Sinai displayed the martyrs as happy and tough fighters for the group. The martyrs often emerged as the human face of the group to inspire supporters to join the militants' cause.

By contrast, the military deemed its own personnel as the protagonist best positioned to protect Sinai. It used intimate/personal distance, positive facial expressions, and direct eye contact to humanize its soldiers, officers, and leaders. The military's media campaign provided viewers a look at the protagonist's eyes and his smile from a close distance. Unlike the militant group, the Egyptian military mostly applied this particular semiotic constellation to photographs featuring injured soldiers accompanied by leaders who visited them in hospitals. The approach suggested a close, imagined relationship to evoke empathy for soldiers facing death in Sinai and for the leaders who care for them in ways that might stimulate more support for a greater military response against ISIS. In images of the battlefield, however, the military's constellation of personalized semiotic elements disappeared, perhaps in order to present the soldiers as parts of a larger assemblage focused on destroying the enemy and securing Sinai or as a result of photo production restrictions during combat.

Another key area over which Wilayat Sinai and the Egyptian military competed in their image campaigns was in the display of the protagonist's strength. The militant group used low camera angles and subjective shots to display warriors in action on the battlefield. The images positioned the viewer to look up to or be level with the protagonist as he attacked the Egyptian security forces in Sinai. Exclusive to the militants' media campaign in the Sinai conflict, this semiotic strategy encouraged positive evaluations of the group's power and viewer identification with ISIS against the state. The first-person shooter POV and OTS techniques in the group's battlefield images were also notable examples of using new technologies (e.g., GoPro cameras) to construct similar scenes to those in popular culture.

The Egyptian military, on the other hand, used a combined strategy of low camera angles and subjective shots to display a different protagonist. The images placed the viewer in a position to look up to military personnel or to navigate the on-the-ground scene from the fighters' perspective. The visual semiotic strategy suggested the relative power position of the military and encouraged viewer identification with the forces as they participated in counterterrorism operations. Nonetheless, the military was much less reliant on this strategy than the militant group. The subjective shots in the military's media campaign hardly even depicted combative actions on the ground. With the availability of GoPro action cameras, the military's choice to avoid subjective shots in combat may well indicate the military's unwillingness to disseminate images that could reveal details of its operations. Notwithstanding these cautionary perspectives, the relative absence of the POV and OTS techniques may have also inhibited the ability of the military's photographic campaign to engage viewers in the online space as it competed with the choices of ISIS.

Wilayat Sinai and the Egyptian military finally competed over the display of the protagonist's activities. The militant group used high camera angles, intimate/personal distance, and OTS shots to introduce its activities away from the battlefield, such as reading, watching videos, and cooking. This semiotic constellation positioned the viewer to look down at objects related to daily life from the militants' perspectives in the barracks. Accordingly, the images placed the viewer in a comfortable position to survey the salient parts of the object, which, if acceptable, might reinforce viewer identification and create closer perceived relationships with the protagonist. Engaging the viewers in these activities behind the front lines could also function as a form of visual entertainment to some curious about the militants' lives outside of combat.

In contrast, the Egyptian military used high camera angles and intimate/personal distance to focus on only a narrow set of the protagonists' activities. The images positioned the viewer to get closer to and look down at particular soldier activities in the field, such as clearing underground storage units and confiscating illegal materials. By using this semiotic strategy, the military presented the objects associated with security threats in Sinai at a comfortable height for exploration, while still encouraging viewers to imagine their close relationship with the soldiers. The military's media campaign, however, lacked subjective OTS shots in its displays of the protagonists' activities. Further, the military focused only on activities that were part of its law enforcement campaigns and avoided depictions of the soldiers' social life. The avoidance of OTS shots to reveal military and social activities is likely a byproduct of the level of secrecy the military typically imposes on the life of its soldiers. As a result, the military presented the activities through shots maintaining the spectatorship role of the viewers without necessarily encouraging their involvement.

Alignment Approaches to the Sinai Conflict

Besides directly competing over human character types and activities in their visual media campaigns, Wilayat Sinai and the Egyptian military aligned in their display of one character type: civilians. The militant group defined civilians who collaborated with the security forces or practiced Sufi Islam in Sinai as spies and/or apostates punishable under their distorted version of shari'a law. It used intimate/personal distance, high camera angles, negative facial expressions, and direct eye contact to emphasize the humiliation of those citizens in death and in the process leading up to it. The visual semiotic constellation positioned viewers to look down at the supporting character lying or kneeling on the ground at a close distance, look him in the eye, and recognize his desperation in the run-up to his execution. ISIS encouraged viewers to imagine having a connection with the civilian facing punishment, recognize their relative impotence in relation to the militant forces, and develop a desire to avoid similar levels of emotional distress in their own lives. Together, the semiotic constellation used in relation to photographed civilians arguably posed a death threat to the viewer and sent a stern warning to those who would violate the group's expected norms of behavior in Sinai.

Meanwhile, the military's media campaign identified civilians who smuggled drugs, cigarettes, or other suspicious materials in Sinai as criminals who deserved the state's punishment. It featured the humiliation of the arrested civilians through the combined use of intimate/personal distance, high camera angles, and direct eye contact. The images typically positioned the viewers to watch nearby citizens kneeling on the ground who looked the viewer in the eye. The semiotic constellation emphasized civilians' weak position and prompted viewer identification with perpetrators to deter future instances of similar illegal activities. The Egyptian military's arrest warning, however, was less poignant than the one the militants offered. Due to the group's frequent blurring of the faces of arrested civilians, the shots restricted the viewer's ability to further connect and interact with the individuals receiving punishments.

Expansion Approaches to the Sinai Conflict

Having directly interacted with the opposing group's media campaigns through strategies of competition and alignment, Wilayat Sinai went further to expand the application of visual semiotic constellations to imagined human subjects outside of the photographic frames. The militant group used POV shots and social/public distance to display vehicular targets on the verge of exploding in IED attacks. Through the use of overlaid red markers, the constellation positioned the viewer to follow distant, approaching vehicles from the perspective of someone standing immediately outside the frame. The double absence of human photo subjects in these images—observer and vehicle driver—encouraged viewers to simultaneously imagine their role as a protagonist marking the target and the role of the antagonist driving the targeted vehicle. Involving the viewer in the meaning-making process may well reinforce the image of the militants as the dominant character type capable of destroying Egyptian soldiers on the ground in ways that also offer steps of empowerment to viewers.

The Egyptian military further engaged in expansion strategies by using POV shots, bird's-eye view, and public distance to display its airstrikes on storage facilities and vehicular targets in Sinai. The semiotic constellation allowed the viewer to look down at the distant targets through the scope of an air force jet. The military encouraged viewer identification with an imagined pilot operating outside of the photographic frame engaged in the targeting of the militants' infrastructure. The strategy of deploying double absence again appeared here, as the images encouraged viewers to assign the role of the protagonist to an unseen fighter pilot in the cockpit and the role of a hidden ISIS militant inside the building or vehicle in the crosshairs. The scenes conveyed the military's dominance over the Sinai airspace and invited viewers to experience the pilots' ability to annihilate militants using airstrikes. At the same time, they portrayed the devastating consequences awaiting those choosing to join ISIS in Sinai.

Concluding Thoughts

This chapter has demonstrated how militant groups and state actors in Arab conflicts utilize visual semiotics to facilitate the message strategies of their media campaigns, focusing on the Sinai conflict at its peak. ISIS generally featured human photo subjects more often than the Egyptian military. The militant group was also more reliant on intimate/personal distance, low camera angles, negative facial expressions, direct eye contact, and subjective shots to depict the militants, collaborators, and citizens in Sinai. The relatively high, strategic use of such visual semiotics reflects ISIS's attempts to imitate visual techniques prominent in Western entertainment media to bolster its online messages. By contrast, the Egyptian military campaign relied more heavily on positive facial expressions in its distributed photographs to humanize its image as a fighting power in Sinai and emphasize unity among its ranks in hospitals and the positive outcomes of its humanitarian operations.

The Sinai photographic warfare reveals that high-context cultures offer competing sides in a conflict more flexibility to integrate localized cues that can augment widely understood meanings of visual semiotics. ISIS and the Egyptian state often assigned intimate/personal distance, direct eye contact, and positive facial expressions as semiotic features of their martyrs. The immediate context complemented that choice by suggesting the martyrs' strength, moral discipline, and austere lifestyle elevated their status as prototypical heroes in a masculine, restrained culture. Moreover, the collectivism of Egyptian society served as an apparently recognized pretext for both sides of the conflict, as they pushed the opponent away from the viewer with more long shots, while using subjective shots to integrate more people into their in-groups. Similarly, the power distance cultural dimension further assigned meanings to semiotic choices. ISIS, for example, apparently understood the local context filled with class inequalities and reverence for the elderly. Accordingly, they used the large power distance in society as a backdrop and high camera angles coupled with negative facial expressions as strategies to project a new social justice reality undifferentiated based on age or kinship. While Western standards of visual semiotics can apply in other cultural contexts, local environments alter the intensity, if not the substance, of their symbolic meanings.

At the same time, the use of visual semiotics in the Sinai photographic warfare exposes alternative ways such tools can function in non-Western cultures. Rather than operating predictably as a means of creating perceived close relationships with and suggesting power, credibility, and/or attractiveness of the photo subject, intimate/personal distance and direct eye contact in ISIS and Egypt's media campaigns often highlighted graphic warnings to viewers by showing photographs of weak, isolated opponents facing death. Here, the perceived spatial and emotional proximity emphasized the photo subjects' humiliation and deviance from the underlying masculine, collectivist culture. Combined, the two semiotic elements functioned as deterrents to viewer identification with opposing collectives rather than as catalysts assumed in Western frameworks.

Also departing from Western assumptions was the use of social/public distance. Rather than depict others and strangers, social/public distance in the Sinai context also emerged as a recurring space to emphasize the unity of the protagonists on the Sinai battlefields. Wilayat Sinai and the Egyptian military both appropriated the semiotic device in alignment with the surrounding culture to present community vanguards, showcase their collective strength on the ground, and ascertain their belonging to the in-group. The cultural context can thus introduce new visual semiotic functions that amplify the communicating group's localized message.

Besides the role of cultural dimensions, many on-the-ground contextual factors arguably contributed to the emergence of new strategic applications of semiotic constellations in state and non-state actors' images. The strained relations between Sinai residents and the government since the 2004 security crackdown, the military's incorporation of destructive airstrikes in the peninsula in recent years, and the increased pressure on ISIS in 2016–17 may explain the militant group's choice to use proxemics and eye contact to emphasize brutal retaliations for its followers to celebrate and its enemies to fear. The isolation of Sinai residents from mainland Egypt, the stereotypical image of Bedouins as traitors and drug dealers, and the deadly attacks that Wilayat Sinai has conducted against Egyptian security forces, civilians, and religious minorities may have all encouraged the military to apply proxemics in graphic scenes that can exaggerate its ability to dominate the Sinai field and kill the outlaws.

Additionally, this chapter has demonstrated that our understanding of the contested online environment can benefit from an examination of the interactions between the constellations of state and non-state actors' use of visual semiotics. This exploration of the Sinai photographic warfare revealed the existence of visual semiotic interactions involving competition, alignment, and expansion strategies. However, these interactive approaches varied according to character type. Through competition, ISIS and the Egyptian state transformed the opponent's protagonist character into an antagonist. They limited the character types qualifying for favorable semiotic treatment to their own individual members. Through alignment, the two reinforced the rigid friend-foe dichotomy by humiliating additional human subjects who failed to abide by the groups' respective guidelines. Through expansion, both campaigns introduced unique destructive methods that unseen protagonists can effectively deploy against hidden enemies. Together, the three strategies helped emphasize clear delineations between opposing characters in conflict. By erasing any mediated middle ground between representatives of the established state and its challenger, visual semiotic contestations can exacerbate localized clashes of ideology.

Future studies of visual semiotics can reveal nuanced constellations operative in cross-cultural conflicts. Because the assumptions of visual semiotics in Western studies do not necessarily apply to all contexts, this area of study requires further testing. Researchers can use content analysis to determine the comparative level of reliance on visual semiotics and the range of human character types across different communicators. The addition of a mixed-methods approach, however, could further understandings of how audiences interpret the semiotic contestations in more depth. A qualitative inductive analysis can help generate new or alternative semiotic constellations and assess the character types that qualify for unique treatments across different local and regional settings. Integrating cultural dimensions that are relevant to the photographic warfare efforts can further supplement the analysis with valuable insights into the potential implications of semiotic choices in non-Western contexts. Studies can also examine competition, alignment, and expansion as interactive strategies, but explore new ones in order to develop a broader framework of visual semiotic interactions in times of conflict.

CHAPTER 5

An Analytic Framework of Visual Contestation

Today's media landscape inhibits states from exercising an absolute monopoly over public communication and fully censoring opposing media content. The online environment allows non-state militant actors to create hubs for media dissemination, relocate message distribution sites during crackdowns, and maintain a direct line of contact with supporter networks. Such capabilities enable militant groups to advocate their own alternative ideologies and present content that further challenges states in the digital sphere.

This book demonstrates the value of comparatively examining the competing visual component of state and non-state actors' media campaigns. A focus on one side's media efforts in a conflict gauges only an isolated visual campaign and misses the rich interactive potentials of the online battlefield. Instead, examining the photographic warfare between the two opposing forces exposes the inherent similarities and differences in their media campaigns, identifies competing messaging tactics to reach the target audience, and detects their principal interactive strategies available for engagement with the other side.

The critical nature of the Sinai conflict at the local, regional, and international levels serves as an excellent exemplar for understanding visual contestation in the digital environment. Besides its religious status as home to the three Abrahamic faiths and its geopolitical significance for world peace, Sinai is a cornerstone in the expansionist ideology of Islamist militant groups in the Arab world. Bordering Gaza and Israel, it is a sought-after place for militants claiming to fight for the liberation of the third holiest site in Islam, Jerusalem. Also, Sinai serves as a strategic supply line and entry point to North Africa by militant groups operating in the Levant, Iraq, and Yemen and wishing to expand the fight westward. Decades of social alienation, economic deprivation, and underdevelopment in large parts of the peninsula, coupled with the lacking security presence at the border areas and the Sinai Bedouins' strong ties

154 Chapter 5

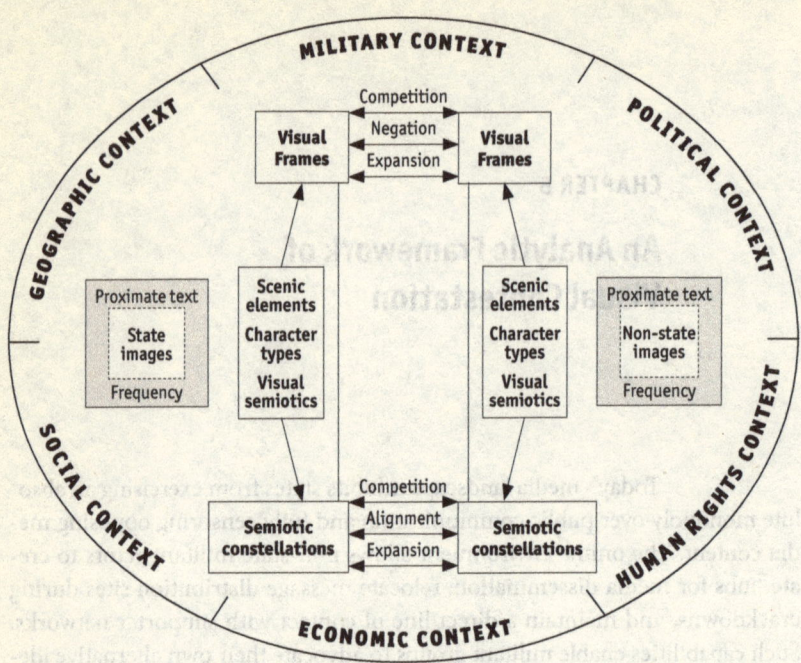

FIGURE 21. The analytic framework of visual contestation by state and non-state actors.

of kinship across national boundaries, further position the site as an ideal location for Egyptian and foreign militants seeking to destabilize the most populous country in the region. Hence, Sinai has emerged as a key focus of ISIS, particularly after the group lost most of its occupied territory in Syria and Iraq by the end of 2017. With Wilayat Sinai as its provincial arm on the ground, many ISIS militants regrouped in the peninsula, fought the Egyptian military, and posed a threat to the entire region that persists today. Complementing the military conflict on the ground, Wilayat Sinai and the Egyptian military have engaged in photographic warfare that shows how state and non-state actors compete visually for audiences in a cluttered online environment.

This book outlines an interactive model of online visual contestation by state and non-state actors based on the research process examining the photographic warfare between ISIS and the Egyptian state at the peak of the Sinai insurgency. The analytic framework is a visual representation of how contemporary media battles have been and are likely to continue to be fought between asymmetric forces in the online terrain. It emphasizes that visual images of non-state militant actors do not exist in a vacuum. It situates the visual contestation itself as part of the overall context. It further highlights the visual characteristics defining the state and non-state actors' opposing media campaigns.

Most importantly, the model underscores key types of visual interactions that can occur between the two media campaigns (see Figure 21). In so doing, it recognizes the critical role that context, content, and form play in understanding how image contestations result in multiple types of interactions.

Situational Context

The model's depiction of situational context provides a broader view of the conflict within which the state and non-state actors' visuals operate. The context interacts with the image campaigns on both sides of the conflict in two complementary ways. First, conditions on the ground can influence viewer interpretations of the opposing visual campaigns. Lack of economic opportunities in a conflict zone, for example, can influence how the audience understands the state's portrayals of new projects or a non-state actor's displays of social services. Second, the visual media campaigns can focus viewer attention and help define portions of reality by limiting what the viewers see in the photographic frames. The selection of particular scenes to depict and others to ignore redefines the context itself in the online environment. The model emphasizes six contextual factors that help explain the competition between state and non-state actors: military, political, human rights, economic, social, and geographic.

Military Context

The military context, in particular, is key to understanding visual contestations between state and non-state actors in conflict. Five military elements are related to changes in the Sinai photographic warfare: the onset of state military operations, the completion of state military operations, the militants' attacks, the participation by local groups on either side of the battlefield, and the loss of top leaders. These factors intersected with the visual conflict in various ways. The onset of local counterterrorism operations was the most impactful on the Egyptian military's photographic campaign. It corresponded with consistent shifts in output, content, and form that emphasized success on the ground. Upon the launch of the second phase of the Martyr's Right Operation, for example, the military reached its highest productivity of image production in 2016, shifted to a reliance on battle aftermath images often displaying no human characters, and adopted a repeated use of long, wide angle shots of destruction. The loss of local leaders, by contrast, had the most crippling effect on the militant group's photographic campaign. The military's killing of senior militant leader Abu Duaa al-Ansari along with dozens of his aides in airstrikes devastated Wilayat Sinai's ranks and likely explains the temporary disruption of the group's media operations and the dissemination of only one image over nearly two months. The military conditions on the ground in Sinai, coupled with the battlefield outcomes, offered crucial insights on the two sides' media decisions in the visual conflict.

Given the broad scope of ISIS's presence and its operations in the Arab world, the regional military context also played a role in the Sinai photographic warfare. Although ISIS's regional attacks did not coincide with changes in the visual contestation between the Egyptian military and Wilayat Sinai per se, the onset and completion of regional counterterrorism operations marked clear shifts in the Sinai media campaigns. As regional forces launched attacks on ISIS in Mosul and Raqqa, for example, Wilayat Sinai increased its use of high-angle, close-up shots of dead enemies to emphasize the group's potency and resistance. Upon the liberation of ISIS's two occupied cities, however, the provincial group in Sinai failed to maintain its steady stream of death images and reduced its photographic output. Simultaneously, the Egyptian military boosted the number of its images, increasingly utilized wide-angle shots of destruction to depict the opponents' losses, and portrayed smiling leaders interacting with their troops. The regional military events and their corresponding visual shifts in Sinai suggest that the Egyptian state may have been in close coordination with the global coalition and that Wilayat Sinai had close linkages to ISIS's central media infrastructure.

Political Context

The political context in the conflict zone also serves as an important backdrop to the visual contestation between state and non-state actors. Situating the Sinai photographic warfare in the context of the post-Morsi period helps understand the underlying tone and symbolism in ISIS and the Egyptian state's opposing campaigns. First Lieutenant General Sedki Sobhi, who assumed the role of minister of defense in 2014, became a major figure in President al-Sisi's administration during the period when the military became increasingly involved in Sinai. The military portrayed Sobhi as the key leader and vanguard of the state's counterterrorism efforts in its Sinai media campaign until mid-2018.

Unlike Wilayat Sinai, which avoided the portrayal of its leadership altogether, the Egyptian state's photographic campaign depicted other ministers, senior security officials, governors, and members of parliament in the field or visiting injured soldiers. The images highlighted the appointment of new leaders in al-Sisi's administration, including Major General Mohamed Fareed, who replaced Major General Mahmoud Hijazy as army chief of staff, and Major Mohamed Abdel Illah, who succeeded Major General Ossama Askar as the military commander of the unified leadership east of the canal in 2017. Like Sobhi, however, the governor of North Sinai, Major General Abdelfattah Harhour, and governor of South Sinai, Major General Khaled Fouda, remained in their positions for longer periods and appeared in campaign photographs documenting the launch of new projects. Thus, the state's images reflected power transitions, introducing the new administration's central characters and their roles in the Sinai conflict; the non-state actor, in contrast, presented its members as part of a nonhierarchical, self-empowered grassroots movement effectively challenging the government forces.

The relationship between the state and its constituents was a key area of political contention evident in the Sinai photographic warfare. Former minister of the interior Habib al-Adli cracked down on Sinai following the 2004 attacks, which further exacerbated the Bedouins' immense frustration with the Egyptian political establishment under Mubarak's rule. Community sentiments erupted in 2011, with increasing violence targeting police forces in Sinai in the postrevolutionary period. The new military strategy in the peninsula during the post-Morsi period further placed more constraints on North Sinai residents, ranging from curfews and forced evictions to home demolitions. But the Egyptian military's media campaign challenged the notion that such conditions resulted in a strained relationship between the state and local Sinai residents. Instead, the photographs depicted Sinai residents rallying around leaders and government representatives in the North as well as Bedouin tribes publicly expressing support for the military in the South.

ISIS, on the other hand, presented its own militants as an alternative and as more favorable political actors in North Sinai. The group's images emphasized the local residents' fear of and respect for Wilayat Sinai through scenes of civilians handing their identification cards to militants at checkpoints, receiving their handout statements, and surrounding them as they destroyed confiscated materials. Thus, in the political arena, the state portrayed a relatively stable political climate in Sinai, while the non-state actor undermined the government's stance by presenting militants as an emerging force in the community.

Human Rights Context

The human rights context contributes to how state and non-state actors approach their visual conflict in the online space. Human rights organizations have reported violations against Sinai residents since 2004, including mass arrests and torture.[1] Addressing the right of freedom from arbitrary arrest and the rights to life and fair trial, the Egyptian military's media campaign pictured smuggling, drug dealing, and supporting terrorists as grounds for arrest and referral to further interrogations. Using displays of dead militants equipped with lethal weaponry, however, it presented fighting alongside the terrorist group as carrying out an act of war that warranted swift killing in response.

Wilayat Sinai applied a different approach in its photographic campaign by stripping soldiers, state collaborators, and Sufi Muslims of their rights to life and a fair trial altogether as a result of their "apostasy." The provincial images showed brutal and humiliating executions of so-called apostates unless they repented and pledged allegiance to ISIS. While the state emphasized its respect for human rights in the Sinai operations, the non-state actor discounted those rights by sanctioning its actions as resulting from a higher power, from religious callings.

The Sinai photographic warfare also addressed civilians' deprivation of basic human rights in the peninsula. As chapter 1 documented, North Sinai residents have suffered a lack of educational opportunities and healthcare facilities for decades. Human Rights Watch's reports also point to the demolition of thousands of homes and the forced eviction of families in the North as part of the military's plan to create a buffer zone since 2013.[2] The Egyptian military specifically tackled the right to education in its online campaign by picturing government officials as they opened new schools and educational facilities in Sinai. However, it avoided any depictions of healthcare beyond the services injured soldiers received in the posted photographs. Furthermore, the military's photographic campaign never directly engaged the issue of evictions at the border areas during the peak of the conflict.

The depictions of Wilayat Sinai's efforts as a solution to the same issues, by contrast, were limited to several images of militant-run clinics in the North. Otherwise, the militant group relied on exposing the destruction of schools, farmland, and civilian property as direct outcomes of the military's actions. It also depicted Sinai civilians evacuating their homes in late 2017, which coincided with public reports announcing the continuation of the military's eviction policy. Hence, in the arena of human rights, the state actor presented its efforts as needed solutions to overcome some of the human rights issues in Sinai and avoided any contentious displays of eviction-related scenes, while the non-state actor attempted to downplay these efforts and undermine the military's credibility by showing its alleged violations.

Economic Context

The economic context interacts with nonmilitary photographs in the visual contestation between state and non-state actors. Economic conditions in North and South Sinai have changed over the years. Building on the infrastructure in South Sinai after the Israeli occupation, Egypt further developed the tourism industry, which in turn provided economic opportunities to local residents. But the more populous North has continued to suffer from economic marginalization. The Egyptian military offered itself as a solution to the economic inequalities in Sinai by highlighting the state's new policies and projects in the North. Egypt's photographic campaign showed ministerial visits marking the launch of new manufacturing and agricultural projects and emphasized the happiness of North Sinai residents as they received food aid from military personnel.

ISIS, on the other hand, failed to provide any solutions that could alleviate poverty in the North. Lacking resources, the militant group instead resorted to several depictions of destroyed farmland reportedly resulting from the state's military airstrikes. In the economic arena, the state displayed a roadmap for North Sinai's economic development, while the non-state actor adopted a victimhood lens portraying the military's actions as destructive to the agricultural sector and the local economy as a whole.

Illegal trade was yet another critical economic issue in the Sinai photographic warfare between the state and the non-state actor. With widespread poverty in North Sinai, underground smuggling emerged as an alternative source of income for the residents. Not only did it become a profitable industry after the Gaza siege of 2007, but it further facilitated the Salafi militancy spillover into North Sinai until the Egyptian military announced its official plan to create a buffer zone in 2013. The military's photographic campaign frequently highlighted its security measures to stop illegal trade and border breaches by showing the discovery and destruction of dozens of underground tunnels.

For Wilayat Sinai, however, the underground industry did not generally appear in the campaign photographs. The militant group's images showed only its crackdown on the smuggling of cigarettes through scenes of confiscation and burning of the packs. This move, which the group framed as a measure to stop religiously prohibited substances, reportedly angered some of the tribal members and played a role in al-Tarabin tribe's decision to side with the military forces. Although the state and non-state actors both pictured their crackdown on illegal economic activity, the apparent motives shifted from national security for the former to religious norms for the latter.

Social Context

The social context also intersects with the visual contestation between state and non-state actors. The Sinai occupation period generated suspicions among many mainland Egyptians who equated the Bedouins' life under an Israeli administration for fifteen years to treason. The involvement of some Bedouins in illegal trade, drug dealing, and smuggling in the post-occupation period added to the cultural stereotypes that further isolated the group from Egypt's social fabric over the years. The Egyptian military reinforced the stereotypes in its images by frequently picturing Bedouins as criminals under arrest for collaborating with militants and for smuggling drugs or other goods across the border. Recurring shots of soldiers confiscating and burning drugs in Sinai further reinforced that image. Nonetheless, the military attempted to balance its mediated crackdown portrayals with other scenes stressing the integration of Sinai residents into the population. In these images, Sinai residents carried Egyptian flags and warmly welcomed military personnel on the ground.

Although Wilayat Sinai's displays of seized contraband cigarettes arguably played a similar role in affirming the image of North Sinai as a hub for smugglers, the group also depicted the Bedouin subgroup as its main constituency. By providing an insider's look into the life of Bedouins, the images highlighted the group's social isolation further by showing a unique, nomadic lifestyle in deserted locations. Although the state and non-state actors' images both propagated preexisting cultural stereotypes of the Bedouins, the former promoted their social integration to reinforce a message of stability, while the latter depicted a social schism to promote the achievement of its goal of challenging the state.

The Sinai visual contestation between the state and the non-state actor also revealed nuanced differences in social demographics. Bedouins, Egyptians from the Nile Valley, and Palestinians constitute the main groups that reside in the Sinai Peninsula. With their origins in the Arabian Peninsula and the Levant, the Sinai Bedouins enjoy strong ties with their fellow tribal members in neighboring countries and often uphold communal identity at a higher level than loyalty to the nation-state. The Egyptian military did not necessarily distinguish between the different groups making up the North Sinai population in its photographic campaign. Although some of the arrested smugglers, dead militants, and civilians were wearing Bedouin clothing, the identity of most depicted characters was not clear.

On the other hand, Wilayat Sinai emphasized the different groups involved in the conflict. Eulogizing its martyrs, for example, the militant group displayed a pool of smiling Bedouin, Nile Valley Egyptian, and Palestinian fighters looking to the viewer before their participation in the militant attacks. The captions presented the martyr's unique origins, despite the appearance of their similar, embodied looks and identical military fatigues. The militant group further identified its local enemies, who often knelt on the ground before executions, by full name and Bedouin tribe. Demographically, the state defined the Sinai conflict in broader terms as an Egyptian war on terrorism and crime, but the non-state actor pinpointed the different cultural identities to emphasize the diverse ethnic and transnational buildup of its ranks and to warn local Bedouins against siding with the military.

Geographic Context

The geographic context breaks up the conflict zone into meaningful locales in the visual contestation between the state and non-state actors. The Sinai Peninsula is a large desert that constitutes about 6 percent of the size of Egypt and that shares land borders with Gaza and Israel to the east. In their visual media campaigns, the Egyptian state and ISIS defined the peninsula's topographic nature and border areas in different ways. Although both sides often depicted the desert as a site of combat, the militant group transformed North Sinai's urban center al-Arish into a battlefield. But Wilayat Sinai also displayed green fields, trees, fruit orchards, and water streams at times as evidence of the peninsula's beauty that must be protected.

The borders further presented a key area of visual contestation. Sinai's northeastern border appeared in the military's images only as a site of underground tunnels that threaten national security. In the militant group's images, by contrast, the border areas constituted scenes of military excavators, airstrikes, destroyed houses, and displaced civilians. Geographically, the state highlighted North Sinai's open battlefields and unsecured borders to justify its intense crackdown on militant activity and on the residents' ties with Gaza, while the non-state actor juxtaposed the beautiful sceneries with the military's destruction to garner support for wide-scale retaliation.

The Sinai conflict images also revealed the nature of the two main divisions in the peninsula. Sinai comprises the northern region, which has housed the militant insurgency in recent years, and the southern region that is imperative for Egypt's tourism industry. Although Egypt and ISIS both depicted the North as the center of the fight, they differed on the display of the southern part of the peninsula. South Sinai appeared in the military's photographic campaign as a secure region juxtaposed to the volatile North. The images showed international leaders taking part in forums in Sharm El Sheikh and Egyptian soldiers securing the streets. Wilayat Sinai, in contrast, failed to disseminate any images of South Sinai. The state thus pictured the southern part of Sinai to ensure viewers of its stability and security as a key tourism hub, while the non-state actor focused only on the northern region perhaps due to the intensity of battle operations and militant recruitment in that sector as well as the militant group's inability to operate freely in the South.

Immediate Context

Two immediate visual contextual factors influence the meaning of the state and non-state actors' images in the model. The proximate text presents the communicator's narration on the scene, while the frequency helps generate areas of emphasis. The image can work in tandem with the text to deliver a common, reinforced message or direct the viewer to the key elements in the scene. For example, several images showing dozens of half-buried IEDs can complement captions describing the military's success in foiling roadside attacks while visually emphasizing the militants' weapon of choice. Thus, interactions between the two contextual variables and the images can alter the viewing experience and the meaning-making process in visual contestations between state and non-state actors.

Proximate Text

The proximate text contextualizes depicted scenes and their components. It is unique in many ways to each image and source. The "apostate" and "takfiri" labels in Wilayat Sinai and the Egyptian military's text, for example, were frequent derogatory identifiers describing the two opposing forces and their belongings in Sinai. Simultaneously, the two sides utilized text to hail their own members as heroes and martyrs. Beyond the labeling of in- and outgroups, the proximate text further described the nature and setting of the on-ground activities. The military used much more text with combat and battle aftermath images, specifying the phase of the Martyr's Right Operation, the locations of the soldiers' actions, the numbers of casualties and arrests, and the types of weapons that had been confiscated or destroyed. It also described nonmilitary activities, such as hospital visits and school openings, by identifying the leaders in attendance, the outcome of the events, and the state's counterterrorism goals. The military spokesman's tendency to post such details may have been an effort to project transparency, given the fines that journalists have to pay in Egypt for reporting terrorism-related information contradicting the military's official statements.

On the other hand, Wilayat Sinai was more succinct in its captions. It used additional labels to describe the types of the attacks, ranging from suicide bombings, suicide attacks, and sniping to IED detonations. It also used captions to pinpoint the exact locations of the attacks within Sinai. But in nonmilitary images, the militant group specified neither cities nor regions but rather broadly presented the Sinai province as the location housing all the scenes of media distributions, feast celebrations, medical workshops, and natural landscapes. The unique locational identification strategy in those images serves as a means to suggest the militant group's control over large swathes of land across Sinai. The group's labels and short captions further prompted the viewer to fill in missing information relevant to the scene. For example, the caption "Targeting the Egyptian apostate army with snipers," which complemented an image of a militant pointing his sniper rifle outside a window, allows the viewer to imagine the target, outcome, and frequency of such attacks. The proximate text in each of the state and non-state actors' photographic campaigns played a critical role in emphasizing the meaning of the images and defining the Sinai conflict at large.

The format of the proximate text further influenced the images' meaning in circulation throughout the online environment. In the Sinai conflict, the proximate text that the Egyptian military used appeared in the form of Facebook posts for the most part. The text in one Facebook post served as a standard description for several images that the Egyptian military would release together as a collective. This format constrained the clarity of the visual message as the viewer had to toggle back and forth between the image and the attached lengthy text. Circulating such images on other digital platforms without the text could further distort the images' meaning. ISIS, by contrast, described each scene using a superimposed caption. In so doing, Wilayat Sinai's images and text together created individual media products that could retain meaning both at the initial point of dissemination and beyond. In short, the differential text-formatting decisions limited the circulation potential of the state's photographic campaign, while allowing the non-state actor's images to operate consistently and efficiently across platforms.

Frequency

The frequency of images serves as a means of presence in the online environment. In 2017, the Egyptian military boosted its online visual presence through a 260 percent surge in photographic output, compared to Wilayat Sinai's images whose frequency remained relatively constant. The frequency of images on both sides did fluctuate in correspondence to events on the ground, however. When the al-Tarabin tribe sided with the state, for example, both the military and the militant group increased their photographic outputs to imply strength on the battlefield. At other times, the militant group could not maintain its visual presence due to apparent disruptions to its media operations, signaling the precariousness of its resources in comparison with those of the state. To make up for these interruptions, the group resorted to disseminating additional images of its more limited attacks to give the impression of a sustained online presence. Despite these ebbs and flows of output, both the state and non-state actors treated visual presence as a necessary tool to convey their strength on the ground.

The Sinai photographic warfare also revealed different levels of visual emphasis on certain content elements over time. The military's media campaign, for example, displayed underground tunnels in over one-tenth of its images to emphasize the state's law enforcement activities at the Sinai border areas, while ISIS visually ignored the tunnels altogether. By contrast, both the state and non-state actors heavily relied on military images but did so in different ways. Of Wilayat Sinai's military images, 70 percent showed impending IED, group, and sniping attacks to highlight its battlefield actions. The military, instead, focused on the resulting destruction, confiscation, and death in about 90 percent of its military images to emphasize dominance and success in battlefield confrontations. The repetitive output of visual images conveyed strategic messages in the state and non-state actors' media campaigns.

Image Components

The image in the model comprises three main components. The scenic elements, character types, and visual semiotics all serve as message fragments that combine to attribute meaning to the photograph. For example, a scene that shows a burning military tank, a militant, and a smile would likely suggest an insurgent's happiness after taking belligerent action against the state. Changing any of these components could alter the meaning of the message.

Scenic Elements

The scenic elements mediate the conflict setting in the online environment. Destruction and presumed death were recurrent elements that shifted over time throughout the Sinai photographic warfare. The Egyptian state and ISIS often presented their military actions and victories through depictions of the ongoing destruction of the opponents' weapons, vehicles, and buildings. The surge in Egyptian counterterrorism operations from 2016 to 2017, for example, translated into more than a 700 percent increase in the military's displays of ongoing destruction. Although depictions of destruction dropped in Wilayat Sinai's images amid decreasing attacks during the same period, they remained a central feature in the campaign. The bulk of the state and non-state actors' images defined Sinai as a devastating battlefield where the enemy forces are always losing.

Death and identity symbols also emerged as frequent scenic elements in the Sinai visual contestation. The two players typically circulated images of corpses, highlighting the lethal consequences to the opponents in major attacks on checkpoints and military bases in Sinai. Operating outside the bounds of battle, the militant group went further by showing Egyptian solders, state collaborators, and Sufi Muslims about to die in public executions to emphasize the deadly beheading and shooting punishments that await its enemies. In the meantime, both sides demonstrated contrasting identities. The military often used the Egyptian flag as a scenic backdrop to both civilian and military gatherings in Sinai. The militant group instead employed the Qur'an, prayers, and the monotheism gesture as religious symbols present in the barracks and on the battlefields. Using scenic elements, the state evoked a sense of patriotism that can justify killing the enemies of the nation-state, while the non-state actor sanctioned its brutality as a necessary part of a holy war.

Character Types

The human character types identify the key actors in the visual conflict. Despite humans appearing in only 56 percent of the Sinai images, the character types set the parameters of the message in each photographic campaign. The Egyptian state and ISIS differed in the portrayals of their own fighters. The militants, for example, emerged as the most recurrent character type in Wilayat Sinai's images, almost always appearing as the powerful, victorious players in the field. The same character type was the least prevalent in the Egyptian military's campaign, whose images presented them as corpses or helpless individuals under arrest. In the meantime, Egyptian soldiers were the most recurrent type and the only competent fighters in the military's images. They were also prevalent in the militant group's photographic campaign, but as weaker individuals under attack, injured, dead, or on the run. In other words, the state dismissed the militants by downplaying both their number and their strength, while the non-state actor bolstered its image by juxtaposing the soldiers' large presence with their defeats.

Some character types were generally limited to only one of the photographic campaigns. Top security officials, for example, were an exclusive character type and the second most recurring one appearing in the military's images. They always appeared as caring leaders in support of their subordinates fighting on the field or recovering in hospitals. In contrast, Sinai civilian collaborators with the state were a key character type that appeared mainly in the militant group's images. The photographic campaign did not display the acts of collaboration themselves, but rather emphasized the deadly consequences for civilians whether on the battlefield or in public executions. Although the military also portrayed Sinai civilian supporters in some of its images, they appeared only as secondary actors ready to receive aid or attend launching events while surrounded by military personnel. Collectively, the state media campaign emphasized the role of its leaders in directing counterterrorism operations, while the non-state actor pictured death threats to local civilians thinking of siding with the military.

Visual Semiotics

Visual semiotic elements associate symbolic meaning to the characters in the scene. Both the Egyptian military and Wilayat Sinai utilized viewer distance, camera angle, facial expressions, eye contact, and subjective shots in much the same way. For example, each side typically presented shots of its opponents at a distance from the viewer to encourage dissociation, while displaying its martyrs and/or injured soldiers at a close distance to prompt viewer connection and empathy. At times, the two groups also photographed their enemies from a close distance, yet only in humiliating situations to send a clear, culture-specific warning. Although both players displayed a group of their fighters and enemies looking directly at the viewer, the immediate context and the local culture conveyed contrasting meanings. Direct eye contact underlined the high status of martyrs as the text underscored the sacrifices they had made. But the same semiotic element also emphasized the vulnerability of opponents kneeling in captivity as they awaited their fate, thus depriving them of any semblance of strength that the Egyptian, masculine culture values. Moreover, the two sides positioned the viewer inside combat scenes using POV shots to prompt identification with their fighters. Without developing unique strategies for their own side in the conflict per se, the state and non-state actors strategically employed semiotic tools and cultural cues in tandem to present a positive image of their members and degrade their enemies.

Nonetheless, the two sides of the Sinai photographic warfare revealed different levels of reliance on particular semiotic elements. In its depictions of human characters, ISIS was generally more dependent on many semiotic tools, including intimate/personal distance, low camera angles, subjective shots, and direct eye contact. By doing so, it constantly reinforced its differential portrayals of the two main character types: militants and soldiers. One key exception involved the use of positive facial expressions, which the military utilized about ten times more than Wilayat Sinai. The military often pictured its own soldiers, leaders, and civilian supporters smiling at hospital visits and food distribution drives. Instead, the militant group limited its use of positive facial expressions to a small number of images showing martyrs before they attacked the military. The state stressed the unity between its military and the population by regularly displaying smiling faces, while the non-state actor emphasized martyrdom as an exclusive pathway to happiness by rarely using the semiotic tool.

Ways Images Interact in State/Non-state Media Campaigns

Interactions between the state and non-state campaigns in the visual contestation model occur at the levels of both content and form. The image components (scenic elements, character types, and visual semiotics) work together to generate the campaign's visual frames (i.e., image content) and semiotic constellations (i.e., image form), which then engage with the opposing communicators' messages in a number of identifiable ways.

Visual Frames

The Sinai photographic warfare revealed three interactive strategies between the visual frames of state and non-state actors: competition, negation, and expansion. ISIS and the Egyptian state each claimed superiority through the use of competing visual frames. In their use of the martyrdom frame, for example, Wilayat Sinai presented religiosity as the sole driving force behind its fallen fighters' sacrifices, while the military emphasized the patriotic, nationalistic motivations of its martyrs.

The two sides also utilized negation to challenge the credibility of the other side by presenting alternate interpretations of events embodied in their visual frames. To negate the military's claimed success from precision airstrikes against militants, for example, the militant group pictured the bombings' destructive outcomes to civilian property, mosques, and lands. To undermine the military's announced accomplishment of opening schools and providing aid for Sinai residents, ISIS displayed images of destroyed schools and evacuated civilians resulting from the state's shelling and eviction policy in the North.

Finally, the state and non-state actor expanded the available means of persuasion by incorporating unique frames of their own. The frame showing military visits to hospitals was a prime example that clearly emphasized the intimate relationship between the leaders and soldiers. Together, the three visual framing interactive strategies explain how opposing content in visual images interacts in the contested online environment.

Semiotic Constellations

The state and non-state actors' semiotic constellations serve as a second site of interaction in the visual contestation model. Three semiotic interactive strategies emerged from the two conflicting sides in the Sinai conflict: competition, alignment, and expansion. Wilayat Sinai and the Egyptian military competed over which characters qualified for a positive semiotic constellation rendering. ISIS used a combination of intimate/personal distance, positive facial expressions, and direct eye contact to symbolize the humanity of its own militants, while the Egyptian military's campaign deployed a similar favorable semiotic treatment to its own soldiers.

The two sides aligned over the identity of a character type that qualified for a negative semiotic treatment. They combined high camera angles, intimate/personal distance, and negative facial expressions to symbolize the humiliation of civilian lawbreakers under arrest. The conception of law was different in ISIS and the Egyptian state's campaigns, however. Wilayat Sinai claimed to uphold sacred commandments, while the Egyptian military stressed the rule of law.

Further, the two groups expanded the use of semiotic constellations by encouraging viewers to imagine character types operating outside of the photographs' boundaries. Egyptian fighter pilots, for example, functioned as a notable protagonist in the military's visual campaign despite their actual absence from the photographs; instead, the campaign encouraged viewers to imagine them through the use of public distance and high-angle POV shots from the cockpit. The three semiotic interactive strategies reveal how visual form serves as another way visual images compete in the online environment.

Implications of the Analytic Framework of Visual Contestation

The proposed interactive model of visual contestation fills a gap in the visual communication literature. Expanding beyond Birdsell and Groarke's visual argumentation framework that accounts for image elements, context, and change over time,[3] this model presents a holistic approach that maps visual conflict onto the three pillars of context, content, and form, as well as the ensuing interactions among them in the online environment. It combines visual framing and semiotic methodologies with contextual analysis and comparative applications. This new approach allows for a comprehensive and nuanced study of visual contestation between state and non-state actors. By applying the model, researchers can further dissect the emerging communicative phenomenon of online visual contestation in other contexts, including competitions between non-state actors or even political campaigns in the media battlefield. Hence, the model serves as a means to assess the implications of online digital technologies for the dynamics of contemporary photographic warfare.

The framework of visual contestation also demonstrates that communicators in visual conflicts interact at the level of image collections. The online environment facilitates the dissemination of digital photographic albums, which explains the high number of images by the Egyptian state and ISIS in the Sinai photographic warfare, reaching an average of one to two images per day at the peak of the conflict. A small sample size can help identify select features and the level of iconicity of individual images in conflict. However, it does not sufficiently reveal the nature of the dialogue between the two communicators online. The visual contestation model captures the individual image, but, most importantly, it accounts for the patterns emerging across content and form in the overall campaigns over time. The resulting visual frames and semiotic constellations are two collections through which the communicators can emphasize select messages and characters in online visual contestations.

The model's visual framing component differentiates between competing narratives. Each communicator creates unique frames highlighting different aspects of the same conflict. The inductive framing analysis identifies those frames and classifies their functions into Entman's four associations: problem definition, causal interpretation, moral evaluation, and treatment recommendation. Two overarching stories thus emerge, each with an underlying rationale and a distinct progression of events. The model further accounts for the interactions between the content elements of the stories. Investigating the interactive strategies between the two visual framing blocks over time can detect changes in how communicators present and adjust their narratives in times of conflict.

Meanwhile, the semiotic constellations component of this model has cross-cultural implications. The state and non-state actors in the Sinai conflict utilized visual semiotics in ways that do not always align with the assumptions of the Western visual grammar. These cultural distinctions are indicative of the polysemic and culture-specific nature of visual semiotics, which can convey different symbolic meanings across audience groups. The model allows for examining how semiotic tools work together with character types and scenic elements to generate context-specific semiotic constellations that are key to the process of message construction. This inductive method helps understand unique, culture-based visual messages in their immediate communicative environment and challenges the assumptions that semiotic devices embody a standardized grammar and set of meanings.

Additionally, the analytic framework of visual contestation has practical implications for institutions and content creators facing the current and future threats that militant groups embody in the digital sphere. States, civil society groups, and nongovernmental organizations can all utilize this approach to better understand the mechanisms through which extremist militant groups construct their media campaigns and to identify their unique strategies of engagement. Creators of entertainment-education projects emphasizing values of social cohesion, exposing militant groups, and warning against joining such organizations can also benefit from this approach. The model's outputs identify the main areas of emphasis in opposing campaigns and the conflicting presentations of character roles that are both key for building counter and alternative narratives. In sum, the visual contestation model can guide the process of transforming prosocial messages into more effective visual narratives relevant to the conflict.

Limitations and Future Areas of Research

The analysis of the Sinai photographic warfare is subject to some limitations that can guide future work. First, the data sets on state and non-state actors' military activities provide useful insights and figures but do not accurately reflect all the conditions on the ground. By counting regional attacks that ISIS has not claimed, for example, the GTD data set provides an exaggerated picture of the group's military activity, which can influence the examination of shifts in the media campaigns. Similarly, the level of secrecy around the state's military operations can prevent researchers from accounting for unpublicized military events, such as covert operations or assassinations of leaders. Second, Wilayat Sinai and the Egyptian military also produce and disseminate videos as part of their media efforts in the Sinai visual conflict. Hence, the findings in this book are representative only of the two groups' most prominent visual medium—photographs—but not their entire visual campaigns. Third, this book has demonstrated that the process of message construction in the Egyptian context involves the use of visual semiotic tools in ways that differ from the assumptions of Western frameworks. Despite underlining how cultural dimensions can alter the intensity of symbolic meanings and even introduce new semiotic functions, this book has not empirically examined how such elements influence the perceptions of Egyptian or Arab respondents.

One area of research needed for improving understandings of visual contestation by state and non-state actors is an expanded focus on contextual variables. Chapter 2 primarily examined military conditions as a lens to investigate the relationship between situational context and visual contestation. This focus on military context, however, is only a useful starting point. The political, economic, geographic, social, and human rights contexts also interact with the media campaigns in the conflict, and the book chapters have examined them only in a cursory way. Future studies should examine these factors as additional lenses for understanding visual contestations over time. These situational contexts may then generate supplementary variables, such as GDP, unemployment rate, or reported cases of human rights violations, to extend the applicability and usefulness of the model.

Another area of research that would help scholars better understand contestation is an expanded focus on visual mediums. State and non-state actors' media utilize videos and infographics that play a role in online visual conflicts. Researchers can further examine visual contestations by sampling the different visual media products. The components of the immediate context (text and frequency) and the image (scenic elements, character types, and visual semiotics) in the proposed model of visual contestation should all apply to videos and infographics. Yet the different visual mediums may introduce divergent elements or interactions that could expand the model.

An area of research that would also enhance the understandings of visual contestation is a cross-cultural examination of the role of visual semiotic tools. Researchers can compare audience responses to semiotic elements in different cultural settings, such as the United States vis-à-vis Arab countries, and account for their technological capabilities, including access to broadband, activity on social media, and use of smartphones. Such experimental studies can thus reveal how similar or different semiotic strategies influence viewers' interpretations of the same image. They may even reinforce the need to develop new culture-based frameworks of visual grammar with set assumptions that do not necessarily align with those of Western studies of visual semiotics.

Furthermore, the interactions between the opposing media campaigns is an area that warrants further study. This book has identified key visual framing and semiotic interactive strategies in the Sinai photographic warfare. Competition, negation, expansion, and alignment emerged from the comparative, inductive approach to the study of visual contestation between ISIS and the Egyptian state. However, these interactions do not necessarily constitute a comprehensive list applicable to every conflict. Each visual contestation is contextual and thus may exhibit unique visual content and form in the online environment. By exploring state and non-state actors' visual frames and semiotic constellations in other settings, future studies might find additional interactive strategies or recognize situational constraints governing the ones identified here. Conflicts between the Taliban and Afghanistan's former government, the PKK and Turkey, Hamas and Israel, al-Qaeda in the Arabian Peninsula and Yemen, al-Shabaab and Somalia, and the West African ISIS province and Nigeria offer interesting opportunities for research about visual contestation. Over time, researchers can develop a broader framework that encompasses a range of potential interactions between opposing online media campaigns in times of conflict.

APPENDIX

Coding Sheet and Intercoder Reliability

This appendix includes the coding instrument used to examine all 1,905 photographs that the Egyptian military and ISIS's Wilayat Sinai disseminated online in 2016–17. It also contains the level of intercoder reliability between the two coders per each variable on a sample of 10 percent of the photographs ($n = 190$).

Coding Sheet

As you code the images, you may consider the headlines, photo taglines, and images. Please record an answer for each of the bolded categories.

Human Features

HUMANS:

Which of the following best describes the number of humans in photograph? (count human parts such as legs if that human is dead or about to act in the photograph)

1. One human exists in the image
2. A small group of humans exist in the image (~2–10)
3. A large group of humans exist in the image (>10)
4. No humans exist in the image

AGE:

What age category best describes the human subject(s) in the image? (choose category that best describes the subject(s) in the photo)

1. Infants (up until 3 years old)
2. Children

3. Adults
4. Mixed
5. Not applicable—no human subjects are in the image

GENDER:

Which gender category best describes the human subject(s) in the photo?

1. Male
2. Female
3. Mixed—the image includes both males and females
4. Not applicable—no human subjects are in the image

BODY POSITION:

Which of the following best describes the body position of the human(s) displayed in the photograph?

1. On knees (not praying)
2. Sitting (if can't discern when riding in vehicles, default to sitting)
3. Standing
4. Laying down
5. Praying (on knees or bent over)
6. Mixed—the humans display a mixture of 1–5
7. Not applicable

Visual Semiotics

VIEWER DISTANCE:

How far is the viewer away from the subject(s) of the photograph?

1. Intimate space (facial close-up)
2. Personal space (1.5–~4 ft)
3. Social/public space (>4 ft)
4. Mixed—some subjects are at one distance; others are at other distances

CAMERA ANGLE:

When taking the picture, the camera is: (note: when coding, move image at your eye level and code accordingly)

1. Low looking up
2. High looking down
3. At the eye level
4. Mixed (use only in cases where multiple photographs are embedded in the image and are shot from different camera angles)

EYE CONTACT:

How would you best describe the eye contact of the human subject(s) in the photograph?

1. Looking directly at the viewer
2. Looking away/mixed
3. Eyes closed or mangled
4. Not applicable—no humans appear in the photograph

FACIAL EXPRESSIONS:

How would you best describe the facial expressions of the human subject(s) in the photograph?

1. Positive (e.g., happy, joyful)
2. Negative (e.g., concerned/angry/troubled/afraid)
3. Unclear (include images that have both positive and negative facial expressions here; also include all images shot from a public distance here)
4. Not applicable—no human subjects are in the image

SUBJECTIVE SHOTS:

1. Embodied point of view (i.e., embodied POV shots that reveal neither the photographer parts nor any props the photographer carries—e.g., sniper shot)
2. Referentially embodied point of view (i.e., embodied POV shots that reveal the photographer's hand/arm and/or a prop that he carries—e.g., shot from right behind a rifle in battle)
3. Over the shoulder (i.e., shots from right behind the subject's shoulder revealing what he sees in front of him)
4. Not applicable

Scenic Visual Elements

DEATH:

Is there presence of the following:

1. Dead human being (note: can be in casket, in body bags, or exposed)
2. Not applicable—no signs of death appear in the photograph

DESTRUCTION:

What features of destruction are present in the image?

1. Presence of fire, explosions, or other acts of destruction in process (must be in the context of destruction; cooking fire, for example, does not fall under this category)

2. Destroyed buildings/bridges/vehicles/religious iconography
3. Not applicable—the image contains no features of destruction

ABOUT TO DIE:

1. Possible
2. Certain
3. Presumed death
4. Not applicable

STATE BUILDING:

Which of the following state-building actions are present in the photograph?

1. Social services/state infrastructure workers (education, health, parks, playgrounds, plumbers, electricians, foot distribution, etc.)
2. Law enforcement/punishment (*hudud*, tobacco, alcohol, stealing, homosexuality, adultery, executions)
3. Economic activity
4. City/natural landscape
5. Media distribution (pamphlets, leaflets, newsletters, and videos)
6. Mixed—more than one of the actions in 1–5 are in the image
7. Not applicable—none of the state-building actions mentioned above are present in the image

INFRASTRUCTURE:

Which of the following infrastructure elements are present in the photograph?

1. Buildings (outside of buildings only)
2. Bridges
3. Vehicles (trucks, planes, ships, trains, tanks)
4. Military weaponry/equipment (AK47s, rockets, RPGs, etc.)
5. Mixed—more than one of the infrastructure elements in 1–4 are present
6. Not applicable—none of the infrastructure elements in the list above are present

RELIGIOUS SYMBOLS:

What symbols of religious practice are present in the photograph?

1. One finger pointing to heaven
2. Reading Qur'an, Qur'anic text, or Qur'ans (don't include text on IS flag)
3. Individuals engaged in prayer
4. Religious iconography/shrines
5. Mixed—more than one of the religious practices described in 1–4
6. Not applicable—none of the religious practices described above are present

FLAG:

Which of the flags below are contained in the image?
1. The image contains at least one ISIS flag
2. The image contains a U.S. flag
3. The image contains an Egyptian flag
4. Other
5. The image contains multiple flags from various entities
6. Not applicable—the image contains no flag

TABLE 7. Intercoder reliability for coding variables in content analysis

Variable	Percentage agreement	Cohen's kappa
Human	98.96	.98
Age	98.96	.97
Gender	99.48	.99
Body position	96.37	.94
Distance	96.89	.95
Camera angle	96.89	.94
Eye contact	97.92	.96
Facial expressions	98.96	.98
Subjective shots	98.44	.86
Death	100	1
Destruction	95.33	.87
About to die	96.89	.94
State building	96.37	.92
Infrastructure	98.96	.98
Religious symbols	100	1
Flags	98.96	.94

NOTES

Introduction. State and Non-state Actors' Visual Arsenals

1. ISIS can be traced back to the al-Tawhid wal-Jihad (Monotheism and Jihad) training camp that Abu Mus'ab al-Zarqawi ran in Afghanistan, before establishing a militant group carrying the camp's name in Iraq in the early 2000s. In October 2004, the group pledged allegiance to bin Laden and thus became known as al-Qaeda in Iraq. After American airstrikes killed al-Zarqawi in 2006, the group declared itself the Islamic State of Iraq and added al-Sham (the Levant) to its moniker in April 2013, before dropping the geographical markers altogether in June 2014 to announce the so-called Caliphate or Islamic State. Yet the acronym ISIS and its Arabic equivalent Daesh tend to be the most commonly used labels for the group.

2. Shaffer, "Natural Gas Supply Stability," 121.
3. Deluca, *Image Politics*, 54.
4. Sontag, *Regarding the Pain of Others*, 7.
5. Von Clausewitz, *On War*, 90.
6. Edwards and Winkler, "Representative Form and the Visual Ideograph," 290; Hagopian, "Vietnam War Photography as a Locus of Memory"; Hariman and Lucaites, *No Caption Needed*, 5; Kraidy, "Projectilic Image," 1194; Perlmutter, *Photojournalism and Foreign Policy*; Zelizer, *Remembering to Forget*.
7. Bitzer, "Rhetorical Situation," 3.
8. Vatz, "Myth of the Rhetorical Situation," 160.
9. See Consigny, "Rhetoric and Its Situations," 179; Turnbull, "Political Rhetoric and Its Relationship to Context," 116.
10. Goffman, *Frame Analysis*; Goffman, *Gender and Advertisements*.
11. Entman, "Framing," 52.
12. Halliday, *Language as Social Semiotic*, 49.
13. Barthes, *Image-Music-Text*, 23.
14. Kress and van Leeuwen, 3.
15. Hall, *Hidden Dimension*; Branigan, *Point of View in the Cinema*.
16. El Damanhoury, "Understanding ISIS's Provincial Propaganda," 11; Milton, "Communication Breakdown"; Winter, "Apocalypse, Later," 116.
17. For an overview of the about-to-die visual trope, its three types (i.e., presumed, possible, and certain death images), and its influence on viewer engagement and perception, see Zelizer, *About to Die*.
18. See Bruce, "Framing Arab Spring Conflict"; Greenwood and Jenkins, "Visual Framing of the Syrian Conflict"; Huang and Fahmy, "Picturing a Journey of Protest or a Journey of Harmony?"

19. Trachtenberg, "Albums of War"; Goldstein, *Capturing the German Eye*; Chouliaraki, "Humanity of War."

20. Wignell, Tan, and O'Halloran, "Under the Shade of AK47s"; Winkler et al., "Medium Is Terrorism."

21. Hochberg, *Visual Occupations*; Ratta, *Shooting a Revolution*; Khatib, *Image Politics in the Middle East*.

22. Seo and Ebrahim, "Visual Propaganda on Facebook"; Hyunjin Seo, "Visual Propaganda in the Age of Social Media."

23. See Kraft, "Influence of Camera Angle"; McCain, Chilberg, and Wakshlag, "Effect of Camera Angle"; Fahmy, "Picturing Afghan Women"; Hardin et al., "Framing of Sexual Difference."

24. Brunner and Deluca, "Argumentative Force of Image Networks"; Azoulay, *Civil Imagination*; Finnegan, *Making Photography Matter*, 14; McLuhan, "Playboy Interview," 1; Mitchell, *Picture Theory*.

25. Messaris and Abraham, "Role of Images in Framing News Stories."

26. Al-Muqrin, "Message to Yemeni Youth."

27. Joscelyn, "Graphic Promotes the Islamic State's Prolific Media Machine."

28. Milton, "Communication Breakdown," 21.

29. Winter, "Apocalypse, Later," 109.

30. Chavez and Levenson, "Terror Suspect Wanted to Attack People."

31. U.S. Department of Justice, "U.S. v. Akayed Ullah Federal Criminal Complaint."

32. Winkler, "Challenging Communities."

33. Holbrook, "Spread of Its Message," 90.

34. O'Neil, "13th Juror."

35. "Israeli Drone Strike Kills Suspected Islamic Militants in Egypt."

36. The Sinai-based group shared the same moniker as al-Zarqawi's Jama'at al-Tawhid wal-Jihad militancy in Iraq. Similarly, the group adopted an extreme interpretation of the concepts of monotheism and jihad, arguing that existing Muslim states are polytheistic for using man-made rather than shari'a laws and that American, Israeli, and Western civilians ought to be fought due their nations' interference in Muslim countries.

37. Al-Furqan Media, "Audio Speech by the Emir."

38. Tahrir Institute for Middle East Policy (TIMEP), "Egypt Security Watch: Quarterly Report: January–March 2017."

39. Halverson, Corman, and Goodall, *Master Narratives of Islamist Extremism*, 164.

40. Mikhail, "Sinai Tribes Take Up Arms."

41. Marroushi, "Dark Clouds over the Sinai"; Masress, "Journalists and Reporters in North Sinai"; Shilad, "Egypt's State of Emergency."

42. Ahram, "Transcript of Counterterrorism Law."

43. Frampton, Fisher, and Prucha, "New Netwar."

44. Powers and O'Loughlin, "Syrian Data Glut."

Chapter 1. Contextualizing the Sinai Conflict

1. Hofstede, "Cultural Relativity of Organizational Practices and Theories"; Hofstede, "Dimensionalizing Cultures." According to Hofstede's framework, collectivist cultures are centered around family, clan, and/or tribe, exhibit a sense of belonging to

the in-group, and respect group norms. Masculine cultures associate toughness, assertiveness, and success with males and show admiration for strong figures. Large-power-distance cultures are unequal, hierarchical, and more respectful of elderly figures.

2. Hall, *Beyond Culture*. According to Hall's framework, high-context cultures are more cohesive, family-oriented societies in which most of the information is implicitly communicated in the context or through symbols rather than in the explicit message. In such cultures, people tend to be polychronic, meaning that they are multitaskers and in need of greater centralization and more absolute control over individuals.

3. Hofstede, Hofstede, and Minkov, *Cultures and Organizations*. In the book, the authors associate a number of characteristics with short-term-oriented cultures, such as possessing universal guidelines about good and evil, deeming social obligations important, respecting traditions, and considering the most important life events as either in the past or taking place now. Meanwhile, restrained cultures are morally disciplined, do not perceive leisure as important, and tend to have more police officers.

4. CAPMAS, "Egypt's Annual Census."
5. Bradley, *Inside Egypt*.
6. International Crisis Group, "Egypt's Sinai Question"; Morrow and Al-Omrani, "Egypt."
7. Shuqair, *Old and New History*, 5.
8. Mubashir and Tawfik, *Sinai*.
9. Shuqair, *Old and New History*, 137.
10. Hussein, *Our Unknown People*, 117–18.
11. Weizman, *Hollow Land*, 98.
12. Gorenberg, *Accidental Empire*, 221–22.
13. Glassner, "Bedouin of Southern Sinai," 50.
14. Sabry, *Sinai*; Hussein, *Our Unknown People*, 135–40.
15. Sharon and Chanoff, *Warrior*, 400.
16. Al-Tahtawy, "Study."
17. Eleiba, "Sinai."
18. International Crisis Group, "Egypt's Sinai Question," 13.
19. Dentice, "Geopolitics of Violent Extremism."
20. Pelham, "Sinai."
21. Abu Mudallala and Al-Agha, "Tunnel Economy in Gaza," 1163.
22. Ashour, "Egypt's North Sinai Post 2011 Revolution"; Pelham, "Sinai," 2.
23. CAPMAS, "1996 Egypt Census."
24. Said, "Tales of Palestinian Fighters in Sinai."
25. Slackman, "30 Are Killed in Sinai."
26. Ashour, "ISIS and Wilayat Sinai."
27. Human Rights Watch, "Egypt: Mass Arrests and Torture in Sinai."
28. Sabry, *Sinai*, 24.
29. Al-Sorani, «Rafah Tunnels.»
30. Abu Mudallala and Al-Agha, "Tunnel Economy in Gaza," 1164.
31. Sabry, *Sinai*, 100.
32. Salafism comes from the Arabic word *salaf*, which means "predecessor." Applied in the context of apolitical Islamist movements, Salafism simply refers to the revival of

Islam as practiced by the first generations of Muslims, including the Prophet Muhammad, his companions, and the followers of the companions. Salafi jihadism, which has been adopted by groups like al-Qaeda and ISIS, on the other hand, is a political ideology that presents activism in the form of militancy and armed jihad as a means to attain a puritanical Muslim society. For a genealogy of the concepts jihad and Salafism, see Bonner, *Jihad in Islamic History*; Lauzière, *Making of Salafism*.

33. Al-Beheiry, "Terrorist Operations."
34. Al-Beheiry, "Terrorist Operations," 2.
35. TIMEP, "Egypt Security Watch: Quarterly Report: January–March 2017."
36. TIMEP, "ESW Month in Brief"; TIMEP, "ESW Week in Brief."
37. TIMEP, "Egypt Security Watch: Quarterly Report: October–December 2016."
38. "Egypt's Coptic Christians Flee Sinai."
39. Gomaa, "Main Directions for Terroristic Activity."
40. Human Rights Watch, "Egypt: Thousands Evicted."
41. Human Rights Watch, "Egypt: Army Intensifies Sinai Home Demolitions"; Human Rights Watch, "If You Are Afraid for Your Lives, Leave Sinai!"
42. Sabry, *Sinai*, 215.
43. Said and Naguib, "Counterterrorism in Sisi's 1st Term."
44. TIMEP, "Egypt Security Watch: Quarterly Report: October–December 2016," 7.
45. TIMEP, "Egypt Security Watch: Quarterly Report: January–March 2017," 7.
46. TIMEP, "ESW Month in Brief: January 2019," 1.

Chapter 2. The Military-Photography Nexus

1. Seo and Ebrahim, "Visual Propaganda on Facebook"; Seo, "Visual Propaganda in the Age of Social Media"; Green, "Advertising War"; El Damanhoury, "Understanding ISIS's Provincial Propaganda"; El Damanhoury et al., "Examining the Military–Media Nexus"; Holiday, Lewis, and Labaugh, "Are You Talking to Me?"; Milton, "Communication Breakdown"; Winter, "Apocalypse, Later"; Melki and El-Masri, "Paris Attacks"; Melki and Jabado, "Mediated Public Diplomacy"; Winkler et al., "Considering the Military-Media Nexus."
2. Based on a Pearson's correlation coefficient test, the monthly photographic outputs by Wilayat Sinai and the Egyptian military exhibited no linear relationship over the two-year period, $r(22) = .20, p > .05$.
3. Zelizer, *About to Die*, 135.
4. TIMEP, "Egypt Security Watch: Quarterly Report: October–December 2016"; Said and Naguib, "Counterterrorism in Sisi's 1st Term."
5. Global Terrorism Database, "ISIL Terrorism Incidents."
6. TIMEP, "Quarterly Report: January–March 2016."
7. Zelizer, *About to Die*, 72.
8. Dearden, "Abu Duaa Al-Ansari."

Chapter 3. The Visual Framing Battle

1. See Parry, "Visual Framing Analysis."
2. Wilayat Sinai's captions are superimposed on the images. There are no URLs to cite for the news briefs and photo reports since they appear in encrypted channels on Telegram.

3. Official Page of Armed Forces Spokesman, "Egyptian Military Statement on a Second Army Operation in North Sinai."
4. Official Page of Armed Forces Spokesman, "Egyptian Military Statement on Third Army's Sinai Operations."
5. Zelizer, *About to Die*, 266–88; Winkler et al., "Images of Death and Dying in ISIS Media," 251; Chouliaraki, "Humanity of War."
6. Official Page of Armed Forces Spokesman, "Egyptian Military Statement on the Killing of 16 Terrorists in North Sinai."
7. Official Page of Armed Forces Spokesman, "Egyptian Military Statement on the Ministers of Defense and Interior's Visit to Sinai."
8. Proverbio, Riva, and Zani, "Observation of Static Pictures of Dynamic Actions," 1; Cian, Krishna, and Elder, "This Logo Moves Me," 184.
9. Wells, "Narratives of Liberation and Narratives of Innocent Suffering," 55; Vail et al., "Aftermath of Destruction," 1069.
10. Newhagen and Reeves, "Evening's Bad News," 25; Pfau et al., "Influence of Television News Depictions," 303.
11. Winkler et al., "Medium Is Terrorism"; Winter, "Apocalypse, Later"; Wignell, Tan, and O'Halloran, "Under the Shade of AK47s."
12. Chouliaraki, "Humanity of War," 315–40; Ohl, "Nothing to See or Fear"; Holiday, Lewis, and Labaugh, "Are You Talking to Me?"

Chapter 4. The Visual Semiotic Battle

1. "Council Decision (CFSP) 2020/20 of 13 January 2020"; U.S. Department of State, "Foreign Terrorist Organizations"; United Nations, "United Nations Security Council Consolidated List."
2. Ministry of Foreign Affairs, "Bahrain Terrorist List (Individuals—Entities)"; "UAE Blacklists 82 Groups as 'Terrorist.'"
3. Hall, *Beyond Culture*; Hofstede, "Dimensionalizing Cultures"; Hofstede, Hofstede, and Minkov, *Cultures and Organizations*; Hofstede, "Cultural Relativity of Organizational Practices and Theories."
4. Combatting Terrorism Center, "Short Summary for the Media Mujahid."
5. Jewitt and Oyama, "Visual Meaning"; Hall, *Hidden Dimension*; Lampinen, Neuschatz, and Cling, *Psychology of Eyewitness Identification*.
6. Gerhardsson, Högman, and Fischer, "Viewing Distance Matter to Perceived Intensity of Facial Expressions"; Cohen, "Defining Identification"; Koga-Browes, "Social Distance Portrayed"; Hjarvard, "Proximity"; Wagenaar and Van Der Schrier, "Familiar Face Recognition."
7. Kang and Heo, "Framing the Enemy."
8. Batziou, "Framing 'Otherness'"; Silva et al., "Distant Other."
9. Official Page of Armed Forces Spokesman, "Egyptian Military Statement on Third Army's Sinai Operations."
10. Official Page of Armed Forces Spokesman, "Egyptian Military Statement on Third Army's Checkpoints in Sinai."
11. Hofstede, Hofstede, and Minkov, *Cultures and Organizations*, 291.
12. Zettl, *Television Production Handbook*; Mandell and Shaw, "Judging People in the News—Unconsciously"; Kraft, "Influence of Camera Angle."

13. Stahl, *Through the Crosshairs*, 55; Amad, "From God's-Eye to Camera-Eye."
14. Kraft, "Influence of Camera Angle," 291; Greer, Hardin, and Homan, "'Naturally' Less Exciting?"; Tiemens, "Some Relationships of Camera Angle"; Mandell and Shaw, "Judging People in the News—Unconsciously," 353; Huang, Olson, and Olson, "Camera Angle Affects Dominance."
15. Fahmy, "Picturing Afghan Women," 102.
16. Meyers-Levy and Peracchio, "Getting an Angle in Advertising," 454; Sammartino and Palmer, "Aesthetic Issues in Spatial Composition."
17. Official Page of Armed Forces Spokesman, "Egyptian Military Statement on Third Army's Operations in Central Sinai."
18. Öhman and Dimberg, "Facial Expressions as Conditioned Stimuli"; Knutson, "Facial Expressions of Emotion"; Forgas and East, "How Real Is That Smile?"; Hess, Blairy, and Kleck, "Influence of Expression Intensity."
19. Baudouin et al., "When the Smile Is a Cue to Familiarity"; Schmidt and Cohn, "Human Facial Expressions as Adaptations."
20. Parry, "Images of Liberation?"
21. Kress and van Leeuwen, *Reading Images*, 89.
22. Palanica and Itier, "Attention Capture by Direct Gaze"; Senju, Hasegawa, and Tojo, "Does Perceived Direct Gaze Boost Detection in Adults and Children with and without Autism?"; Brooks, Church, and Fraser, "Effects of Duration of Eye Contact"; Hemsley and Doob, "Effect of Looking Behavior"; Tankard, "Effects of Eye Position on Person Perception"; Ewing, Rhodes, and Pellicano, "Have You Got the Look?"; Von Grunau and Anston, "Detection of Gaze Direction"; Neal and Brodsky, "Expert Witness Credibility."
23. Tang and Schmeichel, "Look Me in the Eye"; Larsen and Shackelford, "Gaze Avoidance."
24. Batziou, "Framing 'Otherness,'" 49.
25. Official Page of Armed Forces Spokesman, "Egyptian Military Statement on the Martyrdom of Ahmed Abdelhamid Al-Dardiry."
26. Branigan, *Point of View in the Cinema*.
27. Cummins, Keene, and Nutting, "Impact of Subjective Camera"; Fabe, *Closely Watched Films*; Lombard et al., "Presence and Television"; Lombard and Ditton, "At the Heart of It All."
28. Brown, *Cinematography Theory and Practice*.
29. Branigan, *Point of View in the Cinema*, 110.
30. Rose, *Visual Methodologies*; Ortiz and Moya, "Action Cam Phenomenon."
31. Stahl, *Through the Crosshairs*, 63.

Chapter 5. An Analytic Framework of Visual Contestation

1. Human Rights Watch, "Egypt: Mass Arrests and Torture in Sinai."
2. Human Rights Watch, "Egypt: Army Intensifies Sinai Home Demolitions"; Human Rights Watch, "Egypt: Thousands Evicted in Sinai Demolitions."
3. Birdsell and Groarke, "Toward a Theory of Visual Argument."

BIBLIOGRAPHY

Abu Hashash, Mahmoud. "On the Visual Representation of Martyrdom in Palestine." *Third Text* 20, nos. 3–4 (2007): 391–403. https://doi.org/10.1080/09528820600901008.

Abu Mudallala, Samir M., and Wafeek H. Al-Agha. "The Tunnel Economy in Gaza: A National Necessity or an Economic and Social Catastrophe." *Al-Azhar University Magazine in Gaza* 13, no. 1 (2011): 1147–82.

Ahern, Maureen. "Visual and Verbal Sites: The Construction of Jesuit Martyrdom in Northwest New Spain in Andres Perez de Ribas' Historia de los Triumphos de nuestra Santa Fee (1645)." *Colonial Latin American Review* 8, no. 1 (1999): 7–33. https://doi.org/10.1080/10609169984746.

Ahram. "Transcript of Counterterrorism Law." August 17, 2015. https://bit.ly/3dZu8rI.

Al-Beheiry, Ahmed K. "Terrorist Operations: Paths and Characteristics since January 2011." *ACPSS*, January 25, 2017. http://acpss.ahram.org.eg/News/5669.aspx.

Al-Furqan Media. "Audio Speech by the Emir of the Faithful Abu Bakr Al-Baghdadi Entitled 'So Wait, We Too Are Waiting with You.'" Archive.org, December 29, 2015. https://ia800201.us.archive.org/17/items/29122015mediaIS/K1.mp3.

Ali, Sanjar. "Peshmerga Will Not Participate in Western Mosul Operation: Ministry." *Kurdistan* 24, February 22, 2017. http://goo.gl/3eKRnT%0A.

Allen, Lori. "Getting by the Occupation: How Violence Became Normal during the Second Palestinian Intifada." *Cultural Anthropology* 23, no. 3 (2008): 453–87.

Al-Muqrin, Abu Hajar. "A Message to Yemeni Youth." *Sada Al-Malahim* 4 (July 2008).

Al-Sorani, Ghazi. "Rafah Tunnels and Their Economic, Social, and Political Impact." *Al-Hiwar Al-Mutamidin*, December 14, 2008. http://www.m.ahewar.org/s.asp?aid=156356&r=0.

Al-Tahtawy, Rasha. "Study: Reviving 'the Frozen' Sinai Development Project Needs 300 Billion Egyptian Pounds." *Al-Masry Al-Youm*, August 26, 2012. http://www.almasryalyoum.com/news/details/159467.

Amad, Paula. "From God's-Eye to Camera-Eye: Aerial Photography's Post-Humanist and Neo-Humanist Visions of the World." *History of Photography* 36, no. 1 (2012): 66–86. https://doi.org/10.1080/03087298.2012.632567.

Andén-Papadopoulos, Kari. "Citizen Camera-Witnessing: Embodied Political Dissent in the Age of 'Mediated Mass Self-Communication.'" *New Media & Society* 16, no. 5 (2013): 753–69. https://doi.org/10.1177/1461444813489863.

Ashour, Karim. "Egypt's North Sinai Post 2011 Revolution: The Nexus between Ungovernability Dimensions and Terrorism." American University in Cairo, May 2016.

http://dar.aucegypt.edu/bitstream/handle/10526/4751/MGA Project- Final Version - Karim Ashour - May 22–2016.pdf?sequence=1.

Ashour, Omar. "ISIS and Wilayat Sinai: Complex Networks of Insurgency under Authoritarian Rule." *DGAP kompakt*, August 2016. https://www.ssoar.info/ssoar/handle/document/54270.

Axel, Brian K. "Digital Figurings of the Unimaginable: Visual Media, Death, and Formations of the Sikh Diaspora." *Journal of Ethnic and Migration Studies* 34, no. 7 (2008): 1145–59. https://doi.org/10.1080/13691830802230471.

Azoulay, Ariella. *Civil Imagination: A Political Ontology of Photography*. London: Verso, 2015.

Barthes, Roland. *Image-Music-Text*. New York: Macmillan, 1978.

Batziou, Athanasia. "Framing 'Otherness' in Press Photographs: The Case of Immigrants in Greece and Spain." *Journal of Media Practice* 12, no. 1 (2011): 41–60. https://doi.org/10.1386/jmpr.12.1.41.

Baudouin, Jean-Yves, Daniel Gilibert, Stephane Sansone, and Guy Tiberghien. "When the Smile Is a Cue to Familiarity." *Memory* 8, no. 5 (2000): 285–92. https://doi.org/10.1080/09658210050117717.

Birdsell, David S., and Leo Groarke. "Toward a Theory of Visual Argument." *Argumentation and Advocacy* 33, no. 1 (1996): 1–10.

Bitzer, Lloyd F. "The Rhetorical Situation." *Philosophy & Rhetoric* 1, no. 1 (1968): 1–14.

Bonner, Michael. *Jihad in Islamic History: Doctrines and Practices*. Princeton, NJ: Princeton University Press, 2008.

Bradley, John R. *Inside Egypt: The Land of the Pharaohs on the Brink of a Revolution*. New York: Macmillan, 2008.

Branigan, Edward. *Point of View in the Cinema: A Theory of Narration and Subjectivity in Classical Film*. Berlin: Walter de Gruyter, 1984.

Brooks, Charles I., Michael A. Church, and Lance Fraser. "Effects of Duration of Eye Contact on Judgments of Personality Characteristics." *Journal of Social Psychology* 126, no. 1 (1986): 71–78. https://doi.org/10.1080/00224545.1986.9713572.

Brown, Blain. *Cinematography Theory and Practice: Imagemaking for Cinematographers and Directors*. 2nd ed. Waltham, MA: Focal Press, 2012.

Bruce, Michael D. "Framing Arab Spring Conflict: A Visual Analysis of Coverage on Five Transnational Arab News Channels." *Journal of Middle East Media* 10, no. 1 (2014): 1–27.

Brunner, Elizabeth A., and Kevin M. Deluca. "The Argumentative Force of Image Networks: Greenpeace's Panmediated Global Detox Campaign." *Argumentation and Advocacy* 52, no. 4 (2016): 281–99. https://doi.org/10.1080/00028533.2016.11821875.

CAPMAS. "Egypt's Annual Census." January 1, 2020. https://www.capmas.gov.eg/Pages/StaticPages.aspx?page_id=5034.

———. "The 1996 Egypt Census." December 1998. https://www.capmas.gov.eg/Pages/Publications.aspx?page_id=7195&Year=23354.

Chao, Tien-yi. "Representations of Female Sainthood and Voluntary Death in Margaret Cavendish's 'The She-Anchoret' (1656)." *English Studies* 92, no. 7 (2011): 744–55. https://doi.org/10.1080/0013838X.2011.622161.

Chavez, Nicole, and Eric Levenson. "Terror Suspect Wanted to Attack People on Brooklyn Bridge, Documents Say." *CNN*, November 2, 2017. http://www.cnn.com/2017/11/02/us/new-york-terror-attack/index.html.

Chouliaraki, Lilie. "The Humanity of War: Iconic Photojournalism of the Battlefield, 1914–2012." *Visual Communication* 12, no. 3 (2013): 315–40. https://doi.org/10.1177/1470357213484422.

Cian, Luca, Aradhna Krishna, and Ryan S. Elder. "This Logo Moves Me: Dynamic Imagery from Static Images." *Journal of Marketing Research* 51, no. 2 (2014): 184–97. https://doi.org/10.1509/jmr.13.0023.

Claiborne, William. "Sinai Reverts to Egyptian Control Today." *Washington Post*, April 25, 1982. http://goo.gl/1PGxAq%0A.

Cohen, Jonathan. "Defining Identification: A Theoretical Look at the Identification of Audiences with Media Characters." *Mass Communication & Society* 4, no. 3 (2001): 245–64.

Combatting Terrorism Center. "A Short Summary for the Media Mujahid on the Subject of Filming." August 28, 2018. https://ctc.usma.edu/pulling-back-the-curtain-an-inside-look-at-the-islamic-states-media-organization/.

Consigny, Scott. "Rhetoric and Its Situations." *Philosophy & Rhetoric* 7, no. 3 (1974): 175–86. http://www.jstor.org/stable/40237197.

"Council Decision (CFSP) 2020/20 of 13 January 2020 Updating the List of Persons, Groups and Entities Subject to Articles 2, 3 and 4 of Common Position 2001/931/CFSP on the Application of Specific Measures to Combat Terrorism, and Repealing Decision (CFSP)." *Official Journal of the European Union*, January 14, 2020. https://eur-lex.europa.eu/legal-content/EN/TXT/PDF/?uri=CELEX:32020D0020&from=en.

Cummins, R. Glenn, Justin R. Keene, and Brandon H. Nutting. "The Impact of Subjective Camera in Sports on Arousal and Enjoyment." *Mass Communication and Society* 15 (2012): 37–41. https://doi.org/10.1080/15205436.2011.558805.

Dearden, Lizzie. "Abu Duaa Al-Ansari: Leader of Isis' Sinai Province Killed in Air Strikes, Egyptian Military Says." *Independent*, August 4, 2016. https://www.independent.co.uk/news/world/africa/isis-leader-killed-air-strikes-bombed-egypt-military-sinai-province-wilayat-abu-duaa-doaa-al-ansari-a7172851.html.

Deluca, Kevin M. *Image Politics: The New Rhetoric of Environmental Activism*. New York: Guilford, 1999.

Dentice, Giuseppe. "The Geopolitics of Violent Extremism: The Case of Sinai." *Iemed*, February 2018. http://www.iemed.org/publicacions-en/historic-de-publicacions/papersiemed-euromesco/36.-the-geopolitics-of-violent-extremism-the-case-of-sinai/image_view_fullscreen.

Doss, Erika. "'Revolutionary Art Is a Tool for Liberation': Emory Douglas and Protest Aesthetics at *The Black Panther*." *New Political Science* 21, no. 2 (1999): 245–59. https://doi.org/10.1080/07393149908429867.

Edwards, Janis L., and Carol K. Winkler. "Representative Form and the Visual Ideograph: The Iwo Jima Image in Editorial Cartoons." *Quarterly Journal of Speech* 83, no. 3 (1997): 289–310.

"Egypt's Coptic Christians Flee Sinai after Deadly Attacks." *BBC*, February 25, 2017. https://www.bbc.com/news/world-middle-east-39085285.

El Damanhoury, Kareem. "Understanding ISIS's Provincial Propaganda : A Visual Framing Analysis of Wilayat Sinai's Imagery in 2016." *Journal of Middle East Media* 13 (2017): 1–31.

El Damanhoury, Kareem, Carol Winkler, Wojciech Kaczkowski, and Aaron Dicker. "Examining the Military–Media Nexus in ISIS's Provincial Photography Campaign." *Dynamics of Asymmetric Conflict: Pathways toward Terrorism and Genocide* 11, no. 2 (2018): 89–108. https://doi.org/10.1080/17467586.2018.1432869.

Eleiba, Ahmed. "Sinai: Atrophied Development." *Ahram Online*, May 2, 2013. http://english.ahram.org.eg/NewsContentP/1/70604/Egypt/Sinai-Atrophied-development.aspx.

Entman, Robert. "Framing: Toward Clarification of a Fractured Paradigm." *Journal of Communication* 43, no. 4 (1993): 51–58.

Ewing, Louise, Gillian Rhodes, and Elizabeth Pellicano. "Have You Got the Look? Gaze Direction Affects Judgements of Facial Attractiveness." *Visual Cognition* 18, no. 3 (2010): 321–30. https://doi.org/10.1080/13506280902965599.

Fabe, Marilyn. *Closely Watched Films: An Introduction to the Art of Narrative Film Technique*. Oakland: University of California Press, 2014.

Fahmy, Shahira. "Picturing Afghan Women: A Content Analysis of AP Wire Photographs during the Taliban Regime and after the Fall of the Taliban Regime." *International Communication Gazette* 66, no. 2 (2004): 91–112. https://doi.org/10.1177/0016549204041472.

Fahmy, Shahira, and Daekyung Kim. "Picturing the Iraq War: Constructing the Image of War in the British and US Press." *International Communication Gazette* 70, no. 6 (2008): 443–62. https://doi.org/10.1177/1748048508096142.

Finnegan, Cara A. *Making Photography Matter: A Viewer's History from the Civil War to the Great Depression*. Urbana: University of Illinois Press, 2015.

Flaskerud, Ingvild. "Redemptive Memories: Portraiture in the Cult of Commemoration." *Visual Anthropology* 25, nos. 1–2 (2012): 22–46. https://doi.org/10.1080/08949468.2012.627830.

Forgas, Joseph P., and Rebekah East. "How Real Is That Smile? Mood Effects on Accepting or Rejecting the Veracity of Emotional Facial Expressions." *Journal of Nonverbal Behavior* 32, no. 3 (2008): 157–70.

Frampton, Martyn, Ali Fisher, and Nico Prucha. "The New Netwar: Countering Extremism Online." Policy Exchange, September 2017. https://policyexchange.org.uk/wp-content/uploads/2017/09/The-New-Netwar-2.pdf.

Francis, Martin. "Cecil Beaton's Romantic Toryism and the Symbolic Economy of Wartime Britain." *Journal of British Studies* 45, no. 1 (2006): 90–117. https://doi.org/10.1086/497057.

Friedlaender, Gary E., and Linda K. Friedlaender. "Saints Cosmas and Damian: Patron Saints of Medicine." *Clinical Orthopaedics and Related Research* 474, no. 8 (2016): 1765–69.

Gerhardsson, Andreas, Lennart Högman, and Håkan Fischer. "Viewing Distance Matter to Perceived Intensity of Facial Expressions." *Frontiers in Psychology* 6, July 2, 2015, 1–8. https://doi.org/10.3389/fpsyg.2015.00944.

Glassner, Martin I. "The Bedouin of Southern Sinai under Israeli Administration." *Geographic Review* 64, no. 1 (1974): 31–60.

Global Terrorism Database. "ISIL Terrorism Incidents in Iraq and Syria 2016–2017." September 2018. https://bit.ly/3sbqqDL.

Goffman, Erving. *Frame Analysis: An Essay on the Organization of Experience.* Boston: Northeastern University Press, 1974.

———. *Gender and Advertisements.* London: Macmillan, 1979.

Goldstein, Cora S. *Capturing the German Eye: American Visual Propaganda in Occupied Germany.* London: University of Chicago Press, 2009.

Gomaa, Mohamed. "Main Directions for Terroristic Activity in Egypt in 2017." *ACPSS*, January 15, 2018. http://acpss.ahram.org.eg/News/16514.aspx.

Gorenberg, Gershom. *The Accidental Empire: Israel and the Birth of the Settlements, 1967–1977.* New York: Times Books, 2006.

Green, Leanne. "Advertising War: Pictorial Publicity, 1914–1918." PhD thesis, Manchester Metropolitan University, September 2015. https://e-space.mmu.ac.uk/600404/.

Greenwood, Keith, and Joy Jenkins. "Visual Framing of the Syrian Conflict in News and Public Affairs Magazines." *Journalism Studies* 16, no. 2 (2013): 207–27. https://doi.org/10.1080/1461670X.2013.865969.

Greer, Jennifer D., Marie Hardin, and Casey Homan. "'Naturally' Less Exciting? Visual Production of Men's and Women's Track and Field Coverage during the 2004 Olympics." *Journal of Broadcasting and Electronic Media* 53, no. 2 (2009): 173–89. https://doi.org/10.1080/08838150902907595.

Hadjittofi, Fotini, and Hagith Sivan. "Staging Rachel: Rabbinic Midrash, Theatrical Mime, and Christian Martyrdom in Late Antiquity." *Harvard Theological Review* 113, no. 3 (2020): 299–333. https://doi.org/10.1017/S0017816020000127.

Hagopian, Patrick. "Vietnam War Photography as a Locus of Memory." In *Locating Memory: Photographic Acts*, edited by Annette Kuhn and Kirsten E. McAllister, 201–22. New York: Berghahn Books, 2006.

Hall, Edward T. *Beyond Culture.* New York: Anchor Books, 1989.

———. *The Hidden Dimension.* Garden City, NY: Doubleday, 1966.

Halliday, Michael A. K. *Language as Social Semiotic: The Social Interpretation of Language and Meaning.* London: Edward Arnold, 1978.

Halverson, Jeffrey, Steven Corman, and H. L. Goodall. *Master Narratives of Islamist Extremism.* New York: Springer, 2011.

Hardin, Marie, Susan Lynn, Kristie Walsdorf, and Brent Hardin. "The Framing of Sexual Difference in SI for Kids Editorial Photos." *Mass Communication and Society* 5, no. 3 (2002): 341–59. https://doi.org/10.1207/S15327825MCS0503_6.

Hariman, Robert, and John L. Lucaites. *No Caption Needed: Iconic Photographs, Public Culture, and Liberal Democracy.* Chicago: University of Chicago Press, 2007.

Hemsley, Gordon D., and Anthony N. Doob. "The Effect of Looking Behavior on Perceptions of a Communicator's Credibility." *Journal of Applied Social Psychology* 8, no. 2 (1978): 136–42.

Hess, Ursula, Sylvie Blairy, and Robert E. Kleck. "The Influence of Expression Intensity, Gender, and Ethnicity on Judgments of Dominance and Affiliation." *Journal of Nonverbal Behavior* 24, no. 4 (2000): 265–83. https://doi.org/10.1023/A:1006623213355.

Higazy, Mourad. "Update: Sinai Province Claims Responsibility for Arish Airport Attack." *Mada Masr*, December 20, 2017. https://www.madamasr.com/en/2017/12/20/news/u/at-least-1-officer-5-militants-killed-in-clashes-outside-arish-airport-following-attack/.

High, Casey. "Victims and Martyrs: Converging Histories of Violence in Amazonian Anthropology and U.S. Cinema." *Anthropology and Humanism* 34, no. 1 (2009): 41–50. https://doi.org/10.1111/j.1548-1409.2009.01022.x.

Himdan, Gamal. *Sinai: In the Strategy, Politics, and Geography*. Cairo: Madbouly Library, 1993.

Hjarvard, Stig. "Proximity: The Name of the Ratings Game." *Nordicom Review*, no. 21 (2000): 63–81.

Hochberg, Gil Z. *Visual Occupations: Violence and Visibility in a Conflict Zone*. Durham, NC: Duke University Press, 2015.

Hofstede, Geert. "The Cultural Relativity of Organizational Practices and Theories." *Journal of International Business Studies* 14, no. 2 (1983): 75–89.

———. "Dimensionalizing Cultures: The Hofstede Model in Context." *Online Readings in Psychology and Culture* 2, no. 1 (2011): 1–26.

Hofstede, Geert, Gert J. Hofstede, and Michael Minkov. *Cultures and Organizations: Software of the Mind*. New York: McGraw-Hill, 2005.

Holbrook, Donald. "The Spread of Its Message: Studying the Prominence of Al-Qaida Materials in UK Terrorism Investigations." *Perspectives on Terrorism* 11, no. 6 (2017): 89–100.

Holiday, Steven, Matthew J. Lewis, and Jack L. Labaugh. "Are You Talking to Me? The Sociopolitical Visual Rhetoric of the Syrian Presidency's Instagram Account." *Southwestern Mass Communication Journal* 30, no. 2 (2015): 1–28.

Huang, Wei, Judith S. Olson, and Gary M. Olson. "Camera Angle Affects Dominance in Video-Mediated Communication." *Short Talk: Communication Media* (April 20, 2002): 716–17. https://doi.org/10.1145/506558.506562.

Huang, Ying, and Shahira Fahmy. "Picturing a Journey of Protest or a Journey of Harmony? Comparing the Visual Framing of the 2008 Olympic Torch Relay in the US versus the Chinese Press." *Media, War & Conflict* 6, no. 3 (2013): 191–206. https://doi.org/10.1177/1750635213495601.

Human Rights Watch. "Egypt: Army Intensifies Sinai Home Demolitions." May 22, 2018. https://www.hrw.org/news/2018/05/22/egypt-army-intensifies-sinai-home-demolitions.

———. "Egypt: Mass Arrests and Torture in Sinai." February 2005. https://www.hrw.org/sites/default/files/reports/egypt0205.pdf.

———. "Egypt: Thousands Evicted in Sinai Demolitions: In Insurgent Fight, Border Families Left to Fend for Themselves." September 2015. https://www.hrw.org/news/2015/09/22/egypt-thousands-evicted-sinai-demolitions.

———. "If You Are Afraid for Your Lives, Leave Sinai!" May 2019. https://www.hrw.org/

report/2019/05/28/if-you-are-afraid-your-lives-leave-sinai/egyptian-security-forces-and-isis.

Hussein, Fouad. *Our Unknown People in Sinai*. Cairo: Family Library, 1996.

International Crisis Group. "Egypt's Sinai Question." January 30, 2007. https://d2071andvipowj.cloudfront.net/61-egypt-s-sinai-question.pdf.

"Israeli Drone Strike Kills Suspected Islamic Militants in Egypt." *Guardian*, August 9, 2013. https://www.theguardian.com/world/2013/aug/09/israeli-drone-strike-suspected-militants-egypt.

Jewitt, Carey, and Rumiko Oyama. "Visual Meaning: A Social Semiotic Approach." In *Handbook of Visual Analysis*, 7th ed., edited by Theo van Leeuwen and Carey Jewitt, 134–56. London: Sage, 2008. https://doi.org/10.1017/CBO9781107415324.004.

Joscelyn, Thomas. "Graphic Promotes the Islamic State's Prolific Media Machine." *Long War Journal*, November 25, 2015. https://www.longwarjournal.org/archives/2015/11/graphic-promotes-islamic-states-prolific-media-machine.php.

Kang, Inkyu, and Kwangjun Heo. "Framing the Enemy: A Proxemics Analysis of US News Magazine Cover Photographs." International Communication Association, May 2006.

Khatib, Lina. *Image Politics in the Middle East: The Role of the Visual in Political Struggle*. London: I. B. Tauris, 2012.

Khosronejad, Pedram. "Introduction: Unburied Memories." *Visual Anthropology* 25, nos. 1–2 (2012): 1–21. https://doi.org/10.1080/08949468.2012.629593.

Knutson, Brian. "Facial Expressions of Emotion Influence Interpersonal Trait Inferences." *Journal of Nonverbal Behavior* 20 (1996): 165–82.

Koga-Browes, Scott. "Social Distance Portrayed: Television News in Japan and the UK." *Visual Communication* 12, no. 1 (2013): 71–96. https://doi.org/10.1177/1470357212462323.

Kraft, Robert N. "The Influence of Camera Angle on Comprehension and Retention of Pictorial Events." *Memory & Cognition* 15, no. 4 (1986): 291–307. https://doi.org/10.3758/BF03197032.

Kraidy, Marwan. "The Projectilic Image: Islamic State's Digital Visual Warfare and Global Networked Affect." *Media, Culture & Society* 39, no. 8 (2017): 1194–1209. https://doi.org/10.1177/0163443717725575.

Kress, Gunther, and Theo van Leeuwen. *Reading Images: The Grammar of Visual Design*. 2nd ed. London: Routledge, 2006.

Lampinen, James M., Jeffrey S. Neuschatz, and Andrew D. Cling. *The Psychology of Eyewitness Identification*. New York: Psychology Press, 2012.

Larsen, Randy J., and Todd K. Shackelford. "Gaze Avoidance: Personality and Social Judgments of People Who Avoid Direct Face-to-Face Contact." *Personality and Individual Differences* 21, no. 6 (1996): 907–17. https://doi.org/10.1016/S0191-8869(96)00148-1.

Lauzière, Henri. *The Making of Salafism: Islamic Reform in the Twentieth Century*. New York: Columbia University Press, 2015.

Lewis, Kelly. "Digitally Mediated Martyrdom: The Role of the Visual in Political Arab Activist Culture." *Journal of Arab & Muslim Media Research* 12, no. 2 (2019): 169–89.

Lombard, Matthew, and Theresa Ditton. "At the Heart of It All: The Concept of Presence." *Journal of Computer-Mediated Communication* 3, no. 2 (1997): 1–27. https://doi.org/10.1111/j.1083.

Lombard, Matthew, Robert D. Reich, Maria E. Grabe, Cheryl C. Bracken, and Theresa B. Ditton. "Presence and Television: The Role of Screen Size." *Human Communication Research* 26, no. 1 (2000): 75–98. https://doi.org/10.1111/j.1468-2958.2000.tb00750.x.

Lukk, Martin, and Keith Doubt. "Bearing Witness and the Limits of War Photojournalism: Ron Haviv in Bijeljina." *Human Rights Quarterly* 37, no. 3 (2015): 629–36.

Mackintosh, Fiona J., and Roberta Quance. "Speaking/Seeing Saints: Norah Borges and Silvina Ocampo Collaborate." *Romance Studies* 22, no. 2 (2013): 149–63. https://doi.org/10.1179/ros.2004.22.2.149.

Mandell, Lee M., and Donald L. Shaw. "Judging People in the News—Unconsciously: Effect of Camera Angle and Bodily Activity." *Journal of Broadcasting* 17 (1973): 353–62.

Marroushi, Nadine. "Dark Clouds over the Sinai: The Military's Brutal North Sinai Campaign Is Targeting Civilians and Militants Alike." *Slate*, October 7, 2013. http://www.slate.com/articles/news_and_politics/foreigners/2013/10/abdel_fattah_al_sisi_s_sinai_campaign_egypt_s_military_is_targeting_civilians.html.

Masress. "The Journalists and Reporters in North Sinai Condemns the Arrest of 'Al-Shorouk' Journalists." September 23, 2013. http://www.masress.com/fjp/86293.

McCain, Thomas A., Joseph Chilberg, and Jacob Wakshlag. "The Effect of Camera Angle on Source Credibility and Attraction." *Journal of Broadcasting* 21, no. 1 (1977): 35–46. https://doi.org/10.1080/08838157709363815.

McDougall, Julian. "Comrades and Curators." *Journal of Visual Literacy* 38, no. 4 (2019): 245–61. https://doi.org/10.1080/1051144X.2019.1611696.

McLuhan, Marshall. "The Playboy Interview: Marshall McLuhan." *Playboy*, March 1969. https://web.cs.ucdavis.edu/~rogaway/classes/188/spring07/mcluhan.pdf.

Melki, Jad, and Azza El-Masri. "The Paris Attacks: Terror and Recruitment." Carter Center, 2016, 28–33. https://www.cartercenter.org/resources/pdfs/peace/conflict_resolution/countering-isis/counteringdaeshpropaganda-feb2016.pdf#page=30.

Melki, Jad, and May Jabado. "Mediated Public Diplomacy of the Islamic State in Iraq and Syria : The Synergistic Use of Terrorism, Social Media and Branding." *Media and Communication* 4, no. 2 (2016): 92–103. https://doi.org/10.17645/mac.v4i2.432.

Messaris, Paul, and Linus Abraham. "The Role of Images in Framing News Stories." In *Framing Public Life: Perspectives on Media and Our Understanding of the Social World*, edited by Stephen D. Reese, Oscar H. Gandy, and August E. Grant, 215–26. Mahwah, NJ: Lawrence Erlbaum, 2001.

Meyers-Levy, Joan, and Laura A. Peracchio. "Getting an Angle in Advertising: The Effect of Camera Angle on Product Evaluations." *Journal of Marketing Research* 29, no. 4 (1992): 454–61. https://doi.org/10.2307/3172711.

Mikhail, George. "Sinai Tribes Take Up Arms against IS." *Al-Monitor*, May 15, 2017. https://www.al-monitor.com/pulse/originals/2017/05/egypt-sinai-tribes-weapons-fight-islamic-state.html.

Milton, Daniel. "Communication Breakdown: Unraveling the Islamic State's Media Ef-

forts." Combatting Terrorism Center, 2016. https://www.ctc.usma.edu/v2/wp-content/uploads/2016/10/ISMedia_Online.pdf.
Milwright, Marcus. «The Martyred Sultan: Tuman Bay II in André Thevet's *Les vrais pourtraits et vies des hommes illustrés*.» *Word & Image* 33, no. 1 (2017): 1–17. https://doi.org/10.1080/02666286.2016.1228279.
Ministry of Foreign Affairs. "Bahrain Terrorist List (Individuals—Entities)." July 14, 2020. https://www.mofa.gov.bh/Default.aspx?tabid=12342&language=en-US.
Mitchell, Thomas. *Picture Theory: Essays on Verbal and Visual Representation*. Chicago: University of Chicago Press, 1994.
Morrow, Adam, and Khaled M. Al-Omrani. "Egypt: Bedouin Take on the Govt." Inter Press Service, June 18, 2007. http://www.ipsnews.net/2007/06/egypt-bedouin-take-on-the-govt/.
Mubashir, Abdo, and Islam Tawfik. *Sinai: The Location and History*. Cairo: Dar al-Maaref, 1978.
Neal, Tess M. S., and Stanley L. Brodsky. "Expert Witness Credibility as a Function of Eye Contact Behavior and Gender." *Criminal Justice and Behavior* 35, no. 12 (2008): 1515–26. https://doi.org/10.1177/0093854808325405.
Newhagen, John E., and Byron Reeves. "The Evening's Bad News: Effects of Compelling Negative Television News Images on Memory." *Journal of Communication* 42, no. 2 (1992): 25–41.
Official Page of Armed Forces Spokesman. "Egyptian Military Spokesman Statement on Al-Ansari." Facebook, August 4, 2016. https://www.facebook.com/EgyArmySpox/posts/872570456207271.
———. "Egyptian Military Statement on a Second Army Operation in North Sinai." Facebook, April 26, 2017. https://www.facebook.com/EgyArmySpox/posts/1048526451945003.
———. "Egyptian Military Statement on the Killing of 16 Terrorists in North Sinai." Facebook, May 30, 2016. https://www.facebook.com/EgyArmySpox/posts/838588312938819.
———. "Egyptian Military Statement on the Martyrdom of Ahmed Abdelhamid Al-Dardiry." Facebook, March 22, 2017. https://www.facebook.com/EgyArmySpox/photos/a.219625808168409/1022824427848539/.
———. "Egyptian Military Statement on the Ministers of Defense and Interior's Visit to Sinai." Facebook, February 12, 2016. https://m.facebook.com/EgyArmySpox/posts/779002165564101.
———. "Egyptian Military Statement on Third Army's Checkpoints in Sinai." Facebook, November 12, 2017. https://www.facebook.com/EgyArmySpox/posts/1175445129253134.
———. "Egyptian Military Statement on Third Army's Operations in Central Sinai." Facebook, March 23, 2017. https://www.facebook.com/EgyArmySpox/posts/1023359544461694.
———. "Egyptian Military Statement on Third Army's Sinai Operations." Facebook, September 8, 2017. https://www.facebook.com/EgyArmySpox/posts/1138430516287929.
Ohl, Jessy J. "Nothing to See or Fear: Light War and the Boring Visual Rhetoric of U.S.

Drone Imagery." *Quarterly Journal of Speech* 101, no. 4 (2015): 612–32. https://doi.org/10.1080/00335630.2015.1128115.

Öhman, Arne, and Ulf Dimberg. "Facial Expressions as Conditioned Stimuli for Electrodermal Responses: A Case of 'Preparedness'?" *Journal of Personality and Social Psychology* 36, no. 11 (1978): 1251–58. https://doi.org/10.1037/0022-3514.36.11.1251.

"Oh, You Media Operative, You Are A Mujahid." *Al-Himma Library*, April 3, 2016. https://bit.ly/3q7JY9u.

O'Neil, Ann. "The 13th Juror: The Radicalization of Dzhokhar Tsarnaev." *CNN*, March 30, 2015. http://www.cnn.com/2015/03/27/us/tsarnaev-13th-juror-jahar-radicalization/index.html.

Ortiz, María J., and José A. Moya. "The Action Cam Phenomenon: A New Trend in Audiovisual Production." *Communication & Society* 28, no. 3 (2015): 51–64. https://doi.org/10.15581/003.28.3.51-64.

Palanica, Adam, and Roxane J. Itier. "Attention Capture by Direct Gaze Is Robust to Context and Task Demands." *Journal of Nonverbal Behavior* 36, no. 2 (2012): 123–34. https://doi.org/10.1007/s10919-011-0128-z.

Parry, Katy. "Images of Liberation? Visual Framing, Humanitarianism and British Press Photography during the 2003 Iraq Invasion." *Media, Culture & Society* 33, no. 8 (2011): 1185–1201. https://doi.org/10.1177/0163443711418274.

———. "A Visual Framing Analysis of British Press Photography during the 2006 Israel-Lebanon Conflict." *Media, War & Conflict* 3, no. 1 (2010): 67–85.

Pelham, Nicolas. "Sinai: The Buffer Erodes." Chatham House, September 2012. https://www.chathamhouse.org/sites/default/files/public/Research/Middle%20East/pr-0912pelham.pdf.

Perlmutter, David D. *Photojournalism and Foreign Policy: Icons of Outrage in International Crises*. Westport, CT: Praeger, 1998.

———. "The Vision of War in High School Social Science Textbooks." *Communication* 13, no. 2 (1992): 143–60.

Pfau, Michael, Michel M. Haigh, Theresa Shannon, Toni Tones, Deborah Mercurio, Raina Williams, Blanca Binstock, et al. "The Influence of Television News Depictions of the Images of War on Viewers." *Journal of Broadcasting and Electronic Media* 52, no. 2 (2008): 303–22. https://doi.org/10.1080/08838150801992128.

Powers, Shawn, and Ben O'Loughlin. "The Syrian Data Glut: Rethinking the Role of Information in Conflict." *Media, War & Conflict* 8, no. 2 (2015): 172–80. https://doi.org/10.1177/1750635215584286.

Proverbio, Alice M., Federica Riva, and Alberto Zani. "Observation of Static Pictures of Dynamic Actions Enhances the Activity of Movement-Related Brain Areas." *PLOS ONE* 4, no. 5 (2009): 1–8. https://doi.org/10.1371/journal.pone.0005389.

Quash, Ben. "'If We Be Dead with Christ': Christian Visualisations of Death." *Studies in Christian Ethics* 29, no. 3 (2016): 323–30. https://doi.org/10.1177/0953946816642993.

Raheja, Natasha. "Warriors of Goja: Pains and Pleasures of the Sikh (Male) Body." *Sikh Formations* 10, no. 2 (2014): 219–31. https://doi.org/10.1080/17448727.2014.941205.

Ratta, Donatella Della. *Shooting a Revolution: Visual Media and Warfare in Syria*. London: Pluto Press, 2018.

Roberts, Hilary. "Photography." *International Encyclopedia of the First World War*, October 8, 2014.

Romani, Gabriella. "Fashioning the Italian Nation: Risorgimento and Its Costumeall'italiana." *Journal of Modern Italian Studies* 20, no. 1 (2015): 10–23. https://doi.org/10.1080/1354571X.2014.973151.

Rose, Gillian. *Visual Methodologies: An Introduction to the Interpretation of Visual Methods*. London: Sage, 2001.

Sabry, Mohannad. *Sinai: Egypt's Linchpin, Gaza's Lifeline, Israel's Nightmare*. Cairo: American University in Cairo Press, 2015.

Said, Omar. "The Tales of Palestinian Fighters in Sinai." *Mada Masr*, December 1, 2017. https://www.madamasr.com/en/2017/12/01/feature/politics/the-tales-of-palestinian-fighters-in-sinai/.

Said, Omar, and Assmaa Naguib. "Counterterrorism in Sisi's 1st Term: Progress Despite Clinging to Tradition." *Mada Masr*, April 1, 2018. https://www.madamasr.com/en/2018/04/01/feature/politics/counterterrorism-in-sisis-1st-term-progress-despite-clinging-to-tradition/.

Sammartino, Jonathan, and Stephen E. Palmer. "Aesthetic Issues in Spatial Composition: Effects of Vertical Position and Perspective on Framing Single Objects." *Journal of Experimental Psychology: Human Perception and Performance* 38, no. 4 (2012): 865–79. https://doi.org/10.1037/a0027736.

Saramifar, Younes. "The South Side of Heaven: A Journey along the Iranian Collective Memory in Iran-Iraq War Memorial Sites." *Anthropology of the Middle East* 14, no. 1 (2019): 125–41.

Schmidt, Karen L., and Jeffrey F. Cohn. "Human Facial Expressions as Adaptations: Evolutionary Questions in Facial Expression Research." *American Journal of Physical Anthropology*, no. 33 (2001): 3–24. https://doi.org/10.1021/nl061786n.Core-Shell.

Senju, Atsushi, Toshikazu Hasegawa, and Yoshikuni Tojo. "Does Perceived Direct Gaze Boost Detection in Adults and Children with and without Autism? The Stare-in-the-Crowd Effect Revisited." *Visual Cognition* 12 (2005): 1474–96.

Seo, Hyunjin. "Visual Propaganda in the Age of Social Media: An Empirical Analysis of Twitter Images during the 2012 Israeli–Hamas Conflict." *Visual Communication Quarterly* 21 (June 2014): 150–61. https://doi.org/10.1080/15551393.2014.955501.

Seo, Hyunjin, and Husain Ebrahim. "Visual Propaganda on Facebook: A Comparative Analysis of Syrian Conflicts." *Media, War & Conflict* 9, no. 3 (2016): 227–51. https://doi.org/10.1177/1750635216661648.

Shaffer, Brenda. "Natural Gas Supply Stability and Foreign Policy." *Energy Policy*, no. 56 (2013): 114–25. https://doi.org/10.1016/j.enpol.2012.11.035.

Sharon, Ariel, and David Chanoff. *Warrior: An Autobiography*. New York: Simon & Schuster, 2002.

Shilad, Justin. "Egypt's State of Emergency May Act to Further Silence Press." Committee to Protect Journalists, April 11, 2017. https://cpj.org/blog/2017/04/egypts-state-of-emergency-may-act-to-further-silen.php.

Shuqair, Naom. *The Old and New History of Sinai and Its Geography*. Beirut: Dar al-Jeel, 1991.

Silva, Miguel F. S., Elena R. Rodriguez, Ana B. Banares, and Maria del Mar L. Talavera. "The Distant Other: The Depiction of Immigration in Four Spanish Daily Newspapers." *Journalism Practice* 11, no. 5 (2017): 592–605. https://doi.org/10.1080/17512786.2016.1155968.

Slackman, Michael. "30 Are Killed in Sinai as Bombs Rock Egyptian Resort City." *New York Times*, April 25, 2006. http://www.nytimes.com/2006/04/25/world/middleeast/25egypt.html.

Sontag, Susan. *Regarding the Pain of Others*. New York: Picador, 2003.

Stahl, Roger. *Through the Crosshairs: War, Visual Culture & the Weaponized Gaze*. New Brunswick, NJ: Rutgers University Press, 2018.

Stamps, Arthur E. "Distance Mitigates Threat." *Perceptual and Motor Skills* 113, no. 3 (2011): 751–63. https://doi.org/10.2466/24.20.27.PMS.114.3.709-716.

Tahrir Institute for Middle East Policy. "Egypt Security Watch: Quarterly Report: January–March 2017." July 2017. https://timep.org/wp-content/uploads/2017/08/ESW-Report-2017-Q1-Web.pdf.

———. "Egypt Security Watch: Quarterly Report: July–September 2016." January 2017. https://timep.org/wp-content/uploads/2016/01/ESW-Quarterly-Report_July-Sep2016_Q3.pdf.

———. "Egypt Security Watch: Quarterly Report: October–December 2016." April 2017. https://timep.org/wp-content/uploads/2017/04/ESW-Report_Q42016_web.pdf.

———. "ESW Month in Brief: January 2019." April 2019. https://timep.org/esw/esw-month-in-brief-january-2019/.

———. "ESW Week in Brief: December 10–December 17, 2018." March 2019. https://timep.org/esw/esw-week-in-brief-december-10-december-17-2018-2-2-2/.

———. "Quarterly Report: January–March 2016." July 2016. https://timep.org/wp-content/uploads/2016/01/ESW-QR-2016-Q1-WEB.pdf.

Tang, David, and Brandon J. Schmeichel. "Look Me in the Eye: Manipulated Eye Gaze Affects Dominance Mindsets." *Journal of Nonverbal Behavior* 39, no. 2 (2015): 181–94.

Tankard, James W. "Effects of Eye Position on Person Perception." *Perceptual and Motor Skills* 31, no. 3 (1970): 883–93.

Taylor, Jeremy E. "The 'Occupied Lens' in Wartime China: Portrait Photography in the Service of Chinese 'Collaboration,' 1939–1945." *History of Photography* 43, no. 3 (2019): 284–307. https://doi.org/10.1080/03087298.2019.1662604.

Terry, Allie. "Donatello's Decapitations and the Rhetoric of Beheading in Medicean Florence." *Renaissance Studies* 23 (2009): 609–38.

Tiemens, Robert K. "Some Relationships of Camera Angle to Communicator Credibility." *Journal of Broadcasting* 14, no. 4 (1970): 483–90. https://doi.org/10.1080/08838157009363614.

Trachtenberg, Alan. "Albums of War: On Reading Civil War Photographs." *Representations* 9 (1985): 1–32.

Turnbull, Nick. "Political Rhetoric and Its Relationship to Context: A New Theory of the Rhetorical Situation, the Rhetorical and the Political." *Critical Discourse Studies* 14, no. 2 (2017): 115–31. https://doi.org/10.1080/17405904.2016.1268186.

"UAE Blacklists 82 Groups as 'Terrorist.'" *Al Arabiya*, November 14, 2014. https://english.alarabiya.net/News/middle-east/2014/11/15/UAE-formally-blacklists-82-groups-as-terrorist-.

United Nations. "United Nations Security Council Consolidated List." May 27, 2021. https://scsanctions.un.org/consolidated/#alqaedaent.

U.S. Department of Justice. "U.S. v. Akayed Ullah Federal Criminal Complaint." December 12, 2017. https://www.justice.gov/usao-sdny/pr/akayed-ullah-charged-manhattan-federal-court-terrorism-and-explosives-charges.

U.S. Department of State. "Foreign Terrorist Organizations." July 14, 2020. https://www.state.gov/foreign-terrorist-organizations/.

Vail, Kenneth E., III, Jamie Arndt, Matt Motyl, and Tom Pyszczynski. "The Aftermath of Destruction: Images of Destroyed Buildings Increase Support for War, Dogmatism, and Death Thought Accessibility." *Journal of Experimental Social Psychology* 48, no. 5 (2012): 1069–81.

Van Duijnen, Michel. "'Only the Strangest and Most Horrible Cases': The Role of Judicial Violence in the Work of Jan Luyken." *Early Modern Low Countries* 2, no. 2 (2018): 169–97. https://doi.org/10.18352/emlc.73.

Vanzan, Anna. "The Holy Defense Museum in Tehran, or How to Aestheticize War." *Middle East Journal of Culture and Communication* 13, no. 1 (2020): 63–77. https://doi.org/10.1163/18739865-01301004.

Vatz, Richard E. "The Myth of the Rhetorical Situation." *Philosophy & Rhetoric* 6, no. 3 (1973): 154–61.

Verkaaik, Oskar. "Notes on the Sublime: Aspects of Political Violence in Urban Pakistan." *South Asian Popular Culture* 11, no. 2 (2013): 109–19. https://doi.org/10.1080/14746689.2013.784052.

von Clausewitz, Carl. *On War*. Edited and translated by Michael Howard and Peter Paret. Princeton, NJ: Princeton University Press, 1976.

Von Grunau, Michael, and Christina Anston. "The Detection of Gaze Direction: A Stare-in-the-Crowd Effect." *Perception* 24 (1995): 1297–1313.

Wagenaar, Willem A., and Juliette H. Van Der Schrier. "Familiar Face Recognition as a Function of Distance and Illumination: A Practical Tool for Use in the Courtroom." *Psychology, Crime and Law* 2, no. 4 (1996): 321–32. https://doi.org/10.1080/10683169608409787.

Walker, Claire. "'Hangd for the True Faith': Embodied Devotion in Early Modern English Carmelite Cloisters." *Journal of Religious History* 44, no. 4 (2020): 494–512. https://doi.org/10.1111/1467-9809.12701.

Weizman, Eyal. *Hollow Land: Israel's Architecture of Occupation*. London: Verso, 2007.

Wells, Karen. "Narratives of Liberation and Narratives of Innocent Suffering: The Rhetorical Uses of Images of Iraqi Children in the British Press." *Visual Communication* 6, no. 1 (2007): 55–71. https://doi.org/10.1177/1470357207071465.

Wignell, Peter, Sabine Tan, and Kay L O'Halloran. "Under the Shade of AK47s: A Multimodal Approach to Violent Extremist Recruitment Strategies for Foreign Fighters." *Critical Studies on Terrorism* 10, no. 3 (2017): 429–52. https://doi.org/10.1080/17539153.2017.1319319.

Winkler, Carol. "Challenging Communities: A Perspective about, from, and by Argumentation." In *Disturbing Argument*, edited by Catherine H. Palczewski, 4–17. New York: Routledge, 2015.

Winkler, Carol, Kareem El Damanhoury, Aaron Dicker, and Anthony F. Lemieux. "Images of Death and Dying in ISIS Media: A Comparison of English and Arabic Print Publications." *Media, War & Conflict* 12, no. 3 (2018): 248–62. https://doi.org/10.1177/1750635217746200.

———. "The Medium Is Terrorism: Transformation of the About to Die Trope in Dabiq." *Terrorism & Political Violence* 31, no. 2 (2016): 224–43. http://dx.doi.org/10.1080/09546553.2016.1211526.

Winkler, Carol, Kareem El Damanhoury, Aaron Dicker, Yennhi Luu, Wojciech Kaczkowski, and Nagham El-Karhili. "Considering the Military-Media Nexus from the Perspective of Competing Groups: The Case of ISIS and al-Qaeda in the Arabian Peninsula." *Dynamics of Asymmetric Conflict: Pathways toward Terrorism and Genocide* 13, no. 1 (2019): 3–23. https://doi.org/10.1080/17467586.2019.1630744.

Winter, Charlie. "Apocalypse, Later: A Longitudinal Study of the Islamic State Brand." *Critical Studies in Media Communication* 35, no. 1 (2018): 103–21. https://doi.org/10.1080/15295036.2017.1393094.

Zelizer, Barbie. *About to Die: How News Images Move the Public*. New York: Oxford University Press, 2010.

———. *Remembering to Forget: Holocaust Memory through the Camera's Eye*. Chicago: University of Chicago Press, 1998.

Zettl, Herbert. *Television Production Handbook*. 8th ed. Belmont, CA: Wadsworth, 2003.

INDEX

Page numbers in italics indicate illustrations; those with a *t* indicate tables.

Abbas, Mahmoud, 30
Abdelghaffar, Magdy, 69, 105
about-to-die visual trope, 8, 44, *60*, 64, 179n17
Adli, Habib al-, 157
Adnani, Abu Muhammad al-, 71, *72*
Afghanistan, 11, 129, 171; Zarqawi training camp in, 29, 30, 179n1
African Trade Investment Forum, 46, 104, 161
al-Arish, 22, 29–31; checkpoint attack of, 45; Christian Copts in, 35; gas pipeline bombing in, 1–6, *5*
al-Jama'a al-Islamiyya, 28
Al Jazeera, 15
al-Matafi checkpoint attack (2017), 45, 47–48, *87*
al-Qaeda, 81, 113; Jama'at al-Tawhid wal-Jihad ties with, 29, 179n1; U.S.S. *Cole* bombing by, 11
al-Rawda, 108, *109*
al-Sabil checkpoint attack (2016), 45
al-Safa checkpoint attack (2016), 45, 46–47, *122*, *123*
al-Salafiyya al-Jihadiyya, 30, 32
al-Shabaab, 171
al-Takfir wal-Hijra (Ex-communication and Immigration Group), 2
al-Tawhid wal-Jihad training camp, 29, 30, 179n1
Ansar al-Jihad (Supporters of Jihad), 2
Ansar Bayt al-Maqdis (Supporters of Jerusalem), 13, 30, 31, 32; gas pipeline explosions by, 4–6, *5*; Israeli drone strike against, 33; as Wilayat Sinai's predecessor, 38
Ansari, Abu Anas al-, 68, 69–70
Ansari, Abu Duaa al-, 35, 68–69, 155–56

Arab Spring (2011), 2, 8, 134
Askar, Ossama, 156
Azzam, Abdullah, 11

Baghdadi, Abu Bakr al-, 13, 33
Barthes, Roland, 7
battle aftermath framing: by Egyptian military, 99, 100t, 101–2, *102*; by Wilayat Sinai, 84t, 88–89, *89*
Beaton, Cecil, 106
Bedouins, 20, 29–31, 74; Egyptian expulsion of, 27; Israeli expulsion of, 23–24; Salafism among, 30, 31; smuggling by, 28, 30, 36, 125, 159–60; tribes of, 22–23, 28
Beer al-Abd checkpoint attacks, 45, 47
Begin, Menachem, 26
Ben-Eliezer, Benyamin, 1–2
Bin Ali, Turki al-, 71–73, *72*
bin Laden, Osama, 29
Black Power movement (U.S.), 90
Bosnians, 22, 23
Boston Marathon bombings (2013), 12
Branigan, Edward, 141
Bush, George W., 107

camera angles, 129–34, *131*, *133*, 146–48
Camp David Accords (1978), 13, 26
Carter, Jimmy, 26
censorship, 10, 15–16
character types, 10, 154, 165
Chechnya, 11
Churchill, Winston, 106
cigarettes, contraband, 74, 93, *94*, 100t, 101, 104; Egyptian military and, 123, 149; shari'a law on, 110, 159
Civil War, U.S., 6, 106
Clausewitz, Carl von, 6
combat framing, 110, *111*; by Egyptian military,

combat framing (*continued*)
99, 100t, *103*, 113; by Wilayat Sinai, 84t, 85–88, *86*, *87*
Coptic Christians, 35
corpses, displays of, 49, 102, 126, 156, 164
counterterrorism operations, 36, 52–54, *53*, 74–76, 112, 164
Crimean War (1853–56), 6
cultural frameworks, 8, 20, 116, 117t, 181n2

Daesh, 179n1. *See also* ISIS
Dahab, 23, 27–30
Demir, Yusuf, 71, *72*, 73–74
Di Zahav, 24, 26, 27
drug trafficking, 76, 159–60; control of, 93, 100t, 101, 104; shari'a law and, 110; tunnels for, 28, 58–59

Eastern Mediterranean Gas (EMG), 2
economic context, 10, *154*, 158–59
EGAS (Egyptian national gas company), 3
Egyptian-Israeli wars, 12–13, 22, 23
Egyptian military, 4–5; counterterrorism operations of, 36, 52–54, *53*, 74–76, 112, 164; displays of combat by, 99, 100t, *103*, 110; framing categories of, 98–109, *99*, *100*, 100t; human portrayals by, 118, *120*; martyrdom framing by, 99, 100t, 110; photo campaign of, *40*, 41t, 42t, *43*, 49–50, 98–109, 100t; social service provision by, *100*, 100t, 108–9, *109*, 136, *137*; visits by public figures, *100*, 100t, 105–8, *107*, *127*, *136*; visual semantics of, 116–17, 121t, 146–52
Entman, Robert, 7, 18, 81, 114
eye contact, 138–41, *139*

facial expressions, 134–37, *135–37*
Fahmi, Sameh, 1–4
Farouk, King of Egypt, 29
Fouda, Khaled, 156–57
framing. *See* visual framing
frequency of images, 10, *154*, 161, 163–64
Friday of Rage (Jan. 28, 2011), 1
Furqan, Abu Muhammad al-, 71, *72*

gas pipeline bombings, 1–6, *3*, *5*, 31–32
Gaza Strip, 30, 153
Gaza War (2008), 30
Global Terrorism Database (GTD), 50, 79, 80
Goffman, Erving, 7

Hall, Edward T., 8, 20, 116, 117t, 181n2; on proxemics, 122, 127
Halliday, Michael, 7
Hamas, 2, 14, 30, 113, 171. *See also* Palestinians
Harhour, Abdelfattah, 156–57
Hashemi, Abu Hajar al-, 35
Hegazy, Mohamed, 37
Hijazy, Mahmoud, 48, 156
Hofstede, Geert, 8, 20, 116, 117t, 180–81n1
human portrayals, 118, 119, *120*; camera angle for, 129–34, *133*; eye contact in, 138–41, *139*; facial expressions of, 134–37, *135–37*; point-of-view shots for, 141–43, *143*
human rights, 10, 20, *154*, 157–58, 170; of Bedouins, 28–30, 37; victimhood images and, 96
Human Rights Watch, 36, 158
hyperemotional images, 106–8, *107*, 114

Illah, Mohamed Abdel, 108, 156
image components, 164–66
immediate context, 161–64
improvised explosive devices (IEDs), 35–36, *44*, 54, 65, 85–86, *86*, 161–62
inghimasi attacks, 35
in-group lifestyle framing, 85t, 97–98, *98*
Iran-Iraq War, 90
Iraqi, Abu Sulayman al-, 71, *72*, 73
Iraq War, 29, 106–7; ISIS attacks in, 50, *51*; Mosul campaign of, 59–66, *62*, 76–77
Isawi, Abu Sayf al-, 71, *72*
Isawi, Mahmoud al-, 71, *72*
ISIS (Islamic State of Iraq and al-Sham), 1, 14, 35, 50, *51*; media platforms of, 39; in Mosul, 59–66, *62*, 76–77; names of, 179n1; publications of, 11; in Raqqa, 59–63, *62*, 66–68, 77; Syrian attacks by, 50–52, *51*; visual campaigns of, 11–12; Wilayat Sinai branch of, 5–6
ISIS Egypt, 52
ISIS Sinai. *See* Wilayat Sinai
Israeli-Egyptian wars, 12–13, 22–27, *26*

Jama'at al-Tawhid wal-Jihad (Monotheism and Jihad), 13, 28–29, 180n36
Jane's Terrorism and Insurgency Centre (JTIC), 79
Janubi, Abu Ali al-, 71, *72*
Jaysh al-Islam, 30
Jerusalem, 14

Karbala, battle of, 90
Khattab, Umar ibn al-, 12
Khodeiri, Mahmoud al-, 2
Kress, Gunther, 7, 138
Kurdish Peshmerga fighters, 76, 77
Kurdistan Workers' Party (PKK), 171

law enforcement framing, 110; by Egyptian military, 99, 100, 100t, 104–5; by Wilayat Sinai, 84–85t, 93–95, 94, 95
Lebanon, 20
Libya, 14, 20, 97
Luxor massacre (1997), 28, 29

Majlis Shura al-Mujahideen fi Aknaf Bayt al-Maqdis (Mujahideen Shura Council in the Environs of Jerusalem), 31–32
Malahi, Nasr al-, 29
Mansour, Adli, 33
martyrdom framing, 110; by Egyptian military, 99, 100t; by Wilayat Sinai, 84–85t, 89–92, 91, 100, 125, 126, 135, 136, 138
Martyr's Right Operation, 16, 17, 36; phases of, 53, 54–59, 58; statistics on, 79, 80
Meshaal, Rayan, 71–73, 72
Mexican-American War (1846–48), 6
military context, 10, 154, 155–56
military-photography nexus, 38–39, 40, 41t, 42t, 77–80
"mind bombs," 2
Morsi, Mohamed, 17–18, 31; ouster of, 21, 33; Sinai visit by, 32
Mosul, Iraq, 59–66, 62, 76–77
Mount Sinai (al-Tor), 12
Mubarak, Hosni, 2, 4, 31, 134, 157
Muqrin, Abdelaziz al-, 11
Muslim Brotherhood, 21, 31

Nashir channel, 16, 17. See also Telegram channels
NEOM megacity project, 23
Netivei Neft oil company, 24
Neviot, 24, 26, 27
Niépce, Nicéphore, 6
Nigeria, 171

Obama, Barack, 107
Operation Eagle, of SCAF, 32
Ophira, 24–27, 25
Ottoman Empire, 21

over-the-shoulder (OTS) shots, 141–49, 143

Palestinians, 12–14; under Ottomans, 21; Second Intifada of, 1, 28; in Sinai, 22–23, 29, 35, 160; visual campaigns of, 8. See also Hamas
Palmyra attack (2016), 50–52, 51
Paris bombings (2015), 8
PeaceTech Lab (NGO), 79
photographic warfare: definition of, 6–7; future research on, 169–71; pillars of, 8–10, 10; understanding of, 7–8; by Wilayat Sinai, 16–17, 17
point-of-view (POV) shots, 141–48, 143–45
political context, 10, 154, 156–57
proxemics, 122–29, 123, 124, 126, 127, 152
proximate text, 10, 154, 161–63

Qatar, 15
Qur'an, 12, 56, 65, 90, 97, 98, 125, 126

Rafah, 24, 29–31; checkpoint attack in, 32, 45, 48–50; eviction policy in, 35, 96; smuggling in, 36, 104
Raqqa, 59–63, 62, 66–68, 77
Rawi, Abu Khattab al-, 71, 72
Rawi, Fawaz al-, 71–73
Religion of Peace, 79–80
Rumsfeld, Donald, 106–7

Sadat, Anwar, 22, 26, 28
Salafism, 30, 31, 159, 181–82n32
Salem, Hussein, 2, 3–4
Saudi Arabia, 20, 23
scenic elements, 10, 154, 164–65
semiotics, 7–8, 10, 154, 166–68. See also visual semiotics
services provision. See social service provision
Sharaf, Essam, 2
shari'a law, 93–94, 110–11; Jama'at al-Tawhid wal-Jihad on, 180n36
Sharm El Sheikh, 22, 27; African Trade Investment Forum at, 46, 104, 161; bombings in, 28, 29, 30
Sharon, Ariel, 24
Shawky, Tarek, 108
Sheikh Zuwayid, 29–30, 31, 35, 36, 44, 45
Shishani, Abu Omar al-, 71, 72
Sinai, 1–6, 3, 5, 10–16; demography of, 22–23,

Sinai (*continued*)
27; etymology of, 21; geography of, *21*, 21–22; history of, 23–37, *34*; Israeli occupation of, 23–27, *26*; Jewish settlements in, 13, 24, *26*; strategic importance of, 10; tourism industry of, 13, 23, 24, 26, 27

Sinai Arab Organization, 24

Sinai Prisoners Defense Front, 30

Sisi, Abdelfattah al-, 15, *37*, 107; Morsi's appointment of, 32; rise to power of, 33–34

situational context, *10*, *154*, 155–61

smuggling, 28, 30, 36, *104*, 125, 159–60

Sobhi, Sedki, 156; Morsi's appointment of, 32; public visits by, 69, 70, 105, *107*, *127*, 136

social context, *10*, *154*, 159–60

social service provision, 111–13; by Egyptian military, 76, *100*, 100t, 108–9, *109*, 136, *137*, 158–59; by Israeli military, 27; by Wilayat Sinai, 83, *84*, 84t, 159

Somalia, 81, 171

Sontag, Susan, 6

spies, 55, 59, 93, *95*

state/non-state media campaigns, 6–7, *10*, *154*, 166–68

Sudan, 14

Suez Canal, 21, 23

Sufism, 30, 35, 93, *95*

suicide fighters, 35, 44, 49

Suleiman, Adel, 27

Sumerians, 21

Supreme Council of the Armed Forces (SCAF), 2–4, 31, 32. *See also* Egyptian military

Syria, 81, 113; ISIS attacks in, 50–52, *51*

Taba bombings (2004), 29–30, 31

"*takfiri* terrorists," 101, 102, 103, 125

Taliban, 129, 171. *See also* Afghanistan

Tantawi, Mohamed Hussein, 32

Telegram channels, 12, 15, 16, *17*, 39, 79

torture, 29, 30, 90, 157

Trump, Donald, 14

tunnels, 142, *144*, 159; destruction of, 32, 36, 52, 54, 76; for drug trafficking, 28, 58–59; as law enforcement challenge, 100t, 101, *104*, 105; as security threat, 30, 110–11, 159, 161; for smuggling, 28, 30, 32, *104*, 130, 159

Turkey, 15, 171

U.S.S. *Cole* bombing (2000), 11

van Leeuwen, Theo, 7, 138

victimhood framing, *96*, 96–97

viewer distance, 122–29, *123*, *124*, *126*, *127*

visits by public figures, *100*, 100t, 105–8, *107*, *127*, 136

visual contestation, 109–13, 168–71; analytic framework of, 8–10, *10*, 153–71, *154*; semiotics of, 146–50

visual framing, 81–82, 112–15; contestation of, 109–13; by Egyptian military, 98–109, *99*, *100*, 100t; Entman on, 7, 18, 81; Goffman on, 7; semiotic constellations and, *10*, *154*, 166–67; by Wilayat Sinai, 82–84, 82–98, 84–85t

visual semiotics, 7–9, *10*, 116–17, 117t, 121t, 146–52, *154*, 165–66; of camera angle, 129–34, *131*, *133*, 146–48; contestation of, 146–50; of eye contact, 138–41, *139*; of facial expressions, 134–37, *135–37*; future studies of, 152; of subjective shots, 141–46, *143–45*; of viewer distance, 122–29, *123*, *124*, *126*, *127*

Wilayat Sinai, 5–6, 13–15, *34*, *35*; Ansar Bayt al-Maqdis and, 33; battle aftermath framing by, 84t, 88–89, *89*; combat displays by, 83, 84t, 85–88, *86*, *87*, 110; death images of, 59, *60*; founder of, 70; framing categories of, 82–84, 82–98, 84–85t; human portrayals by, 118, *119*; local attacks by, 42–46, *43–45*; loss of local leaders of, 68–70; loss of regional leaders of, 71–74, *72*; martyrdom framing by, 84–85t, 89–92, *91*, 100, 125, *126*, 135, *136*, 138; military visual frames of, 83, 84–85t; nonmilitary visual frames of, *84*, 84–85t; photo campaigns of, *40*, 41t, 42t, *43*, 46–52, *51*, *53*; photographic warfare by, 16–17, *17*; predecessor of, 38; social service provision by, 83, *84*, 84t; suicide fighters of, 35; visual semantics of, 116–17, 121t, 146–52

Yamit, 26

Yemen, 81, 153, 171

Youssef, Bassem, 3, *4*

Zarqawi, Abu Mus'ab al-, 29, 179n1, 180n36

Zawahiri, Ayman al-, 4

CPSIA information can be obtained
at www.ICGtesting.com
Printed in the USA
BVHW071738050822
643913BV00012B/251